BALTHASAR FOR THOMISTS

AIDAN NICHOLS, O.P.

BALTHASAR
FOR
THOMISTS

IGNATIUS PRESS   SAN FRANCISCO

Cover design by Roxanne Mei Lum

© 2020 by Ignatius Press, San Francisco
All rights reserved
ISBN 978-1-62164-339-5
Library of Congress Control Number 2020930313
Printed in the United States of America ∞

If there *is* a growth in the understanding of revelation (although it is questionable whether the concept of "growth" is appropriate here), it is primarily in the awareness of how inexhaustible it is.

—Hans Urs von Balthasar, *Theo-drama*

CONTENTS

PREFACE

Thomists have not always welcomed the entry of Balthasarians into a place in the sun in Catholic theology. The rise of Balthasar's reputation in the years of the pontificate of John Paul II coincided with a renaissance of Thomism, notably in France and North America. Rivalry in the search for disciples was predictable. But Thomists have long lived with such rivals, notably in the Franciscan school, and have not deemed their existence an affront. No one theology can exhaust everything that the historic revelation contains, any more than one philosophy can do justice to all the questions raised by divine agency in the world. A healthy competition could assist the fuller emergence of truth. In any case, as the opening chapter of this book will seek to show, Balthasar and Thomas have different aims in producing their respective theologies. One is not comparing like with like, or at least—for my closing chapter suggests one great commonality in theological method—doing so only to a limited extent.

I am grateful to Mark Brumley of Ignatius Press for suggesting I should write this book, which took me back to things Balthasarian after a lengthy interval. In effect, it is an introduction to Balthasar for those whose first allegiance lies with the school of Saint Thomas. It concentrates, therefore, on two sorts of areas. There are areas where Balthasar's thinking is especially indebted to the approach of Aquinas (not without the addition of occasional creative "spin"). There are also areas where, contrastingly, Thomists are most likely to find Balthasar's texts problematic (if also, perhaps, provocative of thought). At the same time, *Balthasar for Thomists* also seeks to give a rounded view of his work by and large. An introduction to Balthasar for Thomists cannot be wholly unlike such an introduction for other people. That is for a very simple reason. There is only one Hans Urs von Balthasar.

Both Aquinas and Balthasar wrote a very great deal, and they did so in a wide variety of literary genres. But the witness of history is that, among Thomas' writings, the *Summa theologiae* is the central text, and

9

though the time span for appreciation is of course far shorter, it can be said of Balthasar that the same role is played for his corpus by the "Trilogy": the sequence of theological aesthetics, theological dramatics, and theological logic which make up a sixteen-volume masterwork. Accordingly, I shall focus on the Trilogy, especially in chapters 2, 3, and 4. Writing of that Trilogy, I give most weight to the opening volume in each case (for the dramatics, the first two volumes), using those "openers" to provide a perspective on the whole. What seem to me the chief doctrinal issues raised by the overall argument of Balthasar's aesthetics, dramatics and logic, will be addressed in chapters 5 and 6. In chapter 7, I look at Balthasar's only book-length study of Saint Thomas, a commentary on some questions of the *Summa theologiae* which, as it happens, raises issues of wider pertinence to Balthasar's own thought. The commentary includes a delicate area for Balthasar studies, the role of the mystics in the transmission of sacred doctrine. A further word should be said about that here.

Balthasar's own *oeuvre* cannot be fully appreciated without reference to the mysticism of Adrienne von Speyr. More than that: a Balthasarian corpus from which all trace of von Speyrianism had been removed would be substantially different—and, as it happens, significantly less problematic for the school of Thomas. That presents a difficulty. Adrienne is not yet acknowledged as among those mystical writers who, being masters of the spiritual life, enjoy some authority in Catholic Christianity as witnesses to the "sense of faith". In the last couple of years, I understand, a beginning has been made in introducing the "cause" of Adrienne von Speyr for recognition by the Church as a holy woman. For that to proceed it will be essential for her *Nachlass*, the papers she left behind, to become available in its entirety, so as to test exhaustively the mettle of her teaching. Balthasar made no secret of his conviction that his work must be considered inseparable from hers.

Despite leaving the Jesuit Society (and a frustrated attempt to rejoin it late in life), Balthasar never cooled in his enthusiasm for the spirituality of its founder, equating Ignatian *indiferencia* with his own favoured theme of *Bereitschaft*, "readiness", which he took to be the quintessentially "Marian" Annunciation attitude. So it seems suitable to dedicate this book to the memory of a great son of Saint Ignatius, Edward Oakes, who died aged sixty-five in 2013. Oakes was a trailblazer among Jesuits in espousing Balthasar's thought. He has an increasing number of successors, but there are few Dominicans to match them. In my conclusion, I express my agreement with the Chicago scholar Cyril O'Regan. Balthasar's thinking about the faith moves on a "Bonaventurian-Thomasian axis". This makes him an honorary member of the Mendicant theological tradition where the Order of Preachers has its own intellectual roots.

The topic broached here—a comparison between two different, yet overlapping, philosophical-theological universes—has doubtless not found in me an adequate expositor. I console myself with the thought that someone had to make a (book-length) start.

Blackfriars, Cambridge
Saints Peter and Paul, 2019

I

Introducing Balthasar for Thomists

My preface has already conceded the point. Introducing Balthasar to Thomists cannot be entirely different from introducing him to sundry folk more generally. Yet it is also possible to pick out certain factors in his formation and life story that underline the Balthasar-Aquinas connexion—or, alternatively, point up the contrasts that make for difficulties in mutual understanding. So this introduction will seek to serve both those ends—the one general, the other particular.

The biography is the work

Balthasar was born in 1908, in the Swiss city of Lucerne, to a rather patrician family (hence the "von" which precedes his surname). The Balthasars had the closest of connexions to the Catholic Church. Through his mother, Hans was related to a Hungarian bishop martyred by Communists. His father was a professional church architect; his sister, a member and eventually the superior general of a congregation of Franciscans.[1] Considered as a family, they were far more on the "wavelength" of his religious and priestly vocation than had been the kinsfolk of Thomas Aquinas, for whom entry into

---

[1] For the only biography at present, see Elio Guerriero, *Hans Urs von Balthasar* (Cinisello Balsamo: Edizioni Paoline, 1991). Manfred Lochbrunner has published more detailed studies of his work as a writer, editor, and publisher, and selections from correspondence with theologians, philosophers, and literary figures: Manfred Lochbrunner, *Hans Urs von Balthasar als Autor, Herausgeber und Verleger* (Würzburg: Echter, 2002); Manfred Lochbrunner, *Hans Urs von Balthasar und seine Theologiekollegen* (Würzburg: Echter, 2009); Manfred Lochbrunner, *Hans Urs von Balthasar und seine Philosophenfreunde* (Würzburg: Echter, 2005); Manfred Lochbrunner, *Hans Urs von Balthasar und seine Literatenfreunde* (Würzburg: Echter, 2007). These should go far to assist an eventual "scientific" biography.

the Dominicans was a cause of tension, not to say outright conflict.[2] Balthasar was educated by Benedictine monks at the abbey of Engelberg, just south of Lake Lucerne. Those monastic, liturgical, and contemplative beginnings to his Catholic education had been shared at Monte Cassino by Thomas, for whose theology, despite its customary austerity of expression, devotion lies always close at hand. Both come across as manifestly pious men—not something that can necessarily be said of all theologians since the transfer of studious theology into the contemporary academic environment. From Engelberg, Balthasar moved on to the Jesuit college at Feldkirch, across the border of eastern Switzerland in the Austrian Voralberg. There he would have followed a curriculum that, in its emphasis on classics, could be compared (at a pinch) to the teenage Thomas' experiences at the University of Naples. But now we come to a major difference between them, and one that is decisive for a parting of the ways. For his own university studies, Balthasar elected not to continue with a classical education, which would have further deepened his knowledge of Greek philosophy and its extension in ancient Rome (the latter chiefly of importance in ethics). Instead, he opted for *Germanistik*, a compound discipline of literature and philosophy centering on works written in the German tongue, which in Balthasar's period as a student—the later 1920s—had moved quite some distance from the largely philological discipline known by that name to the nineteenth century. It was now a remarkably open-ended intellectual enterprise, analyzing and evaluating texts in their philosophical, spiritual, and affective tenor, as somehow indicators of wider cultural trends. Were one to compare this exposure with Aquinas' experience of the mediaeval curriculum of the "liberal arts", a pedagogical abyss would open.[3]

While attending lecture courses in Zurich, Vienna, Munich, and Berlin, the young Balthasar experienced a call to become a priest, and more specifically a Jesuit. In this period, the Jesuits were prevented

---

[2] For Thomas' life, see Jean-Pierre Torrell, O.P., *Saint Thomas Aquinas*, vol. 1, *The Person and His Work*, trans. Robert Royal (Washington, DC: Catholic University of America Press, 1996).

[3] M. Michèle Mulchahey, *"First the Bow Is Bent in Study": Dominican Education before 1350* (Toronto: Pontifical Institute of Mediaeval Studies, 1998).

by the civil law from opening mission houses in Switzerland, a hang-over from the confessional struggle between Swiss Catholics and Protestants (the Sonderbund War) in the mid-nineteenth century. If Balthasar were to become a Jesuit, it could be only in Austria or Germany, and in the event it was in Bavaria. Balthasar did not relish the standard ordination studies furnished in the south German province of the Society of Jesus. Nevertheless, by that route he entered on a patrimony in philosophy and theology distinct from the heritage of the Dominicans. To gauge the extent of that difference is not altogether easy. In the late nineteenth century, with papal encouragement, the Jesuits had rallied to Thomism after the long reign of the eclectic Scholasticism of their sixteenth-century master Francisco Suárez. Balthasar could be openly contemptuous of his official priestly studies, deploring what he considered their spiritual aridity, but this is not to call him impervious to absolutely everything in interwar Jesuit Scholasticism. It would be premature to describe at this point the kind of Thomism that Balthasar would eventually espouse. In some cases the authors he chose to follow as a would-be disciple of Aquinas the metaphysician were not writing until after the Second World War. A complete exploration of Balthasar's Thomism is something well worth doing, but it would need to be carried out by another author with a fuller philosophical training. It would investigate far more fully than is done here the work of, especially, Gustav Siewerth and Ferdinand Ulrich—the first, an almost exact contemporary of Balthasar's; the second, a generation younger. These are figures whose language combines Scholastic vocabulary with the idioms of phenomenology and even Idealism in a manner that is reminiscent of, but carefully counterposed to, the representatives of transcendental Thomism, the brainchild of a number of mid- and later twentieth-century Catholic writers. It may be significant that the Thomists that Balthasar most admired were all laymen (the name of the existentialist Thomist Etienne Gilson needs to be added here), whereas those who embodied both the "manualist" Thomism that he had been fed and the transcendental Thomism that grew up around him were all Jesuits. (His enthusiasm for one specifically Jesuit Thomist of a peculiar stamp, Erich Przywara, was not to last.) It may also be significant that his only attempt at a book-length study of Thomas was for a Dominican project, the annotated German–Latin *Summa theologiae* of

the province of Teutonia. There is certainly no mileage in regarding
Balthasar as an essentially anti-Scholastic theologian. In introducing
his *Theology of Karl Barth*, he noted how while Catholic theologians
were abandoning Scholasticism, Barth was making his way to it, a
fact which could be a cause only for rejoicing since "it permits us to
speak with Karl Barth within our own theological climate."[4]

The beginnings of his immense corpus were, however, markedly
different from any Thomistic conception. In the light of his study of
Germanistik, which issued in a doctoral thesis on the "eschatological
problem" in modern German literature, self-published in Zurich in
1930,[5] Balthasar had come to see the task of theology as "responding",
on revelation's behalf, to the "cultural situation" of a given time.[6] A
contrasting view of the aim of theology—"*sacra doctrina*", Aquinas
would say—would see it as a setting forth of that revelation that uti-
lises, if also corrects, major philosophical texts. On behalf of Christian
orthodoxy, Saint Thomas' task had been one of coming to terms
with the fuller range of philosophical writings from Aristotle and the
Neoplatonists available in his day, often through the mediation of
the Arabs. In its period, this was a contemporary response—but not to
seismic shifts in culture as represented by a variety of media, especially
among the arts. Thomas was answering a strictly intellectual challenge to a church whose self-understanding was inherited from the
Fathers, a Christianity now called into question by the naturalism—
and also the monism[7]—that pagan philosophy embodied. Thomas
realized the help that such philosophical resources could provide, not
only defensively in rebutting objections to faith but constructively
in articulating the contents of faith—given that individuals do not
have the transparency to divine revelation which that same revelation

---

[4] Hans Urs von Balthasar, *The Theology of Karl Barth: Exposition and Interpretation*, trans.
Edward T. Oakes, S.J. (San Francisco: Communio Books; Ignatius Press, 1992), p. xix.

[5] Hans Urs von Balthasar, *Geschichte des eschatologischen Problems in der modernen deutschen
Literatur* (Zurich: Selbstverlag des Verfassers, 1930).

[6] Paul Silas Peterson, *The Early Hans Urs von Balthasar: Historical Contexts and Intellectual
Formation* (Berlin: De Gruyter, 2015), p. 283.

[7] "The initial affinity which Muslim thinkers felt with this philosophy had to do with its
inherent penchant for resolving all things to one source." David Burrell, C.S.C., "Aquinas's
Appropriation of *Liber de Causis* to Articulate the Creator as Cause-of-Being", in *Contemplating Aquinas: On the Varieties of Interpretation*, ed. Fergus Kerr, O.P. (London: SCM, 2003),
p. 75; see pp. 75–83.

enjoys in the mind of God (and the minds of the blessed). The cool, conceptually sober manner of Thomas was as well-suited to this more strictly philosophical task as the suasive, poetic, or mythopoeic manner of Balthasar was to the latter's more broadly cultural endeavour.[8] Catholics who "feel responsibility for preserving intact the deposit of faith", remarked Balthasar, "must make the strenuous effort it takes to learn the languages of the spirit, and not least the 'modern languages'. If they do not, they will only be able to gesticulate or shrug their shoulders if one of their contemporaries should ask the way, perhaps because the only language they know is 'Medieval-ese'."[9]

The contrast drawn above can be overstated. Balthasar also needed to address philosophical issues, and when doing so can be conceptually rigorous, as is apparent not least from the opening volume of his "theological logic". Conversely, Thomas can be imagistic and rhetorical, as is almost inevitable in any theology that deploys biblical and patristic tropes. I shall return to that matter before this chapter ends under the heading "The style is the man". For the present, the more pressing need is to emphasize how the literary manner of Balthasar, more diffuse and more highly wrought than is theologically customary, was owed not simply to the limited, though also honourable, place he gave to the rational metaphysics and ethics of antiquity. More importantly, it followed from the kind of enterprise on which he was engaged. He sought to wrest the imagination of modern Western people from a post-Christian condition to a neo-Christian—let us call it a New Christendom—condition. This entailed recognizing two things. First, to cite his own words, "the Biblical revelation occurs in the same formal anthropological locus where the mythopoeic imagination designed its images of the eternal."[10] The figural is the natural way for the unique events that constitute the divine self-disclosure in history to be expressed.[11] And

---

[8] There are reflections on Balthasar's combination of "figure and metaphysics" in Anne Carpenter, *Theo-poetics: Hans Urs von Balthasar and the Risk of Art and Being* (Notre Dame, IN: University of Notre Dame Press, 2015).

[9] Von Balthasar, *Theology of Karl Barth*, p. 12.

[10] Hans Urs von Balthasar, *The Glory of the Lord: A Theological Aesthetics*, vol. 1, *Seeing the Form*, trans. Erasmo Leiva-Merikakis (San Francisco: Ignatius Press, 1982), p. 145.

[11] Compare in England the démarche of Austin Farrer, *The Glass of Vision* (Westminster: Dacre Press, 1948).

secondly, philosophy must be allowed its proper orientation towards transcendence, since, as he wrote in the same opening volume of his "theological aesthetics", its "*eros* can be a living principle only so long as it can strive for the unconditionally Ultimate, True, Good, and Beautiful.... [Philosophy] necessarily atrophies into formalism when its power and legitimacy to do this are contested."[12] His overall conclusion ran accordingly, "The self-revelation of God, who is absolute being, can only be the fulfillment of man's entire philosophical-mythological questioning as well."[13] For Cyril O'Regan, Balthasar had correctly identified a "nisus" in modern culture which is at once attracted to mythopoeisis and yet is audaciously rational. From his earliest period as an author, "Balthasar essentially puzzles over why the Romantic, Idealist and nihilistic brew after the Enlightenment had seemed to cement the claims of procedural rationality.... The simple answer is that reason had a dynamic towards vision that could not be restrained, a need for a view of the whole that could not be bought off."[14] The "Trilogy", Balthasar's master-work, "assumes this essentially cultural answer."[15] That Trilogy—and Balthasar's corpus of writings more generally—is addressed to this contemporary situation, presenting Christianity as a totality more comprehensive and satisfying than anything that secular modernity could achieve. This is too different a project from Thomas' to count as a rival to Thomism on the latter's own ground (and, of course, vice versa).

Balthasar, however, did not treat the entire development of Western culture since the thirteenth century as in every respect lamentable—in the way that Catholic neo-mediaevalists, especially in France and England, were sometimes apt to do. From the point of view of ultimate commitments (or "eschatology", in his rather idiosyncratic early use of the term), the cultural development that lay behind German literature might be an accelerating declension from Christian truth. Yet, Balthasar could appreciate how that development had sponsored a fuller affirmation of the finite and the personal. In terms of bringing out the intrinsic value of created realities—not

---

[12] Von Balthasar, *Seeing the Form*, p. 144.

[13] Ibid., p. 145.

[14] Cyril O'Regan, *The Anatomy of Misremembering: Von Balthasar's Response to Philosophical Modernity*, vol. 1, *Hegel* (New York: Crossroad, 2014), p. 150.

[15] Ibid.

least the uniquely personal element in the human creation—the patristic and mediaeval periods, for all their greatness, left something to be desired. That is the message of his programmatic 1939 essay, "Scholastik, Patristik und wir",[16] translated by Edward Oakes for the journal *Communio* (which Balthasar co-founded) as "The Scholastics, the Fathers, and Ourselves".[17] Though Balthasar was a forthright critic of secular modernity, he thought that postmediaeval culture had achieved in some of its representatives a higher, and more appropriate, valuation of the finite realm than anything hitherto—more appropriate, that is, *by the standards of the revealed religion itself.* As he put it, "Supernature has appeared in the form of kenosis, therefore precisely in the form of a divine sanctioning of finitude as such."[18] That explains his positive reaction to elements of the non-Christian authors widely read in the Germanic culture of his day, including the poets Rainer Maria Rilke and Stephan George, the sociologist Georg Simmel, and the philosopher Friedrich Nietzsche. A positive evaluation of the finite, and a search, however ill-conceived, for a form of transcendence that would not abrogate that value might be regarded as the common factor joining together these otherwise disparate figures. To Balthasar's young mind, the key to the past retreat—and the possible future advance—of the Church in culture lay in the loss of the sense of transcendence (retreat) and the discovery of the means whereby to restore that sense of transcendence (advance).

Romano Guardini, Balthasar's teacher in Berlin, gave him a model of just how to incorporate literature into theology. Guardini sought to use both literature and cultural analysis in order to preserve the Christian worldview over against the challenges of humanistic autonomy and radical secularization.[19] Balthasar registered Guardini's

---

[16] Hans Urs von Balthasar, "Scholastik, Patristik und wir", *Theologie der Zeit* 3 (1939): 65–104.

[17] Hans Urs von Balthasar, "The Scholastics, the Fathers, and Ourselves", *Communio* 24 (1997): 347–96.

[18] Hans Urs von Balthasar, *Apokalypse der deutschen Seele: Studien zu einer Lehre von letzten Haltungen, III: Die Vergöttlichung des Todes* (Salzburg: Pustet, 1939), p. 395. I have offered an overview of this, and Balthasar's more minor early writings, in Aidan Nichols, O.P., *Scattering the Seed: A Guide through Balthasar's Early Writings on Philosophy and the Arts* (London: Continuum, 2006).

[19] See the tribute volume: Hans Urs von Balthasar, *Romano Guardini: Reform from the Source* (San Francisco: Ignatius Press, 2010).

rejection of the philosophies of Kant and Hegel as departure points for thought—in Kant, that starting point was inimical to the self-revelation of the object; in Hegel, it was oblivious to the inwardness of living things. He also noted Guardini's hostility to doctrinal pragmatism, citing with approval a dictum of the latter: "Only if the mind desires nothing more than truth does it become capable of doing the right thing."[20] Guardini's higher studies in theology had focussed on the thirteenth-century Franciscan theologian Saint Bonaventure. His doctoral thesis commended Bonaventure's Christocentrism, which Balthasar would go on to make his own. Balthasar learned from Guardini's Bonaventure that Jesus Christ "represents in every relation the mediation of God vis-à-vis the world and the world vis-à-vis God".[21] This insistence marks a difference from Thomas, if not in the substance of *sacra doctrina* then in the structure of the theology in which that substance is presented. It also shows that Balthasar was scarcely averse to every version of "Mediaevalese".

Among his nontheological sources, Balthasar would take inspiration from Simmel's notion of human life as ceaselessly going beyond its own form: not, however, into formlessness, since self-transcendence "always takes on another form".[22] That raised the possibility that moderns might find in the "form" of Jesus Christ, rendered imitable—participable—by the Holy Spirit, the ultimate expression of human aspiration, graciously offered them by the self-revealing Word of God. Not that Simmel, a Jew, found Christianity, though he acknowledged his debt to its belief in personal uniqueness. He had died in 1918, leaving, so Balthasar would report in the first volume of "theological dramatics", a corpus of thought for which God "no longer needs to be 'substantialized', since the absolute resides in life itself".[23] But something could be learned even from this. In the closing pages of *Apokalypse*, Balthasar re-described Simmel's notion of the self-transcending character of human life. He

[20] Ibid., pp. 24–25, with an internal citation of Romano Guardini, *Glaubenserkenntnis: Versuche zur Unterscheidung and Ertiefung* (1949; Freiburg: Herder, 1983), p. 142.

[21] Von Balthasar, *Romano Guardini*, pp. 63–64.

[22] Peterson, *Early Hans Urs von Balthasar*, p. 68.

[23] Hans Urs von Balthasar, *Theo-drama: Theological Dramatic Theory*, vol. 1, *Prolegomena* (San Francisco: Ignatius Press, 1988), p. 623.

wrote of an ascending "eros" in the world, a movement of loving desire, as an effect of the descending love of God which made it possible in the first place. This entire proposal could be considered an existentialist version of Thomas' *desiderium naturale* for God.

Here one unusual source (for a Catholic theologian in the interwar years) could balance another. Simmel's influence had the effect of setting a limit to Balthasar's welcome of the neoorthodox "turn" of Karl Barth—the Protestant dogmatician who was his Swiss contemporary—from theological liberalism to full-blooded acknowledgement of the sovereignty of the divine Word vis-à-vis all human thinking.[24] Barth appears in *Apokalypse* as a sign of the crisis of modern humanism, and its need for the self-revealing Word of God to resolve its aporias. For his part, Balthasar accepted Barth's assertion that the revealed Word trumps all human philosophy—but not his treatment of the latter as potential idolatry. In the words of Paul Silas Peterson, to whom I am indebted for this analysis of the mutually correcting influence on the early Balthasar of Simmel and Barth, "According to Balthasar, much of Barth's antipathy towards the classical Catholic metaphysics was rooted in Barth's negative disposition towards the ascent of humanity in its relative autonomy, the double mystery of transcendence and immanence in loving descent and ascent."[25] Barth's emphasis on creaturely passivity suggested a certain disvaluing of creation, which was precisely *not* the message that Balthasar wanted contemporary Christianity to give. By a Catholic adjustment of Barth's thinking on the God–world relationship, and the interrelation of God and man in grace, Balthasar sought to salvage what he considered of paramount importance in Barth's work: Barth's allowing God to be God and his insistence that all the contents of Christian theology must be focussed on Jesus Christ.[26] The passion and beauty generated by these convictions, as found in Barth's mature writing, reinforced Balthasar's

---

[24] D. Stephen Long describes Balthasar's admiration for a Barth "haunted" by Catholicism, and explains both his book and his chosen title by writing, "Balthasar sought to save Karl Barth, not in the sense that he thought Barth needed salvation, but that his theology needed to be expanded without loss by some essential Catholic teachings and practices that radiated from [the Christological] centre, bringing all of creation into its light". D. Stephen Long, *Saving Karl Barth: Hans Urs von Balthasar's Preoccupation* (Minneapolis, MN: Fortress, 2014), p. 287.

[25] Peterson, *Early Hans Urs von Balthasar*, pp. 236–37.

[26] Von Balthasar, *Theology of Karl Barth*, p. 25.

Guardini-derived Bonaventurian Christocentrism—and, one could add, the theocentrism he had learned in the school of Thomas, since for Aquinas all theology is about God, and other realities in relation to God. Balthasar's writing his book on Barth in the opening years of the 1950s could well be taken as the beginning of what I am calling, in O'Regan's wake, Balthasar's "Bonaventurian-Thomasian axis".

The dialectical relation of Balthasar to Barth will strike Thomists as justified. They too wish to give creaturely reality (including human freedom) its full value while simultaneously emphasizing the ultimate agency of God as creation's Source, with Christ as the Way to God as creation's Goal. Put in terms of theological epistemology, natural reason needs completion, if the intended goal of human life is to be met. Beyond such reason there must be appeal to the "First Truth" in its—in *his*—self-disclosure to Israel, in Christ and for the Church. As Balthasar wrote a generation later in *Love Alone Is Credible*, a summary of the theological aesthetics (or as much of it as was complete by 1963): "This glory does not call into question any philosophical image of God, but rather fulfils these fragmentary images in the radiant mystery of love."[27] He meant by that the divine love revealed as the Trinity through the Incarnation of the Word and the gift of the Holy Spirit. That of course goes beyond the simple existence of a divine Cause for the world—though it would be possible to argue, even on Thomasian principles, that the arguments for the existence of such a "philosophers' God" exemplify *manifestatio*: "a rational clarification of a truth of revelation by means of philosophical arguments".[28] (Even Barth could approve of that.) Balthasar's own conjectures would move on rather different lines, suggesting that "Vatican I's teaching that natural reason suffices 'to know with certainty the one true God as our Creator and Lord through creatures'" might belong to a "domain of truths that genuinely belong to creaturely nature yet do not emerge into the light of consciousness until they are illumined by a ray of the supernatural".[29]

---

[27]Hans Urs von Balthasar, *Love Alone Is Credible*, trans. D.C. Schindler (San Francisco: Ignatius Press, 2004), p. 149.

[28]Rudi A. te Velde, "Understanding the *Scientia* of Faith", in Kerr, *Contemplating Aquinas*, p. 71; see pp. 55–74.

[29]Hans Urs von Balthasar, *Theo-logic: Theological Logical Theory*, vol. 1, *Truth of the World*, trans. Adrian J. Walker (San Francisco: Ignatius Press, 2000), p. 13. The internal citation is from First Vatican Council, Dogmatic Constitution on the Catholic Faith *Dei Filius* (April 24, 1870).

Neither the poets nor Barth would have been on the syllabus of Balthasar's Jesuit study houses in Bavaria and France. But then, as a mature student with a doctorate behind him, he never intended to be restricted to that syllabus. During the time allotted for ordination studies, he read not only the prescribed masters Plato and Aristotle, Augustine, and Thomas—the staples of philosophy and theology in the Catholic tradition—but also, less predictably, the vitalist philosopher Henri Bergson, the philosopher of action Maurice Blondel, and the phenomenologist Martin Heidegger, all of whom were beginning to appear on the radar screen of young Jesuits throughout Western Europe. He read too, in continuity with the inspiration of Thomas himself, the Polish-German Jesuit Erich Przywara, who highlighted for him the importance in Thomas' vision of the "transcendentals", category-crossing qualities such as truth, goodness, and unity.[30] Balthasar would add, as Scholastic metaphysicians sometimes neglected to do, a fourth transcendental: "beauty". Przywara also made much of the celebrated Thomistic "analogy of being", the way created being bears comparison with uncreated being—but only analogically so, for the difference between them utterly exceeds the similarity. Balthasar absorbed Przywara's book on this topic, called, suitably enough, *Analogia entis*; the analogy of being was exceptionally important for Balthasar from this time on.[31] Later he became critical of Przywara in the light of the latter's work as it unfolded, and notably of Przywara's study *Summula*, which, he worried, could lead to "Theopanismus", a mitigated form of pantheism, cancelling out the relative autonomy of the finite.[32] That would be, not least, incompatible with an orthodox Christology for which divine and human being—divine and human natures—are united without separation but also without confusion in the single Person of God the Word.[33] His own highly original employment of the *analogia entis*

[30] Notice in this list the absence of beauty, explained by Jan A. Aertsen, *Medieval Philosophy and the Transcendentals: The Case of Thomas Aquinas* (Leiden: Brill, 1996), p. 337.

[31] Erich Przywara, *Analogia Entis: Metaphysics; Original Structure and Universal Rhythm* (Grand Rapids, MI: Eerdmans, 2014), 231. For more on the importance of analogy in Balthasar, and Przywara's influence on his concept of analogy, see Edward T. Oakes, *The Pattern of Redemption: The Theology of Hans Urs von Balthasar* (London: Bloomsbury, 1997), pp. 15–44.

[32] Erich Przywara, *Summula* (Nuremberg: Glock & Lutz, 1947).

[33] Hans Urs von Balthasar, "Erich Przywara", in *Tendenzen der Theologie im 20: Jahrhundert: Eine Geschichte in Porträts*, ed. Hans Jürgen Schultz (Stuttgart-Berlin: Kreuz-Verlag; Olten-Freiburg: Walter Verlag, 1966), p. 355; see pp. 354–59.

sought to synthesize it with Christology in a manner that aligns it with Bonaventure's theological vision.[34]

Balthasar was also influenced by the literary revival in French Catholicism. In the years 1933 to 1937, he discovered a posse of imaginative writers in France, notably Charles Péguy, Georges Bernanos, and Paul Claudel, the latter of whom taught him how it was possible to be entirely "worldly" (compare the discussion of "finitude" above) and yet obedient to God (compare the emphasis on "transcendence"). These were figures whom he both translated and discussed. Long after his immersion in *Germanistik*, he continued to find literature a stimulating resource for theology, a major symptom of the disparity of projects with that of Aquinas which, at one level, disqualifies comparison between them.

The *renouveau catholique* gave birth in time to the *nouvelle théologie*, which for Balthasar meant in part the historian of mediaeval philosophy Etienne Gilson but, more importantly, his senior confrère Henri de Lubac.[35] The "Leonine" revival of Thomism, with its stress on Thomas the philosopher—philosophy had been the primary concern of Leo XIII's 1879 encyclical *Aeterni Patris*—had an unexpected outcome in Gilson's account of Thomist and Bonaventurian Scholasticism, stressing as that account did the primacy of theology vis-à-vis philosophy.[36] This was what commended Gilsonianism to the masters of the *nouvelle théologie* who detected a distinctly rationalist tone in the discourse of their theological elders. Gilson's influence is especially apparent in Balthasar's opting for *esse*, the "act of existence", as (even) more foundational than "essence", which is how that "act" terminates in things, when writing about Thomas' metaphysical revolution in *The Glory of the Lord*, his theological aesthetics. Balthasar aligned himself with Gilson over against the second Scholasticism summed up in the sixteenth-century figure of Thomas de Vio ("Cajetan"). Balthasar's Thomas is the Thomas of the *actus essendi* (which grants

---

[34] See Junius Johnson, *Christ and Analogy: The Christocentric Metaphysics of Hans Urs von Balthasar* (Minneapolis, MN: Fortress, 2013).

[35] See the tribute volume, Hans Urs von Balthasar, *The Theology of Henri de Lubac* (San Francisco: Ignatius Press, 1991).

[36] Etienne Gilson, *The Christian Philosophy of St. Thomas Aquinas* (London: Gollancz, 1957); Etienne Gilson, *The Christian Philosophy of St. Bonaventure* (London: Sheed and Ward, 1940).

the "primal experience of being"[37]) and the convertibility of the "transcendentals"—goodness, truth, unity, beauty—with being itself. This particular intellectual commitment was lifelong. Balthasar might have echoed Gilson's own words in the latter's book on John Duns Scotus: "When one has passed his life in daily marvelling at the act of being, well before knowing its name, how could one conceive the possibility of breathing in another metaphysical climate?"[38] Balthasar's reservations about the second Scholasticism also extended to transcendental Thomism, which he feared could lead to the reduction of theology to anthropology. The most famous name in transcendental Thomism was Karl Rahner. The two men, who belonged to the same "provincial" institution within the Catholic Church, so long as Balthasar remained a Jesuit, appear to have had little early contact. But their increasing celebrity inevitably meant they knew of each other's work. They retained a mutual respect—tempered by polemic. For Balthasar, Rahnerianism, if not Rahner, was a threat to a genuinely theocentric theology (the human "transcendental subject", borrowed from Johann Gottlieb Fichte, was too overwhelming of the object, including the divinely self-revelatory Object); for Rahner, Balthasar (with his insistence on salvation in the confessed name of Christ, not "anonymous Christianity", and his dramatically counterposed trinitarian Persons) was a proponent of remythologisation.[39]

Above all, however, *nouvelle théologie* meant a recall to the Church Fathers. Like Thomas, Balthasar cites the texts of the Fathers as authorities second only to Scripture—as of course any Catholic theologian should. Only towards the end of Balthasar's lifetime did the general run of Thomistic writers register how similarly rich was Aquinas' patristic documentation,[40] though much of the evidence had been

[37] Larry S. Chapp, "The Primal Experience of Being in the Thought of Hans Urs von Balthasar: A Response to Theodore Kepes, Jr.", *Philosophy and Theology* 20, no. 1/2 (2008): 291–305.

[38] Etienne Gilson, *Jean Duns Scot: Introduction à ses positions fondamentales* (Paris: Vrin, 1952), p. 667.

[39] For a German Jesuit's more pacific view of their differences, see Werner Löser, *Geschenkte Wahrheit: Annäherungen an das Werk Hans Urs von Balthasars* (Würzburg: Echter, 2015), pp. 29–49.

[40] See, for instance, the overview in Leo Elders, "Thomas Aquinas and the Fathers of the Church", in *The Reception of the Church Fathers in the West: From the Carolingians to the Maurists*, ed. Irena Backus (Leiden: Brill, 1997), 1:337–66.

known for some while.[41] In the judgment of de Lubac, whose own patristic reading challenged and inspired him, Balthasar so appropriated the mentality of the Fathers as to be in serious danger of joining their number as one untimely born.

> No matter what subject he is treating, and even if he never mentions any of their names, it is very clear that von Balthasar was formed in the school of the Fathers of the Church. With many of them he is on more than familiar terms; he has in many ways become almost like them. For all that, he is no slavish admirer: he recognizes the weaknesses of each and the inevitable limitations that result from the age in which each lived. With his customary frankness he criticizes even those he admires and loves most. But their vision has become his own.[42]

And de Lubac went on to specify the elected affinities.

> It is principally to them that he owes his profound appreciation of the Christian attitude before the [biblical] Word of God. He owes them too that vibrant feeling of wonder and adoration before the "nuptial mystery" and the "marvelous reciprocation of contraries" realized by the Incarnation of the Word. He is indebted to them for that sense of greater universality (in the strictest orthodoxy) because "it would appear at first that the infinite richness of God contracts and centers in a single point, the humanity of Jesus Christ ... but this unity reveals itself as capable of integrating everything."[43]

This rhythm of reflection that combines confidence in received truth with a wide-ranging scope in investigation is also patristic. It is in spontaneous imitation of the Fathers that in him "the crystal of thought takes fire in the interior and becomes a mystical life."[44]

In that list, de Lubac was quite correct to draw attention first to Balthasar's patristically shaped attitude to Scripture. While making use of twentieth-century historical-critical scholarship, he was more concerned to read the Bible holistically, meaning by that both to read the

[41] Gustave Bardy, "Sur les sources patristiques grecques de saint Thomas", *Revue des sciences philosophiques et théologiques* 12 (1923): 493–502; Godefrid Geenen, O.P., "Saint Thomas et les Pères", *Dictionnaire de théologie catholique* XV.1 (Paris: Letouzey et Ané, 1946), cols. 738–61.

[42] Henri de Lubac, "A Witness of Christ in the Church: Hans Urs von Balthasar", in *The Church: Paradox and Mystery* (Shannon, IE: Ecclesia Press, 1969), p. 114; see pp. 103–21.

[43] Ibid.

[44] Cited in ibid., pp. 114–15.

contents of the canon seen as a whole and also to read each portion of Scripture in terms of not only the literal sense of the text but its wider spiritual resonances.[45] Exactly the same could be said of Aquinas' biblical exegesis, too, though in Thomas' case the advantages of modern knowledge of the historical background to a biblical author's text were not available. Compensation was made in the acuity with which Thomas analysed the thought structure of the documents—something particularly clear in his reading of the Pauline epistles.[46] While agreeing that it was incumbent on theologians to "draw for dogmatics whatever conclusions are possible from the new findings [of historical study of the Bible]",[47] Balthasar actually went further than Thomas in his privileging of the spiritual sense. He had drunk deep at the fountain that is Origen's exegesis.[48] He wrote, "The *fruitio* of the *sensus spiritualis* is ... the central act of theology as a science."[49] He was not bothered by the charge of dilettantism; all the influential theologies have been, by modern academic standards, the work of amateurs—the word of course means "lovers".[50] Better still, an "infused habit" of *scientia* as gift of the Holy Spirit should be combined with the "acquired habit" of theological knowledge. "The work of Aquinas, and also that of Anselm, Bonaventure, and Albert the Great, radiates the beauty of a human power of shaping and structuring which has been supernaturally in-formed in this manner."[51]

The distinctive influence of the *nouvelle théologie* may be seen in the way that in Balthasar's patristic studies—notably those of Gregory of

---

[45] See, for instance, Hans Urs von Balthasar, *Theo-drama: Theological Dramatic Theory*, vol. 2, *Dramatis Personae: Man in God*, trans. Graham Harrison (San Francisco: Ignatius Press, 1990), pp. 113–14.

[46] The revival of interest in Thomas as exegete seems to be the work of Henri de Lubac, who devoted a section to Aquinas in *Exégèse médiévale: Les quatre sens de l'Ecriture* (Paris: Editions Montaigne, 1964), II/2, pp. 263–302. For an overview of how Thomas used the Bible, see Wilhelmus G. B. M. Valkenburg, *Words of the Living God: Place and Function of Holy Scripture in the Theology of St. Thomas Aquinas* (Louvain: Peeters, 1999); for an introduction to his comments on individual books, see Thomas Weinandy, Daniel Keating, and John Yocum, eds., *Aquinas on Scripture: An Introduction to His Biblical Commentaries* (London and New York: T&T Clark, 2005).

[47] Von Balthasar, *Seeing the Form*, p. 76.

[48] Hans Urs von Balthasar, ed., *Origen: Spirit and Fire; A Thematic Anthology of His Writings* (Washington, DC: Catholic University of America Press, 1984).

[49] Von Balthasar, *Seeing the Form*, p. 76.

[50] Ibid., p. 77.

[51] Ibid., p. 78.

Nyssa and Maximus the Confessor,[52] but also the anthologies, especially those of Irenaeus and Origen[53]—Balthasar reads the Fathers
very much from the setting of his own evangelical strategies, tailored
as these were to modernity's cultural situation. In Peterson's words,
he drew the Fathers into "a paradigm which is harmonious and sup-
portive of themes from modern philosophy" such as existentialism
and personalism.[54] Thus, for example, from the 1940s onwards, he
saw Maximus, the Aquinas of the Byzantine tradition, as furnishing *avant la lettre* an answer to Hegel, a "philosophical alternative to
the bleeding of the concrete and the multiple".[55] Thus was finitude
affirmed once more.

The *renouveau catholique* in France had a lively interest in mystical
and existential subjectivity, expressed not least in the two Carmelite women mystics, Saint Elizabeth of the Trinity, from Dijon, and
Saint Thérèse of Lisieux, about whom Balthasar wrote book-length
accounts.[56] On his return to Switzerland after priestly ordination
and a spell as an editorial assistant at the Munich-based Jesuit peri-
odical *Stimmen der Zeit*, Balthasar acquired, so to speak, his very
own mystic, in the shape of a Swiss Protestant convert he had
made at the university chaplaincy in Basel. This was Adrienne von
Speyr.[57] Among recipients of mystical graces, she was in his eyes the
most important figure given to the Church in the twentieth century. As herself (with his assistance) the interpreter of those graces,
he considered her a mystical theologian *sans pareil* whose material
simply cries out for incorporation into the body of Catholic doctrinal reflection. She was a hidden influence as early as 1944 in his

[52] Hans Urs von Balthasar, *Presence and Thought: Essay on the Religious Philosophy of Gregory of Nyssa* (San Francisco: Ignatius Press, 1995); Hans Urs von Balthasar, *Cosmic Liturgy: The Universe according to Maximus the Confessor* (San Francisco: Ignatius Press, 2013).

[53] Hans Urs von Balthasar, *The Scandal of the Incarnation: Irenaeus against the Heresies* (San Francisco: Ignatius Press, 1990); von Balthasar, *Origen*. For Balthasar's Origen, also see *Parole et mystère chez Origène* (1957; Geneva: Ad Solem, 1998), turned into a small book from the original article format of 1936–1937.

[54] Peterson, *Early Hans Urs von Balthasar*, p. 323.

[55] O'Regan, *Hegel*, p. 124.

[56] Hans Urs von Balthasar, *Thérèse of Lisieux: A Story of a Mission* (London: Sheed and Ward, 1953); Hans Urs von Balthasar, *Elizabeth of Dijon* (London: Harvill Press, 1956).

[57] Hans Urs von Balthasar, *First Glance at Adrienne von Speyr* (San Francisco: Ignatius Press, 1981).

first work of spirituality,[58] but Balthasar's later theological work is not fully explicable without some grasp of her mystical "showings", especially the "Pascha experiences" which had their centre in her yearly reliving of the descent of Christ into hell. In the final volume of the theological dramatics, the citations from her considerable output are certainly lavish. Though Thomas may cite the mystical Doctors of the Order of Citeaux, notably Saint Bernard of Clairvaux, living as they had in the century before his own, there is nothing in Aquinas comparable to this. What might a Thomist make of it? I shall defer an answer until we have looked at Balthasar's own interpretation of Thomas' treatise on special charismatic graces in the *Summa theologiae*, a task that I pursue in the penultimate chapter of this book.

After the Second World War, Balthasar published *Wahrheit*, his fundamental metaphysics.[59] This is in effect an extended meditation on the content of Thomas' *De Veritate*, the "Disputed Questions on Truth". Republished as "Truth of the World", the first volume of the theological logic, the best part of half a century later, *Wahrheit der Welt* is the primary reason for calling Balthasar a philosophical theologian in the Thomist tradition. Would he have accepted the sobriquet "Thomist"? He would, if it were understood in the sense ascribed to the distinguished American Neo-Thomist William Norris Clarke by the historian of twentieth-century Thomisms Gerald McCool: "For [Norris Clarke], to be a Thomist is not to be a member of a school; it is to philosophize freely and responsibly in the light of a great tradition."[60] For the Balthasar of the early period (but not by the time of the second and third volumes of the theological logic), Thomas is essentially a philosopher. As has been noted by an authoritative observer, "Reducing Aquinas to his philosophy began

[58] Hans Urs von Balthasar, *The Grain of Wheat: Aphorisms* (San Francisco: Ignatius Press, 1995).

[59] Hans Urs von Balthasar, *Wahrheit: Wahrheit der Welt* (Einsiedeln: Benzinger, 1947).

[60] Gerald A. McCool, S.J., "An Alert and Independent Thomist: William Norris Clarke, S.J.", in *The Universe as Journey: Conversations with W. Norris Clarke, S.J.* (New York: Fordham University Press, 1988), p. 20; see pp. 13–48. For the wider context, see Gerald A. McCool, S.J., *Catholic Theology in the Nineteenth Century: The Quest for a Unitary Method* (New York: Seabury, 1977); Gerald A. McCool, S.J., *From Unity to Pluralism: The Internal Evolution of Thomism* (New York: Fordham University Press, 1989).

as early as the fourteenth century and has exercised an influence down
to the present day."[61] Before the appearance of Marie-Dominique
Chenu's *Introduction a l'étude de saint Thomas d'Aquin* in 1950 it might
even be thought a pardonable mistake.[62] Though Balthasar only had
glimmerings of the overall scheme at the time, *Wahrheit: Wahrheit der
Welt* in its Thomist ontology, creatively expanded to do fuller justice
to the concrete, the finite, the personal, was in fact the beginning of
his masterwork, the Trilogy, which it would take him the rest of his
life to complete.

Keen to found with von Speyr a "secular institute" for worldly
monastics, consecrated celibates otherwise living a professional life
in the world, Balthasar would be obliged to leave the Jesuit Society while retaining his personal commitment to the charism of Saint
Ignatius. He would eventually find in the Diocese of Chur, among
whose clergy he was enrolled, a sacerdotal rooting; at Einsiedeln, in
the shadow of another Benedictine abbey, a publishing house for his
writings (as well as those of many other figures whose "missions" in
the Church he admired); in Basel, a continuing home for himself,
even after Adrienne's death. It would become, after his own demise,
the seat of the "Balthasar Archives".

At the second attempt, Pope Saint John Paul II succeeded in get-
ting him to accept a cardinal's hat. He died three days before it should
have been conferred—the date of the consistory was June 29, 1988—
and was buried in the family vault in the precincts of the Catholic
cathedral at Lucerne. Joseph Ratzinger, the future Pope Benedict
XVI, preached the encomium. It had not been an eventful life, but
one where life was absorbed into theological work. Much the same
could be said of Thomas Aquinas.

---

[61] Otto-Hermann Pesch, "Aquinas and Contemporary Theology", in Kerr, *Contemplating
Aquinas*, p. 191, footnote 11; see pp. 185–216. Pesch had summarised the history of Thomism
in "Thomismus: Geschichtliche Durchblick", in *Lexikon für Theologie und Kirche*, vol. 10,
Teufel bis Zypem, ed. Michael Buchberger, Joseph Hofer, and Karl Rahner (Freiburg: Herder,
1965), pp. 157–59.

[62] Marie-Dominique Chenu, O.P., *Introduction a l'étude de saint Thomas d'Aquin* (Paris: Cerf,
1950). The "mistake" was never entirely pardonable, since Aquinas' texts make plain that he
"never thought of himself as a philosopher. Philosophers, *philosophi*, in his vocabulary, are
always the sages and thinkers of Antiquity." Fergus Kerr, foreword to *Aquinas on Doctrine:
A Critical Introduction*, ed. Thomas Weinandy, Daniel Keating, and John Yocum (London and
New York: T&T Clark, 2004), p. x.

The style is the man

Taken overall, it might be thought that Balthasar's way of executing his programme was so different in style from Thomas' that, were it not for the circumstances in which orthodox Catholic theology finds itself in the post-conciliar Church (i.e., the Church after Vatican II), seeking to bring them together would be a highly unnatural proceeding. But this would be to forget not only the different registers that Thomas can himself employ in his minor works, but also the variety of ways in which the *Summa theologiae* itself has been seen in recent scholarship. Just as there is a Scholasticism in the Christian East found at the hands of writers who could also be homiletic rhetoricians and liturgical poets,[63] so in Thomas, the classical theologian of the Latin West, there are openings to the status of a spiritual or sapiential theologian, or even a "theologian-poet".

This new wave starts most decisively with the Fribourg Dominican Jean-Pierre Torrell, for whom Thomas' theology transmits a spirituality. It presents claims of holiness and wisdom that configure in a distinctive manner the virtues of faith, hope, and charity.[64] From a literary point of view, Thomas by no means disdains the use of rhetoric.[65] Whereas the *quaestio* form in the *Summa* derives from canon law, the *trivium*—the initial disciplines of the "liberal arts" (grammar, dialectic, rhetoric)—furnished him with elements of rhetoric for use in philosophy, especially in ethics. In the wake of Torrell's study, others have argued that, building on Augustine, for whom rhetoric is an instrument of *manuductio* (literally "leading", but in this context a participative, developmental process of knowing), Thomas' treatment of such "manuduction" amounts to "performative theosis".[66] For the

[63] Marcus Plested, *Orthodox Readings of Aquinas* (Oxford: Oxford University Press, 2012), pp. 45–57; I have in mind especially John Damascene, the Scholastic nature of whose formal theological writing Plested reaffirms over against the denial that this is so in Andrew Louth, *St. John Damascene: Tradition and Originality in Byzantine Theology* (Oxford: Oxford University Press, 2004), p. 37.

[64] Jean-Pierre Torrell, O.P., *Saint Thomas Aquinas*, vol. 2, *Spiritual Master*, trans. Robert Royal (Washington, DC: Catholic University of America Press, 2003).

[65] Mark D. Jordan, *Ordering Wisdom: The Hierarchy of Philosophical Discourses in Aquinas* (Notre Dame, IN: University of Notre Dame Press, 1986).

[66] Peter Candler, *Theology, Rhetoric and Manuduction or Reading Scripture Together on the Path to God* (Grand Rapids, MI: Eerdmans, 2006).

Canadian Jesuit Gilles Mongeau, Thomas' overall project, not least in the *Summa theologiae*, is to offer a spiritual pedagogy equipping Christians, above all those who are to preach, for lifelong growth in wisdom.[67] This does not seem so implausible if it is remembered that the ancient philosophy on which Aquinas drew was often framed as a spiritual exercise integral to a way of life.[68] Finally, the Flemish Dominican Servais Pinckaers has shown how, for Thomas, speculation and contemplation are cognate terms.[69] *Sacra doctrina* in Thomas is knowledge necessary for salvation, going beyond theology in the strict sense. It is a subalternated science which takes its principles from God's own self-knowledge, as shared by the blessed in heaven. Or put otherwise, in terms that make possible a comparison of Thomas with Karl Barth, it is rooted in the highest wisdom because it derives from God's own truth as revealed in Christ.[70]

Could there be said to be aesthetic and dramatic—and not simply logical—dimensions of Thomas' text? The French Dominican Olivier-Thomas Venard claims there are indeed, in his treatment of Aquinas as "poet- theologian";[71] for while *determinatio* requires precision based on formality, by contrast "analogicity"—and on one view of the matter, analogies are higher-order metaphors, since all our words, even perfection words, are primarily words for creatures—makes possible an ascent to mysteries. Moreover, the opening question of the *Summa theologiae* alerts us to the twin role of argument and metaphor, two methods in the teaching of *sacra doctrina*, each with revelatory warrant. Thus we can expect to find in the "*Summa theologiae* not only causal explanations but also examples, comparisons, oppositions, images, proportional relationships, analogies, and more".[72]

[67] Gilles Mongeau, *Embracing Wisdom: The* Summa theologiae *as Spiritual Pedagogy* (Toronto: Pontifical Institute of Mediaeval Studies, 2015); I am indebted for the references in notes 33–38.

[68] Pierre Hadot, *Philosophy as a Way of Life* (Chicago: University of Chicago Press, 1995).

[69] Servais Pinckaers, O.P., "Recherche de la signification véritable du terme 'speculatif'", *Nouvelle Revue Théologique* 81, no. 17 (1959): 673–95.

[70] Eugene Rogers, *Thomas Aquinas and Karl Barth: Sacred Doctrine and the Natural Knowledge of God* (Notre Dame, IN: University of Notre Dame Press, 1995).

[71] Olivier-Thomas Venard, *Thomas d'Aquin, Poète théologien*, I-II (Geneva: Ad Solem, 2003–2004).

[72] Mongeau, *Embracing Wisdom*, p. 92.

Metaphor may seem very much second-best to the concept for a Thomist author, but not all Neo-Thomists have taken that view. Norris Clarke's explanation runs as follows, basing itself on that key idea of Thomasian—and notably Gilsonian—ontology, the "act of existence".

There is no radical split even between matter and spirit, because both are in the last analysis only different degrees or modalities of the common energy, or force-filled presence, of existence itself. For if the act of existence is the radical underlying ground and bond of all being and each real being is, to the degree that it exists, in some way an image, however imperfect, of the ultimate Pure Act of Existence, then every single being, no matter how lowly in the material domain or lofty in the spiritual, must somehow have deep hidden similitudes and affinities with every other. Here is the underlying metaphysical grounding of metaphor in poetry, literature, and indeed all the arts. For if psyche mirrors nature and nature mirrors psyche, each in its own way, then comparison with either can illuminate the other. Thus "a smiling field" illuminates nature by psyche, whereas "a stormy face" illuminates psyche by nature. This mutual mirroring of psyche and nature seems to me the very heart of metaphor.[73]

While it may be going too far to claim with Venard that Thomas seeks to ground a symbolism reminiscent of Saint Bonaventure in a world of *esse*-derived substances—that really would bring Aquinas close to Balthasar![74]—nevertheless, the language of "fittingness" or "appropriateness" (*convenientia*) in which Thomas frames nondemonstrative arguments is fundamentally aesthetic in its force, hence the actual comparison with Balthasar attempted by the Toulouse Dominican Gilbert Narcisse.[75] In Mongeau's judgment,

Gilbert Narcisse's masterful study has shown that these arguments from fittingness are not merely descriptive but are ways of expressing the aesthetic-dramatic intelligibility of the relations between certain

---

[73] W. Norris Clarke, S.J., "Metaphysical Reflections", in McCool, *Universe as Journey*, pp. 66–67; see pp. 49–92.

[74] Venard, *Thomas d'Aquin*, 1:179.

[75] Gilbert Narcisse, *Les raisons de Dieu: Arguments de convenance et esthétique théologique selon saint Thomas d'Aquin et Hans Urs von Balthasar* (Fribourg: Editions universitaires, 1997).

mysteries.... As Aquinas points out in articles 9 and 10 of the first question [of the *Summa theologiae*'s *Prima Pars*], while such forms of "argumentation" may be weak, when they are rooted in human wisdom, as part of God's *manuductio* in divine revelation, they are supremely effective.[76]

Looking now briefly at the other great *Summa*, Thomas Hibbs found that the overall logic of the *Summa contra gentiles* is "narrative" in the sense of combining causal explanation with a "divine comedy" framework drawn from the biblical narrative; seeming leaps of meaning reflect the contingent nature of creation and Providence.[77] "Narrative" might suggest "epic", which is precisely what Balthasar says he is *not* offering in the theological dramatics, but "divine comedy" is undoubtedly grist to his mill. And if there is here as yet no reference to Christology—and Balthasar is clear, following Barth, that Christology must be the glowing centre of Christian theology, whereas the matter is disputed for Aquinas, owing to the "displacement" of Christ to the final third part of the *Summa theologiae*—nonetheless Mongeau, for his part, is convinced that Christology is in fact the climax of Thomas' spiritual pedagogy in that work.[78] He rallies to the claim of Jean-Marc Laporte that in the *Tertia Pars* a Christological "cone" constitutes the climax of the *Summa theologiae* such that when the work is viewed from "above", Christology is seen to be central, with wider or more preliminary considerations surrounding the "cone" in the form of concentric circles.[79] But of all recent commentators on Thomas' masterwork, Mark Jordan comes closest to the spirit of Balthasar's overall *oeuvre* when he writes, "The *Summa* is read whole when it is enacted as a single theological teaching, with morals at its centre and the Passion of Christ as its driving force, before a community committed to sanctification through mission, with the consolations of sacraments and liturgy, in the illumination of contemplative prayer."[80]

[76] Mongeau, *Embracing Wisdom*, p. 92.

[77] Thomas Hibbs, *Dialectic and Narrative in Aquinas: An Interpretation of the* Summa contra gentiles (Notre Dame, IN: University of Notre Dame Press, 1995).

[78] Mongeau, *Embracing Wisdom*, p. 117.

[79] Jean-Marc Laporte, "Christ in Aquinas' *Summa theologiae*: Peripheral or Pervasive?", *The Thomist* 67 (2003): 221–48.

[80] Mark D. Jordan, "The *Summa*'s Reform of Moral Teaching—and Its Failures", in Kerr, *Contemplating Aquinas*, p. 53; see pp. 41–54.

At the very least, these comments bring Thomas' project, considered in its most formal characteristics, sufficiently close to Balthasar's for comparison not to be thought altogether odd between a strict Scholastic thinker and a modern theologian in the Germanophone literary tradition.

2

The Trilogy: Theological Aesthetics

Though I have suggested that Balthasar's Trilogy is comparable with Aquinas' *Summa theologiae*, the remark was meant to single out the central work in their corpus—in Thomas' case, at least so far as posterity is concerned.[1] The great *Summa* and the Trilogy are generally regarded as preeminent in the two bodies of writing by those equipped to judge. Yet the structure of the two works (or sets of works) could hardly be more dissimilar. As Thomas explains in the Prologue to the *Summa*, his aim has been pedagogical clarity—a carefully constructed introduction to theology for those whose task it was to teach "beginners" in the discipline. Any attempt to use Balthasar's Trilogy for that purpose would surely be doomed to failure. There was at one time, or so I have heard, a proposal, emanating from the late Bishop Eugenio Correcco of Lugano, who, in the pontificate of John Paul II, reerected the faculty of Catholic theology there, to condense Balthasar's writings—which certainly cover every area of theological doctrine—into a manual for seminarians. If so, it was soon abandoned. That is unsurprising—but not because the Trilogy (surely the principal source for such a venture) is rambling and chaotic. Rather, in its three parts—the theological aesthetics, theological dramatics, and theological logic—Balthasar makes three quite distinct "raids" (to borrow a word from T. S. Eliot's *Four Quartets*) on the content of divine revelation.[2] The aesthetics considers that revelation

---

[1] The title, of course, suggests a crowning work of summation, but it may not be original; see Angelus Walz, O.P., "De genuine titulo *Summae theologiae*", *Angelicum* 18 (1941): 142–51.

[2] A fuller treatment of the Trilogy is found in Aidan Nichols, O.P., *The Word Has Been Abroad: A Guide through Balthasar's Aesthetics* (Edinburgh: T&T Clark, 1998); Aidan Nichols, O.P., *No Bloodless Myth: A Guide through Balthasar's Dramatics* (Edinburgh: T&T Clark, 2000); Aidan Nichols, O.P., *Say It Is Pentecost: A Guide through Balthasar's Logic* (Edinburgh: T&T Clark, 2001); a shorter "guide" is Aidan Nichols, O.P., *A Key to Balthasar: Hans Urs von Balthasar on Beauty, Goodness, and Truth* (London: Darton, Longman and Todd, 2011).

as beautiful; the dramatics looks at it as good; the logic scans it as
true. Naturally, there are interconnexions. In Balthasar's message, just
as these three transcendental characterizations of being are mutually
implicative one of another, so aesthetics, dramatics, and logic likewise
coinhere. As laid out in the Trilogy, these three theological modes
build up an overall picture of what Christian revelation is like. "Thus
the *pulchrum*, with which Balthasar opens his trilogy, is the primordial
appearing of love's gratuity, which, as such, contains both the good
(the beautiful is an appearing of *gratuity*) and the true (the beautiful
is an *appearing* of gratuity, which therefore appeals to *logos*)."[3] No
other formal structure is offered than this, unlike with the *Summa*,
where pedagogical concerns have been uppermost—though it must
also be said that no single account of the deep structure of Thomas'
masterwork has won universal scholarly assent.[4] Be that as it may, to
make of Balthasar's conception a manual, suited to the teaching of
"beginners", is scarcely a feasible undertaking.

Edward Oakes, who wrote the best introduction to Balthasar's
theology in English,[5] took the opportunity, on the centenary of
Balthasar's birth, to explain what it was that drew him to his subject.

> A Jesuit teacher of mine mentioned that Balthasar was at that time
> (in the 1970's) working on a massive theological trilogy ... that
> would try to reverse the direction of Immanuel Kant's three famous
> critiques, the *Critique of Pure Reason*, the *Critique of Practical Reason*
> and the *Critique of [Aesthetic] Judgment*. Kant, following in the wake
> of René Descartes, had begun by questioning the human faculties of
> knowing. Only after he had solved the problem to his satisfaction
> did he then go on to discuss ethics. Finally, almost as a kind of after-
> thought, he considered the question of the perception of beauty,
> which he tended to subsume under the concept of the "sublime,"
> that subspecies of beauty that leads to disinterested, unengaged
> contemplation. . . .

---

[3] Adrian J. Walker, "Love Alone: Hans Urs von Balthasar as a Master of Theological
Renewal", *Communio* 32 (2005): 532, footnote 28; see pp. 517–40.

[4] See, for instance, Michel Corbin, *Le chemin de la théologie chez Thomas d'Aquin* (Paris:
Beauchesne, 1974); Ghislain Lafont, O.S.B., *Structures et méthode dans la Somme théologique de
S. Thomas d'Aquin* (Paris: Desclée de Brouwer, 1961).

[5] Edward T. Oakes, *The Pattern of Redemption: The Theology of Hans Urs von Balthasar* (London: Bloomsbury, 1997).

Balthasar was deliberately trying to reverse that direction because of his realization that if Christians do not at first *perceive*, prior to all apologetic arguments, the beauty of revelation, then they will not then be drawn out of themselves to give a proper assent to God's revelation in Christ.[6]

And Oakes gave some hint, at least, of how Balthasar would move on from the beautiful to the good and the true.

That response is what constitutes Christian ethics in the real sense of the word, which deals primarily with our initial yes or no to God's call; only secondarily does it deal with the precepts of the moral law. Finally, only in a life of Christian discipleship will we ever come to see the inherent plausibility of the truth claims of revelation. In other words, we cannot render a judgment on the truth of revelation outside of a prior obedience to Christ's call, which will never come (at least in any lasting sense) until we first are drawn out of ourselves by the beauty of the life of Christ.[7]

This citation neatly introduces the three constituent parts of the Trilogy, dealing as these do with the beautiful, the good, and the true—in that sequence. They will be the object of my three succeeding chapters.

What is the "beautiful"?

Like the lay Thomist philosopher-theologian Jacques Maritain in *Art et scolastique*, the beautiful for Balthasar is as it were the "splendor of truth": *splendor veri*.[8] Maritain made the innovative suggestion, on behalf of the Scholastics, that the sometimes neglected transcendental, beauty, is actually the splendor of all the other transcendentals

---

[6]Edward T. Oakes, "What I Learned about Prayer from Hans Urs von Balthasar", *America: The Jesuit Review*, August 1, 2005, https://www.americamagazine.org/faith/2005/08/01/what-i-learned-about-prayer-hans-urs-von-Balthasar.

[7]Ibid.

[8]Jacques Maritain, *Art et scolastique*, 2nd ed. (Paris: Louis Rouart, 1927), p. 38.

united.[9] In the aesthetics, Balthasar regards this transcendental as not only the splendor, but also the fulcrum of the others. Without it, truth tends to become mere fact, goodness utility. In a retrospective on patristic and mediaeval wisdom, Balthasar asked,

> May we not think of the beautiful as one of the transcendental attributes of Being as such, and thereby ascribe to the beautiful the same range of application and the same inwardly analogous form that we ascribe to the one, the true, the good? The traditional theology of the Church Fathers and even that of the High Scholastics did this unhesitatingly, prompted by a double impulse. First, they possessed a theology of creation which, likewise unhesitatingly, attributed creation's aesthetic values *eminenter* to the creating principle itself. Second, they had a theology of redemption and of creation's perfecting which ascribed to God's highest work the eminent sum of all of creation's values, particularly as concerns the eschatological form of God's work. But this form already begins with the Lord's Resurrection, which for its part pours out its "sublime splendor" (*kabod, doxa, gloria*) over the whole sphere of the Church and of the bestowal of grace.[10]

The main sources of Balthasar's aesthetics of the beautiful "form" are twofold. The first is the mediaeval aesthetics of beauty as radiant form, form that is light-bringing—not simply the structured intelligibility which the word "form" by itself denotes in the context of Platonic and Aristotelian philosophy, but form that is positively splendid, thanks to the goodness and truth it embodies. Thomas had ascribed to beauty three principal characteristics: "integrity", a fullness of intelligibility, which is pertinent to truth; "proportion" or "consonance", denoting a set of ordered relations within the object, and this is pertinent to goodness; and "clarity", an irradiation of splendor. These qualities together make the beautiful "that which, seen, pleases", a happening which typically takes place through form.[11] Balthasar comments, "The form as it appears to us is beautiful only

[9] Ibid., p. 266.

[10] Hans Urs von Balthasar, *The Glory of the Lord: A Theological Aesthetics*, vol. 1, *Seeing the Form* (San Francisco: Ignatius Press, 1982), p. 38.

[11] Thomas Aquinas, *Summa theologiae*, Ia, q. 5, a. 4 ad 1. Umberto Eco, *The Aesthetics of Aquinas* (Boston: Harvard University Press, 1988).

because the delight that it arouses in us is founded upon the fact that, in it, the truth and goodness of the depths of reality itself are manifested and bestowed, and this manifestation and bestowal reveal themselves as being something infinitely and exhaustively valuable and fascinating."[12]

The other principal source for Balthasar's notion of significant form, derived this time from his many-sided investigations of *Germanistik*, is the late eighteenth-, early nineteenth-century Johann Wolfgang von Goethe, a figure poised between Classicism and Romanticism, for whom "form", *Gestalt*, always includes an import (*Gehalt*) that goes beyond even its content (*Inhalt*). That suggests the way a "form" can open fresh dimensions, can direct the gaze to new horizons. Balthasar once remarked that among the philosophers Goethe had played for him the same sort of basic inspiration which—he considered—the founder of the "critical philosophy", Kant, or the first of the German Idealists, Fichte, had played for Karl Rahner, who was Balthasar's principal rival as the twentieth century's outstanding Catholic theologian.[13]

When Balthasar remarks that form at its highest combines "Classical perfection" with "Romantic boundlessness", he surely has Goethe at the back of his mind.[14]

Balthasar regularly thinks of such form as the ingathering of materials that are then unified in a person who pours them out again, transformed, as the expression of himself.[15] This is in effect a personalistic or, if one prefers, "existentialist" version of the "hylomorphism" or matter-form unity of Aquinas' cosmology and anthropology. The free spirit belongs essentially with its "keyboard", the body, and manifests its interiority there in sensuous fashion.[16] That is a pertinent point if the "form" in which Balthasar will be supremely interested is that of the Person of Jesus Christ.

Furthermore, the self-same concept can also be placed in analogous fashion on the level of Being itself, the level of *esse*, of the most

---

[12] Von Balthasar, *Seeing the Form*, p. 118.
[13] Michael Albus, "Geist und Feuer: Ein Gespräch mit Hans Urs von Balthasar", *Herder-Korrespondenz* 30 (1976): 72–82.
[14] Von Balthasar, *Seeing the Form*, p. 118.
[15] Ibid., p. 20.
[16] Ibid., p. 21.

fundamental ontology, which, thanks precisely to analogy, spans the
abyssal distance between God and the world. Uncreated Being can
find its expression in form through taking up and giving out again the
resources of created being.[17]

The form of Christ

The alerted reader of the opening volume of *The Glory of the Lord*
may perhaps sense already that what these opening pages of the
theological aesthetics are building up to is an account of the "shape"
of the life, death, and Resurrection of Christ considered as the incarnate divine Word, who in his actions and words renders coherent
the diverse elements of Old Testament revelation and in so doing
transforms those elements into something greater: the "new" and
everlasting "covenant" of the Gospel revelation (Mt 26:28). Thus
the world is illuminated by a fresh, and definitive, disclosure of
God. The final two volumes of the aesthetics, on the Old Covenant
and New Covenant, respectively, will seek to lay out along these
lines a novel version of the "argument from prophecy": the universal apologia for Christianity in patristic and mediaeval writers,
including, of course, Thomas.[18]

More widely—and taking in now not just history but the entire
cosmos—a form that "unites God and man in an unimaginable intimacy" would rightly deserve to be called "primal".[19] The chief content of dogmatic theology is the "wonderful exchange and marriage"
between God and mankind in "Christ as Head and Body".[20] And
precisely as primal—just because it is so archetypal—it can also be
reflected in imaging forms, the lives of those the Church of Jesus
Christ calls "the saints". For this reason, Balthasar will place considerable emphasis on the "authority" of the saints for Christian theology

[17] Ibid., p. 29.
[18] Hans Urs von Balthasar, *The Glory of the Lord: A Theological Aesthetics*, vol. 6, *Theology: The Old Covenant* (San Francisco: Ignatius Press, 1990); Hans Urs von Balthasar, *The Glory of the Lord: A Theological Aesthetics*, vol. 7, *Theology: The New Covenant* (San Francisco: Ignatius Press, 1989).
[19] Von Balthasar, *Seeing the Form*, p. 25.
[20] Ibid., p. 126.

and practice. Not that, at Balthasar's hands, there is ever any danger of the saints having to complement Christ, much less of their competing with him for our attention. Jesus Christ is central to the form of revelation not as a "particular section ... which would need to be filled out by other more peripheral aspects", but, rather, "the reality which lends the form its total coherence and comprehensibility, the 'wherefore' to which all particular aspects have to be referred if they are to be understood."[21]

To see Christ in this way as central to the form of revelation of God to the world—and, above all, to see in this way his Paschal Mystery, which sums up the meaning of his Incarnation and life and directs attention to his Parousia—requires, for Balthasar, two things. Those perquisites are a *conversio ad phantasmata*, or "turning to the phantasms", and the grace of the Holy Spirit. In Thomas' epistemology, to which the Latin phrase just quoted refers us, the "agent intellect"—a term Thomas borrowed from Aristotle—must explore the sensuous realm so as to disengage the "intelligible species", which are the things of the real world as entering human minds. This entails an illumination, and so the presence of a "light" (the metaphor is more Platonist than Aristotelian). Such "natural light" (*lumen naturale*) is, for Thomas, already a participation in the divine light whereby God knows all things. Likewise, in the theologically aesthetic scanning—better, *contemplation*—of the form of Jesus Christ, there is needed, according to Balthasar, both attention to what the incarnate Son did and said in our flesh—the sensuous materials—and also enlightenment by the Holy Spirit, which enlightenment at one and the same time reaches our minds and hearts from within *and* springs forth from the form we see placed before us.[22] Here the light in question is of a different magnitude. It is *lumen fidei*, the "light of faith". Illuminating grace comes to its recipients from the Spirit, interiorly, and issues from the Son, exteriorly, in his wondrous epiphany. It is not hard to see here another version of the Thomist theology of the act of faith,[23] especially as found in those disciples of Thomas

---

[21] Ibid., p. 463.

[22] Ibid., p. 30.

[23] See, for instance, Benoit Duroux, O.P., *La Psychologie de la Foi chez saint Thomas d'Aquin* (Paris: Desclée de Brouwer, 1963).

who have emphasized the *eyes* of faith, as these "eyes" are trained on Jesus Christ, the centre of revelation.[24] Such perception entails being rapt—a being caught up into what has been perceived. An apprehension of the divine beauty in the form of Christ and a consequent enrapture—these two movements in their inseparability—constitute for Balthasar the essential framework in which the theological virtues of faith, hope, and charity live, move, and have their being.

It should not be thought, however, that Balthasar is a fideist for whom the assessing of the data and arguments in apologetics is at best a waste of time. There would be a massive departure from the spirit of Thomism if the rational preamble of faith were ditched in the name of sheer "fiducial" faith and a deliberate "sacrifice of the intellect". Rather, as Balthasar carefully formulates matters, "apologetics secretly (though knowingly to be sure) carries with it all dogmatic theology as it sets out to convey and to make plausible to one who does not yet believe the image of divine revelation. This image really becomes plausible, however, only for the person who sees the true contours of its total form dawn before the eyes of his spirit."[25]

To Balthasar's mind, the discipline of apologetics, giving primacy to *verum* (truth) and *bonum*, the true and the good, runs a risk of becoming unilateral in one of two directions. Either it concentrates on the demonstrative power of the objective signs of revelation (miracles, the fulfilment of prophecy) or it focusses on the intimate experience that revelation grants of an "innermost fulfillment and the quieting of ... unrest".[26] There is here an unfortunate bifurcation. It can be overcome—this at any rate is Balthasar's claim—only by "introducing ... the thought forms and categories of the beautiful. The beautiful is above all a *form*, and the light does not fall on this form from above and from outside, rather it breaks forth from the form's interior."[27] Here objective and subjective evidence come together as

---

[24]Prominent here would be Pierre Rousselot, though the language of *fides oculata* is Thomas' own, taken from Augustine. See Pierre Rousselot, *The Eyes of Faith, with Answers to Two Attacks* (New York: Fordham University Press, 1990). While praising Rousselot, Balthasar also worries, however, that he did not do sufficient justice to the inherent "efficacy of the objective evidence" of the revelatory form. Von Balthasar, *Seeing the Form*, p. 177.

[25]Von Balthasar, *Seeing the Form*, p. 127.

[26]Ibid., p. 151.

[27]Ibid.

one. The "central question" of apologetics, or as it has been called in twentieth-century Catholicism "fundamental theology", is at root an aesthetic one: how to perceive that wonderful form.[28]

Hence, the meat of the crucial opening volume of the theological aesthetics is devoted to the subjective *and* objective "evidence" for the impact of Christ's glorious form on individuals.[29] The light of faith makes possible in the subjective evidence the experience of faith, but only the form of revelation, Christ-centred and mediated by Scripture and the Church, can serve as faith's true correlative in objective reality. Here "the subjective is totally dependent on the objective evidence".[30] The expression brings about the impression—the couplet *expressio/impressio*, found throughout the doctrinal discussion in the theological aesthetics, is owed by Balthasar to Bonaventure: they are "the basic concepts that characterize the whole of Bonaventure's aesthetics, distinguishing him from the tradition".[31]

The transformative impress of that form turns on its origin in the plan of the Holy Trinity for human salvation. "Only the mysteries and sacraments of Christ's revelation effect what they signify"[32]— this statement refers in Balthasar's text to the Tridentine canons, but behind those canons lie Thomas' teaching on the causality of the sacraments as signs of Christ, and, more primordially, of Christ's humanity as sign of the divinity of the Logos, through whom, in the Holy Spirit, the Father invests his saving love on earth.[33] Balthasar's theological realism—shared with Aquinas—makes him keen to stress that the consequent "rapture" of the "perceiver" is not just psychological. It is a "movement of man's whole being away from himself and towards God through Christ".[34] Still, this would not occur without

[28] Ibid., p. 173.

[29] On "subjective evidence", see ibid., pp. 129–427; for "objective evidence", see ibid., pp. 429–684.

[30] Ibid., p. 156.

[31] Hans Urs von Balthasar, *The Glory of the Lord: A Theological Aesthetics*, vol. 2, *Studies in Theological Style: Clerical Styles* (San Francisco: Ignatius Press, 1984), p. 271.

[32] Von Balthasar, *Seeing the Form*, p. 123.

[33] The best Thomist account of sacramental theology by an Anglophone writer is Colman O'Neill, O.P., *Meeting Christ in the Sacraments* (Staten Island, NY: Alba House, 1964); Colman O'Neill, *Sacramental Realism: A General Theory of the Sacraments* (Wilmington, DE: Michael Glazier, 1983).

[34] Von Balthasar, *Seeing the Form*, p. 121.

internal changes. Balthasar appeals to Thomas' biblical commentaries as testifying to the "interior instinct and attraction" of the saving revelation, whereby is generated a *connaturalitas*, or "essential kinship", with divine realities—implying ultimately (but here the source is more Meister Eckhart than Thomasian) "the gracious insertion of the creature" into the Son's own generation from the Father.[35] Balthasar appeals for support to the treatise *De revelatione* of the "sacred monster of Thomism" Réginald Garrigou-Lagrange in his statement that "the sole authentic motive for Christian faith is God's uncreated act of revelation, the internal Word of God, with which the believer's spirit comes into contact in a most simple act which unites him directly with the Primal Truth."[36]

The sensibility of the Spirit

Such subjective evidence is brought together with the objective evidence, thanks to the economy of the Holy Spirit. Already in the theological aesthetics Balthasar anticipates the assertions of the closing volume of the theological logic, *The Spirit of Truth*. "The Holy Spirit is, in identity, *both* the Spirit of God's objective revelation in the Christ and of the objectification of the Christ-form in the existential form of the Church—her offices, charisms, and sacraments—*and* the Spirit of Christian subjectivity as faith, hope, and love, and it is only in this Spirit that we can say '*Kyrios Jesous*'."[37] The "new connaturality of the soul with divine things" has real "effects on the sphere of consciousness" albeit in "indirect and successive" fashion, in dependence on the "readiness" of each of the faithful—the term used, *Bereitschaft*, having for Balthasar distinctly Marian connotations.[38] It may be that Thomas would not think of the Blessed Virgin in this specific context; yet, Balthasar's description of those "real effects" is entirely Thomasian. "No sharp line can be drawn where the infused virtues,

[35] Ibid., p. 162.

[36] Ibid., p. 212. My reference is to Richard Peddicord, O.P., *The Sacred Monster of Thomism: An Introduction to the Life and Legacy of Reginald Garrigou-Lagrange, O.P.* (South Bend, IN: St. Augustine's Press, 2005).

[37] Von Balthasar, *Seeing the Form*, pp. 194–95.

[38] Ibid., p. 248.

with their vital centre in *caritas*, begin to unfold consciously as 'the gifts of the Holy Spirit'. Ontologically, these gifts are already contained in the gift of grace itself and the new inclination and readiness that are bestowed with it. But it is up to the believer and the lover to allow this inclination to gain an ever-increasing ascendancy in his life of faith."[39] Balthasar employs a key conception in his vocabulary, that of "attunement" (*Stimmung*) to elucidate how, for Thomas, the Gifts of the Holy Spirit actually work in making individuals correspond with God in Jesus Christ. Thomas' account of the Gifts is complemented by his theology of the "missions" of Son and Spirit where the divine Persons bring about in human souls the loving wisdom which is a participation in the triune life.[40] That, for Balthasar, is the basis of the "experience of faith" which furnishes him with the rest of his "subjective evidence". Balthasar's outlook was markedly sacramental and ecclesial; so he does not forget here the indebtedness of that experience to the sacraments of Baptism and the Holy Eucharist (largely unconscious, although these sacramental acts have a "noetic" side to them),[41] and the taking up of the believer into the "Church's manner of feeling", a *sentire cum Ecclesia* which goes well beyond simple adhesion to doctrine for it comes to its fullest expression in the "bridal" response to the Bridegroom—the Lamb that was slain—of the Mother of God and the saints.[42] That is unmistakably Balthasarian, yet not incongruous when compared with the programmatic statement of Mark Jordan about the spirit of the *Summa theologiae* cited at the end of chapter 1.[43]

For Balthasar, the experience of the mystics is an intensified prolongation of the ordinary experience of faith. Christian experience can have these two modes—mystical and ordinary—since neither

[39] Ibid.
[40] Ibid., p. 294.
[41] Ibid., p. 249.
[42] Ibid., p. 256.
[43] For the combination of ecclesial and mystical elements in a sacramental context, one might compare the Thomas texts brought together in Gilles Emery, O.P., "The Ecclesial Fruit of the Eucharist in St. Thomas Aquinas", *Nova et Vetera* 2, no. 1 (2004): 43–60. On the Marian dimension, what one will never find in Aquinas is anything comparable to the statement that the "offiical liturgical prayer of the Church" is "always Marian prayer". Hans Urs von Balthasar, *The Threefold Garland: The World's Salvation in Mary's Prayer* (San Francisco: Ignatius Press, 1985), p. 23.

of them is primary. The truly "archetypal experience" is "the encounter with God in the Bible".[44] This may remind the Thomist reader that Aquinas, too, the *magister in sacra pagina*, considered Holy Scripture the principal reference point of all Christian understanding. For Balthasar, this means in the first place Jesus' archetypal experience of God *secundum humanitatem*, and this he describes as a "super-faith which is one with the vision of the Father".[45] That description is, for Thomists, inevitably controversial: Thomas would not ascribe the theological virtue of faith to Christ, precisely owing to his possession, as only-begotten Son, of the vision of God. There will be more to say on this in chapter 5, for some of the pertinent Balthasar texts are found outside the aesthetics. For the moment it may be noted that Balthasar understands this "super-faith" (expressed elsewhere as "exemplary 'faith' ")—note the quotation marks, a mark of distinction from the ordinary theological virtue[46]) as "one" with the *visio*, not an alternative thesis. As Balthasar will write in the dramatics, "We shall have to be very careful in our use of the term; we must not give the impression that Jesus' attitude to his Father is nothing more than the perfection of that general attitude of faith found in the Old or New Testament."[47]

In the second place, "archetypal [biblical] experience" means the Old Testament experience of God as preparing the way for the Incarnation. Balthasar is no Marcionite.[48] He always does justice to the place of the Old Testament in the canon, just as Thomas saw the task of *magister in sacra pagina* as extending to Old Testament books (thus his extant lecture materials on Isaiah and Job), and gave the Old Law

---

[44] Von Balthasar, *Seeing the Form*, p. 301.

[45] Ibid., p. 305.

[46] Hans Urs von Balthasar, *Theo-drama: Theological Dramatic Theory*, vol. 3, *Dramatis Personae: The Person in Christ*, trans. Graham Harrison (San Francisco: Ignatius Press, 1992), p. 16.

[47] Ibid., p. 170.

[48] Anthony Sciglitano, *Marcion and Prometheus: Balthasar against the Expulsion of Jewish Origins in Modern Christian Thought* (New York: Crossroad, 2014). Balthasar's "anti-Marcionite agenda" is, for Sciglitano, directly related to his "capacious view of Christianity" (ibid., p. x), which itself allows for authentic dialogue not only with Judaism but also with other religious traditions, thanks to three factors: the analogy of being, the Alexandrian doctrine of the "seeds of the Logos", and Balthasar's own extension thereof in his pneumatology (ibid., p. 155)—all this without, however, surrendering the Christian claim to uniqueness or pandering to the "pluralist" view that religions are so many encodings of the "same" salvation experience.

a place of honour—not least as figuration of Christ—in his lengthy treatment of it in the *Secunda Pars* of the *Summa theologiae*; not unfittingly, he was asked on his deathbed by the monks of Fossanuova to provide them with an oral commentary on the Song of Songs.

In the third place "archetypal biblical experience" means the "God-experience of the disciples as eye-witnesses": a "faith in Christ and, with Christ, in God", which is also a "total human vision of Christ and in Christ of the Father in the Holy Spirit",[49] among those witnesses Balthasar giving primacy to the Mother of the Lord. To Balthasar's mind, these archetypal experiences are participable by the later Church as Bride and Body of Christ—indeed, they were undergone for her sake, since she is the new Israel of God. There is, I think, nothing in Saint Thomas' thought to correspond to this—indeed, it is an authentically new acquisition of Catholic theology.

Of these various levels of archetypal experience, it can also be said that they are what make possible a reading of the "spiritual" meaning of the Old Testament and New Testament, which, at Balthasar's hands in *The Glory of the Lord*, prepares the way for the account of the Bible's more "literal" meaning in the two closing volumes of the aesthetics. He thus exemplifies the two modes of interpretation which Thomas, as other mediaevals, practised as a biblical theologian, though, to be sure, elements of historical-critical method are used in the making of spiritual interpretation in volume 1 of the aesthetics just as a speculative construal of the literal sense enters into the more historical reading in volumes 6 and 7. The right word, no doubt, is "post-critical".[50] For Thomas, the literal—understood as the authorial—sense must have primacy, since it is the immediate effect of biblical inspiration. Balthasar would not dispute that insistence in so many words. Instead he would add that "the centre of

---

[49] Von Balthasar, *Seeing the Form*, p. 305.

[50] W. T. Dickens, *Hans Urs von Balthasar's Theological Aesthetics: A Model for Post-Critical Biblical Interpretation* (Notre Dame, IN: University of Notre Dame Press, 2003). Dickens concentrates on the two last volumes of the aesthetics, seen as "the nearest thing to an extended example of scriptural exegesis in his entire theological corpus" (ibid., p. 23). Dickens was eventually persuaded that "Balthasar's views and uses of scripture" in that work "while remaining conversant with historical criticism and generally abiding by its fruits, are compatible with those features of the pre-modern approaches to the Bible that helped sustain the sort of biblical fluency and imagination among Christians that today is in such short supply" (ibid., p. 237).

gravity of the letter lies in the spirit itself, in its christological sense, which is precisely the sense of the dying and rising of Christ in so far as it becomes an event for us and in us."[51]

But however "spiritual" the interpretation, Balthasar never loses sight of the fact that it concerns a "hearing" and "seeing" of the divine, something whose implications are fully explored in his account of the "spiritual senses"—elevated equivalents of the five senses of mankind's natural "sensorium".[52] This is not as esoteric as it might at first sound. There is, after all, a combination of sensory and suprasensory in all apprehension of material things: compare the Aristotelian understanding of knowledge of the "species" of material singulars as integrated by Aquinas in his account of encounter with being. The "sensorium" is mankind's most fundamental way of experiencing the world, a world in which, with the Incarnation, God has now taken form. Revelation has taken place in the sensuous realm, meaning that the physical and spiritual senses can open onto each other—not without some equivalent to a "death and resurrection" moment, dying to one mode of perception and rising to another. Balthasar ascribes to Origen the patristic theology of the spiritual senses but finds its New Testament source in the well-trained perceptive faculties of the closing verse of chapter 5 of the Letter to the Hebrews.[53] It is Bonaventure, however, in whom that theology reaches its full flowering (with a late fruiting in Ignatius Loyola). Saint Thomas has this doctrine too, so Balthasar notes, instancing his commentary on the Letter to the Philippians (where, seemingly, Aquinas relies on Origen's homilies on Leviticus).[54] Why this is relevant to theological aesthetics becomes apparent in Balthasar's summary of its claims. "The senses are the exteriorization of the soul and Christ is the exteriorisation of God."[55] The "exterior"—the realm of the senses, the realm of the Incarnation—is, then, where man and God meet. Though Aquinas

[51] Von Balthasar, *Seeing the Form*, p. 548.

[52] See Mark McInroy, *Balthasar on the Spiritual Senses: Perceiving Splendor* (New York: Oxford University Press, 2014).

[53] Heb 5:14: "Solid food is for the mature, for those who have their faculties trained by practice to distinguish good from evil."

[54] Thomas Aquinas, *In Phillipenses* 2, lect. 12; see von Balthasar, *Seeing the Form*, p. 380, footnote 185.

[55] Von Balthasar, *Seeing the Form*, p. 407.

may not have made much of the narrower theme, the wider motif is admirably Thomasian. Along with the claim of ontology that where there is anything there is God, it figures as the chief message of G. K. Chesterton's *St. Thomas Aquinas* (famously described by Gilson as the best short account of Thomism ever penned). "As compared with a Jew, a Moslem, a Buddhist, a Deist, or most obvious alternatives, a Christian *means* a man who believes that deity or sanctity has attached to matter or entered the world of the senses."[56]

The glory of the Lord

So far, the discussion has been about subjective evidence—the light of faith and Christian experience. To bring about the requisite change in subjectivity, the impact needed has already been specified: it is Christ's "glorious" form. For Balthasar, "glory" is the divine perfection that has as its analogy in creation the "beautiful"—whether we think of the latter as the work of nature or the work of human art. "Beyond all creaturely hopes and expectations ... the revelation in Christ was to bring together in one divine and human Head everything heavenly and earthly, which is thus endowed by grace with a crown, the radiance of whose glory, belonging to the *Kyrios* of the world, was to shed its rays over the whole of creation."[57] Encouragingly enough, Karl Barth—hardly someone inclined to minimize the difference between the divine and the worldly—had already identified "beauty" as an "indispensable 'auxiliary concept'" in discussion of the biblical "glory".[58] This confirmed what Balthasar knew from the Catholic tradition. "Beauty" is a divine name for patristic and mediaeval writers. It suffices to look at, for instance, Denys and Aquinas.[59] But the glory embodied in the supremely beautiful form that is the "event" of Jesus Christ, taken in its entirety, turns out

---

[56]G. K. Chesterton, *St. Thomas Aquinas* (1933; London: Hodder and Stoughton, 1943), p. 31; emphasis in original.
[57]Von Balthasar, *Seeing the Form*, p. 431.
[58]Ibid., p. 53.
[59]Brendan Thomas Sammon, *The God Who Is Beauty: Beauty as a Divine Name in Thomas Aquinas and Dionysius the Areopagite* (Eugene, OR: Pickwick, 2013).

to be—so the Paschal Mystery informs us—nothing other than the divine Love, which took pity on a humanity estranged from God, brought it back to the Father through the Son's pierced heart, and bathed it in streams of mercy by the Holy Spirit. The Balthasarian equation, among the divine attributes, of glory and love—specifically cruciform and thereby trinitarian love, for the man on the Cross is the trinitarian Son—is pivotal for the theological aesthetics and indeed for the Trilogy at large. And though alongside the Passion, a mystery of humiliation, Balthasar gives great weight to the descent into hell and, moreover, does full justice to the mysteries of exaltation—the Resurrection, Ascension, and the sending of the Spirit at Pentecost— while he also emphasizes the unity of the Paschal Mystery as a whole, nevertheless it is for him the Cross of Christ that is the manifest centre of it all.

From the point of view of aesthetics, the supreme form is an "unform", for the humiliated Lord in the sweat, blood, and death cry of his Passion is as far from conventionally beautiful as any hideous thing on earth could be. Yet the "un-form" is, in truth, the "super-form", since here the glory of the divine Love streams forth, to transfigure mankind and, ultimately, the very cosmos itself.[60] While this language of "un-form" and "super-form" is Balthasar's own, it is not hard to see that the trio of form, unform, and superform corresponds—as an account of the Passion—to Thomas' trio of the *via affirmativa, via negativa, via eminentiae*, in all "proper" language about God. Not till the theological dramatics, however, will Balthasar unfold his fuller theology of the Atonement, where we shall discover, among other things, that only a plethora of terms and images, taken from both the New Testament and Church tradition, is able to do justice to this unique transaction. Saint Thomas had precisely the same reaction.[61]

Meanwhile, one conviction steadied Balthasar in his resolve to venture upon this "aesthetic" masterpiece. The view that the entire divine economy of creation, redemption, and consummation amounts to an expression of the divine glory (analogue of beauty) had left its

---

[60] Von Balthasar, *Seeing the Form*, p. 460.

[61] Aidan Nichols, O.P., "St. Thomas Aquinas on the Passion of Christ: A Reading of *Summa Theologiae* IIIa., q. 46", *Scottish Journal of Theology* 43 (1990): 447–59.

mark, he thought, on countless authors in Church tradition, who found they could not write about that economy without imparting beauty through their very texts. The second and third volumes of the theological aesthetics offer twelve short, yet substantial, monographs, from both "clerical" and "lay" theologians—the latter for the most part "poet-theologians"—as examples of how this is so.[62] These monographs are more to the point than might appear. The reason: for mainstream figures in the Christian intellectual tradition to have "espoused themes central to a theology of glory argues in favour of such a theology"—such a theology as Balthasar is seeking to practice now.[63] Christopher Steck helpfully lists some common indicators among the themes of the glorious twelve: "the ever-greaterness of God, the *eros* of human longing which Christ awakens, the orientation of nature to the advent of grace, the sacramentality of the world's images, the shattering of human understanding before the 'whylessness' [i.e., the sheer gift quality, the gratuity] of God's love as revealed in Christ".[64] There is reason to think that the studies of Irenaeus and Bonaventure are especially indicative of Balthasar's own theological construction in *The Glory of the Lord* and beyond.[65]

As the final chapter of this book will suggest, Balthasar was determined to be no less a comprehensive thinker about the "all" than was Aquinas. He could not be content with a "positive" theology that ended up simply outlining what, as a matter of fact, the Christian tradition has believed.

He needed to address the largest possible questions and show how that tradition both engaged them and answered them. It was for this

[62] Von Balthasar, *Studies in Theological Style*; Hans Urs von Balthasar, *The Glory of the Lord: A Theological Aesthetics*, vol. 3, *Lay Styles* (San Francisco: Ignatius Press, 1986).

[63] Christopher Steck, S.J., *The Ethical Thought of Hans Urs von Balthasar* (New York: Crossroad, 2001), p. 10.

[64] Ibid.

[65] For Irenaeus, see Kevin Mongrain, *The Systematic Thought of Hans Urs von Balthasar: An Irenaean Retrieval* (New York: Crossroad, 2003); and for Bonaventure, Junius Johnson, *Christ and Analogy: The Christocentric Metaphysics of Hans Urs von Balthasar* (Minneapolis, MN: Fortress, 2013).

Irenaean recapitulation meets Bonaventurian exemplarism in Christology. Yet in *The Glory of the Lord* itself Balthasar draws attention more especially to Denys the Areopagite and John of the Cross as embodying a *rapture* expressed in negative theology which never loses contact with the *perception* of the visible form of the divine appearing in salvation history, as found in positive theology. Von Balthasar, *Seeing the Form*, pp. 124–25.

reason that after the twelve sample studies in theological aesthetics, historically conceived, he turns in the fourth and fifth volumes of *The Glory of the Lord* to the most general message of myths, metaphysicians, and "makars"—the old Scots word for poets. "The Bible is full of statements about God's glory, and the passages and vistas are far more numerous than most believers realize.... It is precisely this universality of the biblical glory that necessarily must confront that other universality, the universality of the human spirit, already to hand in the world from the fact of Creation, the spirit which of its nature is open to understand the being of all that is."[66] This, of course, gives Balthasar's thought its most fundamental affinity with that of Aquinas. To be effectively missionary, the Christian must offer the world not only the "biblical glory" but also the "metaphysical depth of being".[67] So the faithful Israelite, singing the creation psalms to God, "was the responsible guardian of the glory of covenant *and* of creation".[68] Balthasar surveys how the Greeks of the archaic Hellenic and Hellenistic periods, and their Roman disciples, saw the radiance of the divine in the world, as attested by myth, philosophy, and dramatic poetry, for the men of antiquity, in all these genres, presupposed what he calls on their behalf a "theological a priori". The divine was—they assumed—involved when beauty is found. When at the start of the patristic epoch, the Gospel entered into dialogue with the Gentile world, three "themes" deriving from this background began to be owned by Christians. Balthasar lists them as "the theme of the procession and return of creatures from God and back to God"; "the theme of *eros* as the fundamental yearning of the finite creature for transcendence in God as the primordial unity, the primordial beauty"; and "the theme of the beauty of the spiritual soul", Christianised as the engracing (or direct infusion) of the virtues by the freely given love of God, and leading thereby to the "marriage-feast" of the end of the ages.[69] It was presupposed that natural theology and biblical theology went

---

[66] Hans Urs von Balthasar, *The Glory of the Lord: A Theological Aesthetics*, vol. 4, *The Realm of Metaphysics in Antiquity* (San Francisco: Ignatius Press, 1989), p. 11.

[67] Ibid., p. 14.

[68] Ibid., p. 17.

[69] Ibid., pp. 321–22.

hand in hand—until, that is, the combined effect of the Renaissance and Reformation spoiled things, generating in due course a purely philosophical aesthetics incapable—in the early modern and modern context—of re-creating the conviction of the ancients that all reality is *kalon*, beautifully good.[70]

Balthasar accords the thirteenth-century Scholastics the accolade of at last thinking through the philosophical-theological grounding of *pulchrum* in all God-derived reality—thanks to their development of a doctrine of the transcendental determinations of being. Though Thomas, except when writing as a participant in the "Dionysian renaissance" (the revival of interest in the *Corpus areopagiticum*), has no special focus on the transcendental of beauty, the ontology he was able to forge by creative modification of high mediaeval reflection on being nevertheless furnished what to Balthasar's eyes is the right solution. All the epithets the ancients had used for *kalon* come home in Thomas' account of nonsubsistent being—the way *esse*, the act of existing, gives itself away in enabling things to be, while at the same time having no essence of its own in which to be at rest. Drawing on a variety of Thomas' texts—the two *Summas*; the *Disputed Questions on Truth* and the *Disputed Questions on the Power of God*; the commentaries on Boethius' *De hebdomadibus* and Denys' *The Divine Names*—Balthasar describes *esse non subsistens* as "the first *created* reality proceeding from God, by participating in which all beings really are, something 'abundant, simple, not-subsisting', 'universal', 'flowing', participating in an infinite manner and thence in itself infinite, lending form inexhaustibly".[71] This *is* the "kingdom of beauty", itself transparent to a mysterious "hidden primordial ground", "radiant *glory*": the glory of the sovereignly free God who is, therefore, elevated above such being, yet elects to sanction its pouring out on all that is.[72] "The metaphysics of Thomas is thus the philosophical reflection of the free glory of the living God of the Bible and in this way the interior completion of ancient (and thus human) philosophy."[73] Balthasar will return to this entire analysis at the end of volume 5 of the aesthetics as simply

---

[70] Ibid., p. 324.
[71] Ibid., p. 374.
[72] Ibid., p. 375.
[73] Ibid., p. 407.

essential to any Christian metaphysics for the modern age. It remains the site of glory in metaphysics, and crucial to the Christian task.[74]

That being is "something united" can be recognized by any metaphysics. But that the one is true, not illusion, and good, not its opposite, is a different matter. The "likeness" between nonsubsisting being and *ipse esse subsistens*—God himself—means that being is true, just as the divine "positing" of such created being means that God "does the good and in so doing reveals the goodness which he is", so being is good likewise.[75] Readers of the opening volume of the aesthetics will not be surprised to learn, as they reach the fourth and fifth volumes, that only the Holy Trinity can guarantee a world so constituted. "If the positing of something really united points back to the creative ultimate cause, to God the Father, then likeness, truth, correspondence point to the eternal *aequalitas* in God the Son who is the exemplary (or transcendently formal) cause of the genuineness of being able to be opposite, and only then can the judgment of being good reveal the love between original and copy as the unifying Spirit who offers a meaningful goal for the whole process."[76] The circumincession of the transcendentals turns on the circumincession of the trinitarian Persons. The first circumincession reflects the origins of the Persons and hence can rightly be invoked to describe the second.[77] Balthasar expects the reader to notice how, in this perspective, the trio of *unum* (one), *verum* (truth), and *bonum* (beauty) leaves no room for the addition of a fourth member, *pulchrum* (goodness), for there are no further divine Persons to invoke. Indeed. *Pulchrum* "oscillates" between the transcendentals—a mobile image, unlike my own more static suggestion of the transcendentals' "fulcrum", though the latter has the advantage of onomatopoeic memorability. The beautiful is the "final, ineffable preciousness of being".[78]

The glory of God is the endless streaming forth of beautiful love. Finding it embodied in the utterly selfless generosity of Saint Francis,

---

[74] Hans Urs von Balthasar, *The Glory of the Lord: A Theological Aesthetics*, vol. 5, *The Realm of Metaphysics in the Modern Age* (San Francisco: Ignatius Press, 1991), pp. 613–34.

[75] Von Balthasar, *Realm of Metaphysics in Antiquity*, p. 376.

[76] Ibid., pp. 376–77; translation slightly altered.

[77] On this, see Angela Franks, "Trinitarian *analogia entis* in Hans Urs von Balthasar", *The Thomist* 62, no. 4 (1998): 533–59.

[78] Von Balthasar, *Realm of Metaphysics in Antiquity*, p. 377.

Balthasar could suppose that the Franciscan school—with Bonaventure its supreme master—was best suited to grasp the further theological implications of Thomas' ontological discovery.[79] At the end of volume 4 of the aesthetics, Balthasar offers in the person of the *Poverello* of Assisi a hint for the succeeding volume, the volume that continues the story of metaphysics to the Kantians and Marxians of his own day. Western philosophy will not prove able to sustain the high point it reached in Thomas. Thomas' discovery of the kenotic character of being (*esse* in giving itself is at once fullness and nothingness, for "existence" does not, as such, exist)—his realisation of how, in this, being is the likeness of the divine goodness,[80] an expression of the Holy Trinity and the preparation for the descent of the Logos in Incarnation and Atonement, stooping down for the sake of man's salvation to Cross and tomb—will, however, continue to be recognized, not in its own terms in philosophical academies, but transposed into biography, in the lives and spirituality of the saints.

What Balthasar tries to show in volume 5, by setting forth the spirituality of a host of figures from the Rhineland mystic John Tauler to the French Jesuit Jean-Pierre de Caussade, is that the self-abandoned person who relies totally on God—the saint—is a kind of personalized version of *esse* in its outpouring. He is a personalized version of the way in which, for Thomas, being in its dependence on God only consolidates itself—essentialises—in giving itself away to beings. The saint, not the cosmos, now becomes the epiphany of glory. In the late mediaeval period, a picture of what it is to be a saint emerges—a portrait of selfhood as "total self-giving prodigality", consciously modelled on not only the incarnate atoning Saviour but the Holy Trinity itself. The mystics think of the individual as finding his identity—being himself—ecstatically, through a going out (*ekstasis*) in contemplation towards God and in apostolic service towards others (and such "apostolic" ecstasy shows precisely the fruitfulness of the original "contemplative" ecstasy towards God). The mystical saints (and, owing to the Gifts of the Holy Spirit, what saint is not "mystical"?) exhibit a form of throwing themselves away lavishly

---

[79] Ibid., pp. 378–81.

[80] Cf. Gustav Sieweth, *Das Sein als Gleichnis Gottes* (Heidelberg: Kerke, 1958), nonsubsistent *esse* is the "parable" of God.

just as does—in the Thomasian ontology—being itself. In this way the mystics not only guide us to the heart of the biblical revelation but "solve" the problem of metaphysics. The subsequent history of Western metaphysics, from nominalism through rationalism and Idealism to Marxism and beyond, is rehearsed by Balthasar only to show how it is trumped in advance.

Yet in the final pages of volume 5, "Our Inheritance and the Christian Task",[81] Balthasar also recognizes that we cannot simply leave the cosmos as a more or less meaningless stage on which meaningful acts are by exceptional people occasionally performed. It is not enough for the self-giving glory of God to manifest itself at these few scattered points; we need to know as well that it really is the universal foundation of the whole world and its history: hence the perduring importance of Thomas' teaching and an insight not as such attained by Thomas (only by certain of his twentieth-century disciples)—namely, the convertibility of being and love. The latter may seem a singularly implausible claim. It will be considered in the last chapter of this book, for it is bound up with the "underlying principle" of Balthasar's entire theology. Here it may suffice to point out that having and giving are inseparably connected.

Back to the Bible

In the concluding volumes of the theological aesthetics—volumes 6 and 7—Balthasar turns again to the Bible in the hope that, by the light of what has preceded in *The Glory of the Lord*, we shall see how, through the New Testament's amazing consummation of the Old, the mystery of all creation, man included, received its definitive interpretation as the hidden presence of absolute love, to which in its luminous, bountiful, and exuberant character beauty's qualities of clarity, integrity, and proportion by analogy belong. See too how the recipients of God's revelation receive thereby the call to make the divine visible in charity, the specifically Christian love of neighbour which is, as Balthasar puts it, "something quite distinct from a good and morally upright model for inter-personal conduct. [This love]

---

[81] Von Balthasar, *Realm of Metaphysics in Modern Age*, pp. 613–56.

occurs always as the focal point, as the demonstration and realization of a love which itself wholly transcends man, and thus also as an indicator of that love which man cannot ascribe to himself since it has long since showed itself to him as that which is ever greater than himself."[82] "Ever-greater", *je grösser, semper maior*: that refers to the inexhaustible, self-dispossessing energy of the triune love, gestured towards in the prophets of the Old Covenant, those servants in whom the Lord of Israel expressed his burning passion,[83] but, at the turn of the ages, actually manifested, beyond all human expectation, in the mission of the Son—whose Incarnation, death, and descent into hell flesh out in the art of a divine narrative the very essence of the Holy Trinity—the absolute love which God is and in which Christ's glory also consists.[84] This is the "narrative" that Thomas Hibbs found subjacent to the surface structure of the *Summa contra gentiles* (see chapter I above). It is the same story that the Liturgy of the Church tells out yearly, above all in its climactic concentration in a "Triduum" from the Thursday of Holy Week to Easter Day—a connexion Balthasar makes more explicit in the liturgically entitled "Theology of the Three Days", later republished as *Mysterium Paschale*, where the climactic mysteries of humiliation and exaltation of the Word are expounded in a fashion no longer focussed on, though by no means dispensing with, theological aesthetics.[85] In Jesus, the image of God which for Israel is man[86] and the glory of God which for Israel is God himself[87] come wondrously to coincide.[88] The unfolding of Jesus' story—his life, death, and Resurrection—exhibits to us what that is going to mean if God's glory really is his unconditional love now freely exposing itself in vulnerable fashion to a sinful world.[89]

[82] Ibid., p. 649.

[83] Von Balthasar, *Old Covenant*, pp. 225–300.

[84] Von Balthasar, *New Covenant*, pp. 115–263.

[85] Hans Urs von Balthasar, *Mysterium Paschale: The Mystery of Easter*, trans. Aidan Nichols, O.P. (2000; repr., San Francisco: Ignatius Press, 2005).

[86] Von Balthasar, *Old Covenant*, pp. 81–143.

[87] Ibid., pp. 31–86.

[88] Von Balthasar, *New Covenant*, pp. 264–385.

[89] In these four last paragraphs, I reuse, modified, some material originally published as Aidan Nichols, O.P., "Von Balthasar's Aims in His Theological Aesthetics", *Heythrop Journal* 40 (1999): 409–23, and republished in Aidan Nichols, O.P., *Beyond the Blue Glass: Catholic Essays in Faith and Culture* (London: Saint Austin Press, 2002), 1:87–106.

It only remained, in the theological aesthetics, for Balthasar to consider what shape the wider human response to all this must have: the "glorification of the divine glory through the creature which receives and answers it".[90] The final volume's last part is self-professedly a "book of the Holy Spirit".[91] The glorification in question is a life of charity as the Spirit "makes the life of love well up, not in front of us nor above us, but in us": only the third trinitarian Person can do this since, being "the glorification of the love between Father and Son, wherein God's true glory disclosed itself to us, it is likewise only he who can bring about glorification in the world".[92] It is a fittingly Thomasian conclusion, for several reasons. There is the signal role of *caritas* in Aquinas' account of the Christian life. There is the place he gives (following Augustine) to the Spirit as the love of the Father and the Son whence charity proceeds. And there is the gloss he offers in his commentary on Saint John's Gospel, at 14:19 ("Because I live, you will live also"), where Thomas declares that the Lord "says this because our glorified life is produced by the glorified life of Christ".[93]

[90] Von Balthasar, *New Covenant*, p. 385.
[91] Ibid., p. 389.
[92] Ibid.
[93] Thomas Aquinas, *In Joannem* 14, lect. 5.

3

The Trilogy: Theological Dramatics

According to Christopher Steck, "In turning now to examine the dramatic interchange of freedoms in salvation history, we do not discard the aesthetics of *The Glory of the Lord*. We rather redeploy von Balthasar's aesthetic ideas with a view to how they apply to dramatic form."[1] Balthasar himself had made a close connexion between the aesthetics and the dramatics. "Right at the heart of the aesthetics, the 'theological drama' has already begun. 'Catching sight' of the glory, we observed, always involves being 'transported' by it.... Now we must allow the encountering reality to speak in its own tongue or, rather, let ourselves be drawn into its dramatic arena. For God's revelation is not an object to be looked at: it is his action in and upon the world, and the world can only respond, and hence 'understand', through action on *its* part."[2] He was aware that some readers of the theological aesthetics—which, as we have seen, is a particular kind of Christocentric fundamental-cum-dogmatic theology—had reacted adversely. Had he not caused the "picture of Christ to ossify into an icon"?[3] He protested. The beautiful form, presenting itself to us, exhibits graciousness and calls forth gratitude, a "dialogue" of a silent kind, perhaps, but one that is eloquent because it is expressive. That already implies action. "The form and the word within it awaken and summon us; they awaken our *freedom* and bid us attend to the call that comes to us from the form."[4] As the term "call" suggests,

---

[1] Christopher Steck, S.J., *The Ethical Thought of Hans Urs von Balthasar* (New York: Crossroad, 2001), p. 34.

[2] Hans Urs von Balthasar, *Theo-drama: Theological Dramatic Theory*, vol. 1, *Prolegomena*, trans. Graham Harrison (San Francisco: Ignatius Press, 1988), p. 15; emphasis in original.

[3] Hans Urs von Balthasar, *Theo-drama: Theological Dramatic Theory*, vol. 2, *Dramatis Personae: Man in God*, trans. Graham Harrison (San Francisco: Ignatius Press, 1990), p. 21.

[4] Ibid., pp. 28–29; emphasis in original.

where free response to gratuitous disclosure is concerned, "being transported" entails some sort of "election". "No one is enraptured without returning, from this encounter, with a personal mission."[5] A movement must be made from the beautiful to the good—the good as not only perceived but *enacted*.

Transition to dramatics

Here comes the transition to the theological dramatics. As the name suggests, "theological dramatics" concerns the interplay of divine and human agency in the action that is salvation history. "One can say that on the most general and formal level drama supposes the nego-tiation between distinct centres of freedom and intentionality with outcomes that are prospectively open."[6] That statement sums up Bal-thasar's presentation of what "theatre" is in his prolegomena to the dramatics, which occupies the entirety of its first volume. There Bal-thasar explained the background to this second part of the Trilogy. His aim was "to find and assess an appropriate analogy between the drama of worldly existence (which attains visible form in the the-atre) and the divine-human drama (theo-drama)".[7] In other words, it is another attempt to locate an analogy between God (and divine agency) and the world (and human agency). This is comparable to that between glory and beauty explored in the theological aesthetics, or indeed to the most foundational of all such analogies, especially prominent as it is in the Thomist tradition, that between uncreated Being and created being—to which Balthasar will revert, in a version of his own, in the concluding part of the Trilogy, the theological logic. Balthasar has it in mind that free agency is intrinsically con-nected to the transcendental *bonum*. "There is nothing ambiguous about what God does for man: it is simply *good*. Theo-drama is con-cerned with the good."[8] But does good necessarily imply the "dra-matic", especially in an age when the theatre is not central to culture,

---

[5] Ibid., p. 31.

[6] Cyril O'Regan, *The Anatomy of Misremembering: Von Balthasar's Response to Philosophical Modernity*, vol. 1, *Hegel* (New York: Crossroad, 2014), p. 151.

[7] Von Balthasar, *Prolegomena*, p. 66.

[8] Ibid., p. 18; emphasis in original.

as it was for classical Greece, Elizabethan England, golden-age Spain, and the ducal court at Weimar? It might seem not. But Balthasar thinks the idea of "theatrical action" inescapable in human life. "Life manifests a fundamental urge to observe itself as an action exhibiting both meaning and mystery."[9] If all theatres were abolished by the *diktat* of a global political authority, the children, if not the adults, of the world would keep drama alive.

The better to grasp the idea of the "world stage", Balthasar makes three distinctions. The first is the "distinction between the (temporal-spatial) finitude of the performed play" (owed ultimately to mortality, which puts an end to all decision-making) and "its non-finite meaning".[10] Drama is concerned with individuals seeking the good—or, at any rate, their good as they see it—with all its multiple gradations. "It has a vanishing point that, itself unattainable, is the absolute Good indicating the direction in which we are to strive; and it has a concrete stopping point on the way, namely, our best course of action under the circumstances."[11] In tragedy, these two points are made to coincide (notably in the martyr play, which also has its secular parallels). In comedy, aspiration is directed only to "a relative happiness that, at best, can symbolize the absolute Good and testify to a belief in it". But, comments Balthasar, "precisely this reveals the questionable nature of the Good that can be attained on earth."[12] The modern (i.e., postclassical) genre of tragicomedy seeks to combine features of both, claiming that this most fairly describes earthly life. But if anything, that category raises the question even more acutely: "How can the Good appear on stage if its ultimate criteria seem to be slipping away?"[13]

The second useful distinction for theo-drama is the "distinction between the 'I' and the allotted role".[14] In discussing "role", Balthasar asserts the limits of that personalism to which Catholic theology, he was otherwise keen to say, should give its proper due. "It is an illusion

[9] Ibid., pp. 78–79.
[10] Ibid., p. 250.
[11] Ibid., p. 414.
[12] Ibid.
[13] Ibid., p. 451.
[14] Ibid., p. 252

to imagine that thinking and philosophizing in 'personal' categories can answer the question, 'Who am I?'. At most it can make us more pressingly aware of the question."[15] The "problem of every philosophy of the subject" is that "the acting 'I' cannot be, cannot become itself, except through the medium in which it plays, its instrument, which again, cannot be isolated from the environment in which it lives."[16] The self must accept its limits, lived out as roles—and Balthasar scans the work of a number of philosophers, psychologists, and sociologists to suggest how this is so. But then how can these roles, if they are not identical with the "I"—for the "I" is not simply a bundle of roles, their sum total—not be so many forms of the alienation of the self? Against the Averroist view of the single agent intellect active in all men, Saint Thomas, who waged warfare as "a Christian fighting for the value of the individual",[17] was, unfortunately, not "in a position to lead the battle for the Christian dignity of the individual to a triumphant conclusion".[18] A combination of Aristotelian and Neoplatonist influences was, in this instance, by no means ideal. The self individualized by matter (courtesy of Aristotle) and yet the "more intelligible the more it is abstracted from matter and generalised" (courtesy of the Neoplatonists) is in a poor way.[19] That is so, thinks Balthasar, despite Thomas' passionate defence of the view that divine Providence extends not just to genera and species but to individuals as well. That is perhaps an obvious inference from the sayings of the Lord in the Sermon on the Mount, but Thomas had to maintain it in the teeth of the pagan philosophical tradition generally—and that was nearly all of the philosophy that existed in his day. In the twentieth century, it would be widely admitted by Thomists that there was here something of a lacuna in Aquinas' thought. Examples would be, in France, the lone lay Thomist Jacques Maritain, in his 1947 study *La Personne et le bien commun*, which sought to distinguish between "person" and (mere) "individual",[20] and in Poland, in the

[15] Ibid., p. 484.
[16] Ibid., p. 481.
[17] Ibid., p. 549.
[18] Ibid., p. 551.
[19] Ibid.
[20] Jacques Maritain, *La Personne et le bien commun* (Paris: Desclée de Brouwer, 1947).

context of the "Lublin School" of phenomenologically oriented Thomism, the writers who contributed to the collection *Person and Community*, among them Karol Wojtyła, later Pope John Paul II.[21] Although in his study of the "spirit" of mediaeval philosophy, Gilson had argued for the existence of a "Christian personalism" in the Middle Ages;[22] in Balthasar's opinion, the closest that thinkers in the Western philosophical tradition had really come to a solution of what he saw as the fundamental problem—how the unique "I" can be constituted despite its mediation by social roles—were the loosely connected "dialogical" thinkers, notable among whom were Martin Buber, Franz Rosenzweig, and Ferdinand Ebner, all stimulated by the biblical conception of divine address ("I"-"thou") to man. They were, so Balthasar tells the reader, essential to his project in this part of the Trilogy.

If we had not discovered this unique "name" (Rosenzweig) of the individual addressed by God and endowed with his personal name, the irreplaceable human being, the "absolute, unique instance" (Ebner), we would not have been justified in attempting a theory of theodrama, for the unique God would have lacked a partner. The fact that this partner came to light in the field of biblical theology, transcending all the approaches made by mysticism, philosophy, psychology and sociology, is no surprise, since from the outset he himself is a product and an element of that dramatic tension that unfolds exclusively, in our view, in the realm of the Bible. Moreover, the man who is a serious co-actor with God will be able, for his part, to contribute to the unfolding of this dramatic tension.[23]

But most of the twentieth-century dialogical thinkers were Jews, whereas, for Balthasar, "only in Jesus Christ does it become clear how profoundly this definitive 'I'-name signifies vocation, mission. In him the 'I' and the role become uniquely and ineffably one in the reality of his mission, far beyond anything attainable by earthly means."[24]

[21] Karol Wojtyła, "Thomistic Personalism", in *Person and Community: Selected Essays*, ed. Andrew N. Woznicki (New York: Peter Lang, 1993), pp. 165–75.

[22] Etienne Gilson, *L'esprit de la Philosophie médiévale* (Paris: Vrin, 1932), pp. 195–215.

[23] Von Balthasar, *Prolegomena*, p. 645.

[24] Ibid., pp. 645–46.

Here Balthasar expected Thomists to adjust their antennae—despite his critical remarks about Thomas' weak doctrine of humanly personal uniqueness. For was it not Thomas who identified "mission" and "procession"—divinely personal uniqueness—in the case of the incarnate Word? "In Christ the *processio* within the Godhead, which constitutes the Son as the Father's dialogue partner, is identical, in God's going-out-from-himself toward the world, with the *missio*, the sending of the Son to mankind," a *missio* which itself is "completed by the sending of the Spirit into the world, proceeding from both Father and Son".[25] It is that same Holy Spirit who, "given to men to enable them to be and act in a God-ward manner", can really mediate—close a breach—between person and role, doing so precisely in the passing on to man of "missions". Here in the notion of divinely distributed missions, the doctrine of man as in the image of God, crucial to the sixth and seventh volumes of the theological aesthetics, is "taken to its ultimate conclusion" and the aesthetic becomes dramatic.[26]

The third serviceable—indeed, essential—distinction Balthasar puts forward at the start of his prolegomena to theo-drama is the "distinction between the actor's responsibility for his performance and his responsibility to a director", which opens up the wider question of a distribution of labour in the theatre.[27] In any production there must be not only an *author*, who holds the "ontological primacy",[28] since he "stands at the point where the drama (which is to unfold between the individuals and their freedoms) comes into being as a unity".[29] There must also be, of course, the *actors*, through whom the playwright's work, hitherto "*potentially* drama", "becomes *actual*",[30] for the "material" of this art is "the actor's entire physical, emotional and spiritual self".[31] But also needed is the *director* since "between the dramatic poet and the actor there yawns a gulf that can be bridged only by a third party who will take responsibility for the play's performance, for making it present here and now",[32] a "party" who, "should know how to

[25] Ibid., p. 646.
[26] Ibid., p. 647.
[27] Ibid., p. 254.
[28] Ibid., p. 270.
[29] Ibid., p. 268.
[30] Ibid., p. 281; emphasis in original.
[31] Ibid., p. 287.
[32] Ibid., p. 298.

awaken's the actor's creative energies ... so that the characters really form an ensemble in the spiritual sense".[33] The trinitarian caste of this trio is obvious: author as Father, director as Holy Spirit, actors as including centrally in their number the principal protagonist of the drama, Jesus Christ.

They will be engaged on production of their play in something like a philanthropic work of redemption. All this effort is for the sake of an *audience* for whose benefit the performance is taking place. Balthasar stresses how that audience's presence, as in the theatre at large, is "not passive—quite the reverse, if the performance is to succeed it must be active, a willingness to enter into the action";[34] for the performance to "win our unreserved involvement—for it excludes any neutral 'observation'—it presupposes that we are unreservedly ready to be carried wherever it takes us".[35] The audience, like any audience, has certain "expectations". In the broadest terms, these are that the drama will "point to the intention of the author, and beyond him to the horizon of all meaning whatsoever".[36]

That "horizon" is what enables Balthasar, for the first time in the *Prolegomena* volume, to set forth the specificity of *Christian* drama on the stage.

In Greek tragedy it was possible for a god to step out of the invisible background of watching deities and appear on stage; he could proclaim divine thoughts and intentions, but only as an individual, not on behalf of the entire divine world. Christ, the Son of God, is not just *any* incarnation: he is the sole incarnation, revealing God's whole mind. God the Father, who sends him, remains in the background as the real "spectator" before whom "the great theatre of the world" is performed; but since Father and Son are one, this role of spectator on God's part cannot be separated from his entering into action on the stage. And when the Spirit proceeds from the Father and the Son and is breathed into the Church of Christ, something of God himself speaks in the mouths of the actors.[37]

[33] Ibid., pp. 300–301.
[34] Ibid., p. 306.
[35] Ibid., p. 309.
[36] Ibid., p. 314.
[37] Ibid., p. 319.

So, with a "dramatic dimension that bursts forth from the Absolute itself", the "horizon" gives the play an "ultimate destination, acting alongside man, from within"—though the meaning in question makes its appearance in a "hidden manner, discerned by faith, in and through the stumbling block of Christ's Cross".[38]

The upshot of Balthasar's theologically dramatic explorations will be a characterization of existence, in the light of the Cross, as "simultaneously a liturgy of worship and a battlefield".[39] That shows the huge weight he gives in *Theo-drama* to the Johannine Apocalypse, where the "power of self-giving love ... speaks in the tones of implacable judgment".[40] Theological aesthetics recurs as theological dramatics when the glorious supra-form of the Crucified and Risen One is reexpressed in terms of divine and human freedom. Ultimately, such theological dramatics will not only lead to theological logic (love's "ontologic"); it will turn into doxology. The "self-giving and self-surrender of the triune God provide the grammar of prayer that sounds endlessly in heaven".[41]

And here is where the analogy between the theatre and the redemptive action of God might be thought to break down. "A dramatic dimension that comes from God's horizon and is implanted in the world, comprehending and judging everything within the world and leading it to its redemptive meaning, is so unique and exuberant that it can only be reflected in a fragmentary and broken way on the stage."[42] There is incorrigible mystery here—but not mystification. For Balthasar the cataphatic deserves more prominence than the apophatic, since what we are dealing with is not concealment but unveiling, not eternal stasis but temporal (and "supra-temporal") enactment.

Thus, whatever the differences between theological aesthetics and theological dramatics, and however we envisage the correction and/ or refiguration of vision initiated by the move towards a dramatic scopus, and its analytic commentary in *Theo-Logic*, the trilogy speaks with one voice concerning both the necessity of apophasis and its

[38] Ibid., p. 320.
[39] Von Balthasar, *Dramatis Personae*, p. 33.
[40] Ibid., p. 35.
[41] O'Regan, *Hegel*, p. 455.
[42] Von Balthasar, *Prolegomena*, p. 320.

secondariness.... Mindful in general that the discourse of apocalyptic is a discourse of symbols—thus of signs that present the reality they represent—and mindful in particular that the governing symbol of apocalypse, that is, the Lamb slain before the foundation of the world, is incorrigibly kataphatic, Balthasar sets limits to apophasis. He does so, however, while remaining convinced that his own work illustrates just the kind of commitment to the apophatic modeled in Pseudo-Dionysius, Maximus, and Bonaventure, sufficient to resist Hegelian *Begriff* [in its highest form the absolute "idea" which constitutes the truth of both existence and essence], whose vocation is to internalize and neutralize that which would exceed language and the concept.[43]

But if the analogy with theatrical performance limps, something entirely predictable on the principle of God the "ever greater", that does not deprive it of serviceability for laying out the shape of divine redemption in the volumes of the theological dramatics that follow. Balthasar intends to show how each and every human "fate"—every human life—can be given meaning by relation to the drama of God in Christ.

Within the drama of Christ, every human fate is deprivatized so that its personal range may extend to the whole universe, depending on how far it is prepared to cooperate in being inserted into the norma-tive drama of Christ's life, death and Resurrection. Not only does this gather the unimaginable plurality of human destinies into a concrete, universal point of unity: it actually maintains their plurality within the unity, but as a function of this unity. This is the aim of an organic integration of all individual destinies in Christ (Ephesians 1:3–10), which is simultaneously the commissioning of the organic fullness of vocations and tasks by the organizing centre (Ephesians 4:7–16).[44]

It is a reading of the Letter to the Ephesians that supplies us with, at one and the same time, a theology of catholicity and a doctrine of the communion of saints; these would be themes allowing a compar-ison with, once again, Thomas' biblical commentaries where, writing on Ephesians itself, he finds in the Ascension of the Lord the source

---

[43] O'Regan, *Hegel*, p. 446.
[44] Von Balthasar, *Dramatis Personae*, p. 50.

of the diversity of gifts that make up the "many different states and functions in the Church".[45] More widely, the reading suggests how Christian revelation is "dramatic *at its very core*".[46] So, Balthasar now considers in turn the departure point of theo-drama in the "dramatis personae" (this occupies the second and third volumes of the theological dramatics), followed by the course of the action (the fourth volume), and lastly its final *dénouement* (the fifth).

Balthasar's theo-dramatic method

The second volume of the dramatics has, in effect, its own "prolegomena" which considers, however, not the character of drama as inferred from the historic practice of the play in various cultures (this was the task of volume 1), but the reasons why Christian theology requires reference to drama in order to do justice to the self-revelation of God. Here Balthasar's concern is with three necessarily interrelated topics: the nature of theology, the principles of biblical interpretation, and the structure of theological proof. Students of Thomas' concept of *sacra doctrina* in the opening question of the *Prima Pars* of the *Summa theologiae* will be familiar with these interconnexions. Notoriously, Thomas can use the term *sacra doctrina* for all four of divine revelation, the content of faith, theological construction, and what the Bible says. In the words of Thomas Gilby, "His distinctions between revelation, the Holy Scriptures, the habits of faith and of theological science as an intellectual virtue and as a gift of the Spirit, lack nothing in preciseness, yet it seems that the *sacra doctrina* of which he speaks in the first question of the *Summa* covers every cognitive reponse to the Word of God in simple and learned alike."[47]

If in that question Thomas comes within hailing distance of Balthasar on "theo-drama", it is probably by virtue of Aquinas' "active" sense of *doctrina* as *disciplina*—the moulding of believers by revelation which sets them on the path of entry into the vision of God.

[45] Thomas Aquinas, *In Ephesios* 4, lect. 3–4.

[46] Von Balthasar, *Dramatis Personae*, p. 51; emphasis in original.

[47] Thomas Gilby, O.P., "Sacra Doctrina", in *St. Thomas Aquinas, Summa Theologiae*, vol. 1, *Christian Theology*, Ia.1 (London: Eyre and Spottiswoode, 1964), p. 65; see pp. 57–66.

According to Balthasar, *one* of the ways in which the notion of theological dramatics can assist, or improve, the concept of theology is by preventing the latter from denoting "teaching" seen as simply the rehearsal of facts and ideas drawn from the revelatory deposit.[48] Of course, that deposit includes teachings, and very importantly so (Balthasar is hardly an antidoctrinal theologian). But the word "teaching" does not in itself convey as fully as possible the sheer impact of God's revelatory agency with its entry in power into the lives of individuals there to demand from them—and also to furnish for them from its own resources—a suitably robust response. In matters of biblical hermeneutics, Balthasar finds the comparison with drama needful in order to avoid what he terms an "epic" reading of Scripture, which simply lays out the narrative of the biblical story as if from a distance—rather than presenting the divine Agent, in whose hands Scripture is a living instrument, as initiating and sustaining an interaction with the hearers of the Word that continues today, and in each believer, until the end of time.[49]

Balthasar's choice of a superordinate principle in theology coheres with these statements. The supreme test of theological truth lies in its resistance to any diminishment of the "dramatic character of the Christian event".[50] "Theological proof" will, in interpreting divine revelation, typically subserve a "totality" that "presses toward *communio*"—a significant word, since Balthasar made it the name of the theological journal he helped to inspire. "Communio" is glossed here as "the primal mystery, namely, that God, out of his freely bestowed love, allows that which is not God to participate in all the treasures of his love, and this comes about in a reciprocity which, in Christian revelation, has again to be grounded in God (in the Trinity), yet without abolishing the creatureliness of the creature".[51] That licences, thinks Balthasar, the "daring integrations embraced by Catholic faith"—*too* daring at Balthasar's hands some Thomists might be tempted to say![52] The reader will encounter a

---

[48] Von Balthasar, *Man in God*, pp. 54–62, 67–70.
[49] Ibid., pp. 102–15
[50] Ibid., p. 115.
[51] Ibid., p. 127.
[52] Ibid.

number of audacities before the five volumes of the theological dramatics are concluded.

This other sort of "prolegomena" leads, then, into the heart of the second volume of the dramatics, concerned as this is with the "themes" of dramatic theology as these unfold on the "stage" of heaven and earth where infinite and finite freedoms have their interplay—not forgetting, however, that the "finite freedom" in question is not that of angels but of members of the human race (a little study of man, inspired by Maximus Confessor, will conclude the volume).

Theology must be shared by an inner participation in the drama of the divine-human interplay; so, unsurprisingly, its historic motifs have included God's "lawsuit" against the covenant people, apparently lost in the death of the Messiah but won in his Resurrection (here, however, Balthasar adduces only contemporary exegetes); the "classical" or patristically predominant Atonement theology of Christus Victor (revived in dogmatics notably by the Swedish Lutheran Gustaf Aulén—Balthasar chides him for failure to do justice to the other Atonement models, including Anselm's);[53] and the notion of "holy warfare", sharing with Christ in redemptive struggle, prominent since Origen in spiritual theology. The historic treatment of these themes by no means amounts to an overall "theological dramatic theory", but they suffice to show that Christian thought has not eschewed dramatic elements.

The topic of the drama's "stage" can be polished off even more rapidly. "What really traverses and fills the stage between heaven and earth comes from God alone: his wisdom (Proverbs 8:1–9:6), his Word, which is sent out to traverse the earth, yet touching heaven (Wisdom 18:16)."[54] Yet, "if ultimately everything comes from God, if only heaven is active and earth is merely passive, there can never be a drama."[55] The doctrine of grace would dissolve into "extreme Predestinationism"; Christology would become Monophysite. But no: grace gives man a "special receptivity" and on that

---

[53] Gustaf Aulén, *Christus Victor: A Study of the Three Main Types of the Idea of the Atonement* (1953; London: Society for the Promotion of Christian Knowledge, 2003).

[54] Von Balthasar, *Man in God*, p. 182.

[55] Ibid., p. 184.

basis a fruitfulness for heaven (cf. Is 61:11), so much so, indeed, that "heaven becomes dependent on earth", and earth "seems to give birth to heaven".[56] These claims, followed up, would take Balthasar into all three of the remaining volumes of his dramatics—volume 3, insofar as they imply a Chalcedonian Christology; volume 4, insofar as they touch on the means of the Atonement, the great "action" of the theo-drama; and volume 5, insofar as they imply a particular understanding of the Trinity and man's final home there, "the last act". As Balthasar explains, in relation to this climactic study of homecoming to the triune Lord, "Later we shall have to reflect on how this self-emptying ('poverty' Second Corinthians 8:9; 'kenosis' Philippians 2:7) on the part of heaven is in accord with its nature; that is, it does not betray a weakness but rather manifests its fullness and its freedom to be itself, even on earth and *in* earth."[57] Balthasar's Siewerth-derived version of Thomism will suggest the ontology that can justify what he considers an orthodox version of kenoticism—to be applied not only to the Word incarnate but to the entire divine Trinity. In context, however, these comments serve to illustrate a more modest claim especially germane to a study of divine action—namely, that "the New Testament relationship between heaven and earth can only be illuminated *dramatically*."[58] Indeed, "heaven and earth have been created as distinct realms with a view to a drama in which each pole has its own, proper, positive role to play."[59] In the last analysis, accordingly, the "stage" is "assimilated into the spiritual dimensions of the actors themselves".[60]

And these actors are God and man, the bearers of, respectively, infinite and finite freedom. Here Balthasar's discussion has quite a high philosophical content, since on the face of things the appearance of God on the stage of the world looks more like the behaviour of the mythological deities of Hellenic polytheism than anything coverable by the rationally refined concept of the divine One. But prima facie is not always a good guide. An Incarnation of the deity

[56] Ibid.
[57] Ibid.; emphasis in original.
[58] Ibid., p. 185; emphasis in original.
[59] Ibid., p. 187.
[60] Ibid., p. 188.

is not so rationally indefensible if it is reasonable to suppose that
the absolute One is free, with an infinite freedom, able to bring
forth centres of finite freedom in what is not itself, and also—most
important—that such bringing into existence of finite freedom does
not so limit as actually to annul the infinitude of the freedom that
did the bringing forth in the first place. For Balthasar, "God shows
his almighty power particularly by imparting authentic selfhood to his
creatures", a highly Thomasian thought.[61] The power of the First
Cause is the better attested the fuller the range of the secondary causality exercised by those whose existence it has effected, and whose
activities testify to the *continuing* fruitfulness of that cause. So, as Balthasar writes, with specific attention to the issue of freedom: "We,
for our part, with our finite freedom, must indeed designate ourselves as the 'others' when we think of our relation to God; but we
cannot draw the conclusion that we are the 'others' as far as God
himself is concerned. The question we ought rather to ask is this:
Since we owe everything (including our freedom) to the 'everything' that God's freedom represents, can we be the 'others' when
seen from God's vantage-point? Does he not recognize and affirm us
in him and not outside him?"[62]

Up to this point, using both the "philosophy that is immanent
in [Christian] theology" and "the accumulated reflections of non-
Christian humanity", a rebuttal of the accusation of "return to mythology" seems perfectly possible. But the doctrines of the Fall and the
Atonement have not yet been factored in, and these will reveal a
heightened contrast between infinite and finite freedom. They will exhibit, moreover, the "abyss that opens up between the holiness of infinite freedom and the plight of finite freedom that has fallen into sin".[63]
If that adds to the original problem, there is also, in the shape of the
doctrine of the Trinity, a way of mitigating the difficulty from which
Balthasar started out. The theologian must "deepen philosophy's 'the
Other as non-Other', in the direction of the Trinitarian mystery of
'the Other in the non-Other', that is, in the One divine Being".[64]

---

[61] Ibid., p. 192.
[62] Ibid., p. 193; emphasis in original.
[63] Ibid., p. 194.
[64] Ibid.

The alterity of the creature vis-à-vis the Creator has as its archetype a primordial, uncreated alterity in God himself: the Word who is the Father's vis-à-vis in the Holy Spirit. But the Atonement theology of the dramatics must await volume 4, and the triadology, volume 5. Even the Christology must be delayed to volume 3, but Balthasar lifts a corner of the curtain when he writes that for the Christ of the Council of Chalcedon, notably as interpreted by Saint Maximus, "infinite freedom indwells finite freedom, and so the finite is perfected in the infinite without the infinite losing itself in the finite or the finite in the infinite."[65]

The character of finite freedom

Meanwhile, Balthasar needs to get a better grip on the very idea of finite freedom. He begins by making the point that a single finite freedom is inconceivable—both the finitude and the corporeality of free finitude require its social mediation, a context in relations with human others. This is not just an empirical observation. Seeking to reconcile the thinking of the Augustinian and Thomasian traditions on the soul's presence to itself,[66] he finds that in the "primal experience" of being, one can distinguish between its mode of being and its grasp of universal being but not separate them.[67] Not through moral generosity but because in knowledge of self the light of being renders the statement unavoidable, one can say, "I am unique, but only by making room for countless others to be unique."[68]

He then goes on to draw a distinction—with far-reaching implications—between freedom as "autonomous motion" and freedom as "consent". The first ("autonomous motion") is inevitable in human living; the second ("consent"), the desirable but by no means assured outcome of a life. "The manner and degree of our 'self-realization' remain open, and it is up to man himself to decide what, ultimately, constitutes freedom and under what form it should

[65] Ibid., p. 201.
[66] Ibid., pp. 207–8, footnote 2.
[67] Ibid., p. 209.
[68] Ibid.

be striven for"—there we have "autonomous motion".[69] Possibly—but not certainly—someone may also see that "finite freedom, if it remains alone and is posited as absolute, is bound to become the hellish torment of a Tantalus if it is not permitted to attain full development in the self-warranting realm of absolute freedom." There, only "consent"—consent to God—will serve our turn.[70]

Balthasar's discussion of these two senses of finite freedom constantly reverts to "Fathers"—notably to Irenaeus, to Nyssa and Maximus (both in critical dialogue with Origen), to Augustine (with whom he brackets Bonaventure), and, not least, to Thomas. The patristic (and high-mediaeval) tradition knows well of the two forms of human freedom that Balthasar has identified. The Fathers affirm man's "autonomous finite freedom operating within an encompassing Providence" over against determinism and Gnosticism.[71] Their doing so is vital in a positive sense for theo-drama and not simply in a negative sense to ward off insanity. It is "precisely man's freedom to choose that makes him a genuine partner in dialogue with God".[72] Saint Irenaeus' notion that fallen man discovers by painful experience how, owing to evil, he must cleave the more firmly to the good will have quite a future ahead of it among the Greek Fathers. Balthasar finds the way that Thomas summarises this tradition[73]—in its Western embodiment, it derives from Augustine's writings against the Manichaeans—bringing him to the verge of the second meaning of finite freedom: "consent"—consent, namely, to the infinite freedom in which finite freedom can find its fullest expansion. "When [Thomas] says that every free will only seeks things under the aspect of the good, and to that extent seeks throughout the whole breadth of being ... for the absolute Good, God; and that in this process it is determined by itself alone, and thus is undetermined in its choice of the path along which the good is to be sought—he is already on the threshold of the second question", freedom as consent.[74]

[69] Ibid., pp. 212–13.
[70] Ibid., p. 213.
[71] Ibid., p. 217.
[72] Ibid., p. 221.
[73] See Aquinas' discussions of freedom of the will as such and freedom, more specifically, of choice in the Disputed Questions on Truth, qq. 22, 24.
[74] Von Balthasar, Man in God, p. 225.

Balthasar considered that the way Thomas sees the relation between these two senses of finite freedom favours Henri de Lubac's interpretation of Thomas on the issue, much disputed in mid-twentieth century Catholic theology (as also today), of nature and the supernatural.[75]

> Because the *"motus"* [motion] of freedom is inseparable from the *"causa sui"* [autonomous operation], because there is thus in the will a natural longing (*desiderium naturale*) for complete, exhaustive self-possession, which would have to coincide with the "possession" of being as such, we arrive at the Thomist paradox.... Man strives to fulfil himself in an Absolute and yet, although he is *"causa sui"*, he is unable to achieve this by his own power or by attaining any finite thing or finite good. Precisely this, according to Thomas, constitutes man's dignity.[76]

The natural is made for the supernatural—though Thomists who worry about the threat this claim may carry for the gratuitousness of grace will be pleased to hear Balthasar say that this does not "mean that God 'owes' it to natural man to raise him to the state of grace; God only 'owes' it to himself to be faithful to the order and consistency of his unitary world plan."[77]

The second sense of finite freedom is profound, and unsuspected by most people, including most Christians, unless they happen to have read Augustine on Paul, or Thomas on—in effect—Augustine. It is also, for Balthasar, a specifically New Testament discovery. "Only in the preaching of Jesus and the post-Easter meditation upon it in the light of the Holy Spirit does the womb of the Father's divine freedom

---

[75] Henri de Lubac, *The Mystery of the Supernatural* (1967; New York: Crossroad, 1998). Balthasar was not fully satisfied by de Lubac's account; see Hans Urs von Balthasar, *The Theology of Henri de Lubac* (San Francisco: Ignatius Press, 1991), p. 63. The same reservations are expressed in Hans Urs von Balthasar, *The Theology of Karl Barth: Exposition and Interpretation*, trans. Edward T. Oakes, S.J. (San Francisco: Communio Books; Ignatius Press, 1992), pp. 297–98.

[76] Von Balthasar, *Man in God*, pp. 225–26. Thomas uses the phrase *causa sui* here as the nominal equivalent to John Damascene's adjective *autoexousios*: this has nothing to do, of course, with the divine "self-positing" of the rationalist philosopher Baruch Spinoza and subsequent Idealist theology.

[77] Hans Urs von Balthasar, *Theo-drama: Theological Dramatic Theory*, vol. 3, *Dramatis Personae: The Person in Christ*, trans. Graham Harrison (San Francisco: Ignatius Press, 1992), p. 257.

open so wide and so deep that we begin to suspect what 'the fulfillment of finite freedom in infinite freedom' might mean."[78] The verse
of the Letter to the Romans on "God's love [which] has been poured
into our hearts through the Holy Spirit" (5:5) is as important for Balthasar as it is for the Augustinian–Thomist tradition. The Holy Spirit
'brings about two things at the same time: he liberates finite freedom so
that it may embrace its own, ultimate freedom; and he does so by initiating it into a participation in infinite freedom".[79] Gregory of Nyssa
has his own version of Augustine's more autobiographically triggered
teaching: finite freedom springs from a source in infinite freedom,
and its aim is to "realize itself by assimilation to it".[80] Thomas' own
view, in Balthasar's opinion, lies "structurally closer to Gregory".[81]
Its starting point is certainly not existential *angst*, as with Augustine,
but serene ontological enquiry into the "mediation of Being, which
permeates and is at work in all finite being, the most unique [such as
the human person] as well as the most general".[82] "Finite freedom, as
autoexousion ... is by no means alienated but rather inwardly fulfilled
by consenting to that Being-in-its-totality which has now unveiled
itself as that which freely grounds all things, as that which, in infinite
freedom, creates finite freedom."[83]

Freedom infinite

It is time to move on to infinite freedom for itself. To Balthasar's
mind, despite certain intimations in Plotinus' account of the One,
the biblical revelation is the only source worth consulting. A "natural sense of finitude" is worlds away from the "Christian sense of
creatureliness", whose objective correlate is the "sole Will of infinite
freedom, which as such is a Will of wisdom and salvation".[84] Balthasar makes use of the *Prima Pars* of Thomas' *Summa theologiae* to clarify

[78] Von Balthasar, *Man in God*, p. 229.
[79] Ibid., p. 230.
[80] Ibid., p. 236.
[81] Ibid., p. 239.
[82] Ibid.
[83] Ibid., p. 242.
[84] Ibid., p. 254.

how the ground of *totum esse*, the world's total reality, can only be infinite Being which as such is "equally infinitely self-illuminating and self-possessed and hence is absolutely free in itself".[85] But if that is pure Thomism, what now follows is sheer Balthasarianism, and it has to do with the freedom not so much of the divine nature as of the divine hypostases, and not so much—or so fully—in connexion with the origin of those hypostases (though also that) as with their relations of communion. In connexion with the origin of the Persons, Balthasar writes: "God is not only by nature free in his self-possession, in his ability to do what he will with himself; for that very reason, he is also free to do what he will with his own nature."[86]

The generation of the Son and the spiration of the Spirit are the upshot. Self-surrender, in the origination of the hypostases, is for God "part of [the] bliss of absolute freedom".[87] In the communion— the continuing relations—of the Persons there must be, if God truly is absolute freedom, so Balthasar continues, eternally enduring "areas of infinite freedom" between them. "Something like infinite 'duration' and infinite 'space' must be attributed to the acts of reciprocal love so that the life of the [intratrinitarian] *communio*, of fellowship, can develop ... in terms of love and blessedness."[88] Here Balthasar introduces the themes of not only the mutual acknowledgement of one Person by another, but also mutual adoration, reciprocal petition, surprise, and wonder. These are motifs which cannot but startle more conventional doctrinal theologians when used as expressions descriptive of the trinitarian relationships. Balthasar's justification for these claims is that "the hypostatic modes of being constitute the greatest imaginable opposition one to another (and thus no one of them can overtake any other), in order that they can mutually interpenetrate in the most intimate manner conceivable."[89] The Persons require the "distance" the relations of opposition found in their origin give to them so as to be maximally "intimate", one to another,

---

[85] Ibid., p. 255, with reference to Thomas Aquinas, *Summa theologiae* Ia, q. 45, a. 1, corpus, and a. 4 ad 1 (hereafter cited as *ST*).
[86] Von Balthasar, *Man in God*, p. 256.
[87] Ibid.
[88] Ibid., p. 257.
[89] Ibid., p. 258.

in the trinitarian *perichoresis*, or coinherence, whereby each abides in the other and exists in no other way. But at the same time, Balthasar also seeks to reassure those same anxious theologians by insisting in the very next sentence that each Person is "co-determined by the *ordo processionis* and the trinitarian unity", a way of saying he is not proposing an unmitigated Romantic anarchy in thinking about God.[90] The single mind and will of God are exercised in three hypostatically distinct modes. Their ontological (not simply moral) unity is not denied ("the trinitarian unity"); their order, which turns on the Father as source of the Son and, with the Son, of the Spirit, is essential (the *ordo processionis*). Having entered this clarification, Balthasar goes on to make the daring claim that, on the basis of his triune freedom, "God is always *greater than himself.*"[91]

That conclusion follows for Balthasar from the basic assertion that the "law", or internal norm, of the triune life is self-surrender, a "letting-be" in love, the ground of endless fruitfulness in the communion of Persons. Here too is why in the last analysis finite freedom can find in the triune life not its own negation but its true fulfilment. The world's own origin lies, yes, in the "realms of creatable being opened up by divine omnipotence" (compare Thomas on the power of God), but "more deeply [it is found] in the trinitarian 'letting-be' of the hypostatic acts."[92] More specifically, the world finds its place in the divine Son. Here Balthasar seeks to explain the "hymn" on the primacy of the Christ "in" and "for" whom "all things were created", according to the Letter to the Colossians (1:15–17). It is an opportunity for an enhanced Bonaventurianism. In an especially rich passage Balthasar writes,

The world can be thought of as the gift of the Father (who is both Begetter and Creator) to the Son, since the Father wishes to sum up all things in heaven and on earth in the Son, as head; thus the Son takes this gift—just as he takes the gift of Godhead—as an opportunity to thank and glorify the Father. Having brought the world to its fulfillment, he will lay the entire kingdom at his feet, so that God (the

[90] Ibid.
[91] Ibid., p. 259; emphasis added.
[92] Ibid., p. 266.

Father) may be all in all; as for the Spirit, he is given the world by both: he *is* eternally the reciprocal glorification of Father and Son, but now he can implement it in and through the creation.[93]

Indeed, the remaining volumes of the dramatics show how this came about, through the Incarnation and the Paschal Mystery.

The play enacted

To enact the play the players must step forward. So far, as Balthasar admits, the characterization of "finite freedom" has been so abstract that, for the most part, it might just as well as have been angels rather than humans he was talking about.[94] There has been a reason for this. The essence of man is not really available until we see it deployed in the dramatic action of life—not least the life that is engagement with God. Even then, all is hardly plain sailing. "In Christian anthropology ... it remains an open question how much of man's original 'essence' has been retained in the 'scene' currently enacted"—a reference, in context, to the spectrum of opinions on the point that were put forward at the Council of Trent.[95] Rooted in the cosmos, both spirit and body, man and woman, individual and community, "man the indefinable" in the present condition of post-lapsarian "brokenness" or "inner torn-ness" has to cope with too many damaged dimensions ever to achieve a proper totality,[96] or synthesis,[97] though in his freedom he is responsible for doing just that. But a Creator who freely shows his favour to mankind draws man to that endlessly desirable condition by making it possible *in* God, *through* Jesus Christ, overcoming in so doing the "last barrier", which is death.[98] This is the course the play follows, emulating in its own dramatic medium the trajectory towards *beatitudo* described by

[93] Ibid., p. 262, with internal allusions to Eph 1:10; 1 Cor 15:24, 28; Jn 16:13–15.
[94] Von Balthasar, *Man in God*, p. 335.
[95] Ibid., p. 336.
[96] Ibid., pp. 343, 359.
[97] Ibid., p. 364.
[98] Ibid.

Thomas in the *exitus-reditus* pattern of the *Summa theologiae*—and the *Summa contra gentiles*, with its "comedic" narrative (something we have noted in considering the "stylistic" affinities of Balthasar and Aquinas towards the end of chapter 1 above).

In volume 3 of the dramatics, Balthasar furnishes concrete description of the main characters of theo-drama, who, in a sense, are only two: Christ Jesus and Mary-Israel-Church, with the "authorities and powers" (angels, whether holy or fallen) playing ancillary, yet in no way dispensable roles. And yet, as the subtitle of this volume makes plain, the cast is not complete until some account has been made of the way *anyone* affected by the plot can play a part, "The Person in Christ". "In theo-drama [Christ] is not only the main character but the model for all other actors and the one who gives them their own identity as characters."[99]

And first, then, Christ. "If Christ is the living point of unity of the divine Sophia in its manifold realizations in the world, and if he is ultimately the place where this Wisdom not only 'hovers over' the created world (in the form of Providence) but actually touches and penetrates it, it follows that, from the outset (Alpha) he is envisaged as the consummating protagonist ... of the entire drama."[100] Put in terms of the nature-grace or natural-supernatural relationship: the "Christ-principle" is the "Adam-principle's" own inner principle—which means it is unnatural for the Adam-principle to seek self-rooting, though at the same time the Christ-principle itself can neither be inferred nor predicated, for its implications—divinization—are "utterly overwhelming".[101] A gift of this sort can only be grace (the Augustinian-Thomist "operative grace") which "also needs to be freely accepted, through a certain influence on the recipient by the same grace" (the Augustinian-Thomist "prevenient grace").[102] And here "the first event to be dramatic in the real sense is the history of the Word's becoming flesh: for the Incarnation takes place in the nature of the old Adam, which is to be transformed by the entire Christ-event into what, henceforth, will be the Christ-principle

99 Von Balthasar, *Person in Christ*, p. 201.
100 Ibid., pp. 20–21.
101 Ibid., p. 35.
102 Ibid.

operating in history. What is created is not a new human being: the same nature that belonged to the old Adam is now, through the drama of the life, death and Resurrection of Jesus, carried over into the state of the new Adam."[103] A new space of divine-human freedom ("acting area") is thus opened up for fresh roles to be enacted and a *dénouement* of a wholly unexpected kind to be prepared.

In Balthasar's opinion this will entail from the Annunciation onwards something certainly unexpected for classical Latin theology: an "inversion" in the ordering of Son and Spirit in the economy. For Thomas the ordering of the economic Trinity continues at all points the ordering in the absolute or immanent Trinity. The principle of the union of Godhood and manhood in Christ is the second trinitarian Person, while the third trinitarian Person acts—as we should expect—"third" following "second", subsequently endowing the Son's humanity with all grace.[104] In Balthasar's theological dramatics, contrastingly, for the purposes of the Incarnation economy, the Spirit will precede the Son, beginning with the Annunciation, when the Son lets the Spirit bring about his enmanment in the Virgin. Of course, as Balthasar says, there "can be no question of the Incarnation interrupting the common spiration of the Spirit by Father and Son, otherwise the Spirit could not exist in and over the Son".[105] But the Spirit, breathed forth eternally as the love of Father and Son, has, for Balthasar, a "twofold face": he is not only the "objective form of [the shared] subjectivity [of Father and Son]"; he is also the "objective witness to their difference-in-unity or unity-in-difference".[106] It is the latter aspect of his being in the absolute Godhead that makes possible his place now as directing the drama, mediating as he does the Father's will to the Son.

For his part, the role of Christ himself is nonexchangeable; "his mission coincides with his person, so that both together constitute God's exhaustive self-communication."[107] Once, with the conclusion of the Paschal Mystery, the economic need of the "trinitarian

---

[103] Ibid., p. 37.
[104] *ST* IIIa, q. 7, a. 13.
[105] Von Balthasar, *Person in Christ*, p. 187.
[106] Ibid.
[107] Ibid., p. 150.

inversion" is met, then at Pentecost the Son can begin to send the
Spirit from the Father in the way that befits the Spirit's other face, as
the objective form of the united freedom of Father and Son. "The
Spirit has always borne witness that [Christ] is the unique and peerless
Son of the Father. But the Son, in inaugurating the acting area for
the theo-drama on the basis of his Resurrection, can impart the Spirit
to the players in such a way that they too, in an analogous way, can be
seen to be unique."[108] These are Balthasar's equivalents of the "invisible missions" of Son and Spirit of which Aquinas speaks.[109] Through
their totality in ongoing history, "the whole world drama", the Son
"becomes the Omega that—precisely because he is the Alpha—he
always is".[110]

Apart from the chief protagonist (in whom—"in Christ"—all roles
are summed up), the other principal actor is the one I described as
"Mary-Israel-Church", or, in more properly Balthasarian terms, the
bearer of "woman's answer". Mary encapsulates the role of Israel and
the Church in the theo-drama as the womanly representative of the
first and the matrix of the second. The Church is "from Mary";[111]
though in discussing such themes of Church agency as the call of the
nations (against "national messianism", presumably of the Polish or
Russian varieties),[112] the continuing challenge of nonbelieving Jewry
(an unavoidable "spiritual duel"),[113] and intra-Christian divisions
(there cannot be an "abstract catholicity"),[114] the Marian focus perhaps inevitably dissipates—and so does, for the most part and maybe
as a consequence, the model of "theo-drama" within which these
otherwise stimulating discussions are embedded. Mary's own role
as the Yes-sayer par excellence necessarily adds to a Christological
Mariology an ecclesiological counterpart. Her consent to be *Theoto-
kos*, the God-bearer (Christological), constitutes for Balthasar's dramatics the foundation for her fontal role in relation to the community

---

[108] Ibid., p. 51; cf. ibid., pp. 263–82, where Balthasar describes what it may mean for anyone to be "chosen and sent forth".
[109] *ST* Ia, q. 43, arts. 5–7.
[110] Von Balthasar, *Person in Christ*, pp. 201–2.
[111] Ibid., pp. 351–53.
[112] Ibid., p. 422.
[113] Ibid., p. 401.
[114] Ibid., p. 446.

of disciples (ecclesiological). "No mission can be more unrestricted and universal than that which gives the Yes that God looks for, the Yes to his all-embracing plan."[115]

But insofar as her *dramatis persona* is her very own person, the Virgin comes on stage already in Balthasar's theo-dramatic account of Christ and his mission—and does so in a way that entails a dispute with Thomas. In Aquinas' account of the "acquired" human knowledge of Jesus (as distinct, then, from his "infused" knowledge, the knowledge that is transferred from the Logos to his human mind, hypostatically united as that mind was to the Word), he thought it appropriate that the Saviour should learn from natural objects, by means of the five senses, for things are directly created by God, but inappropriate for him to learn from human teachers.[116] For Balthasar, the "logic of the Incarnation" is against this, for it goes against an "elementary truth of human nature".[117] Unless a child is awakened to consciousness of its "I" by the human "thou" of his mother, it "cannot become a human child at all".[118] Balthasar is open to the notion that this "awakening" may have been prenatal, thus allowing for Jesus' self-awareness as the humanly embodied Son of the Father from the womb, as Pope Pius XII had proposed in his 1943 encyclical *Mystici Corporis Christi*, following Aquinas.[119] But however that awakening is dated, he qualifies it as not only humanization but spiritual initiation—and adds that, in the case of the mother of the Child Jesus, it cannot but imply a high Mariology. For Balthasar, Jesus' personal self-consciousness is in the first place "mission-consciousness"—he knows himself as the One sent by the Father in the context of the interplay of God and Israel in the Old Testament. Mary will have been his initiator to this awareness too on the basis, at the least, of what was communicated to her at the Annunciation. She could initiate him into the "religious tradition that looks to the fulfillment of Israel's hope and ... teach it to the Child".[120] Balthasar

---

[115] Ibid., p. 300.

[116] *ST* IIIa, q. 12, a. 3, corpus and ad 2.

[117] Von Balthasar, *Person in Christ*, p. 175.

[118] Ibid. No doubt Balthasar would agree that "mother" there includes anyone who plays in an infant's regard the maternal part.

[119] Ibid., pp. 175–76, footnote 21.

[120] Ibid., p. 176.

might have added that Mary's Immaculate Conception, not affirmed by Thomas, would have guaranteed her capacity to transmit her own infused knowledge quite as reliably, when received by Jesus as acquired knowledge, as does the (also divinely caused) existence of natural things. Her role, in Balthasar's view, would suffice to bring from a state of latent awareness to a condition of explicitness the consciousness bestowed with the very existence of Christ's humanized Person. He had "been given a mission, not accidentally, but as a modality of his eternal personal being".[121]

The heart of the theological dramatics is "the Action"—that is, the Passion of the Lord, which has its issue in his Exaltation, for the slain Lamb is the Victor. Though the saving work of God in Christ begins with the Incarnation, it has its climax in the Paschal Mystery and, above all, in the Passion—for the descent is the Passion's obverse, and the Resurrection its outcome. In recent Catholic theology, so Balthasar thought, "it may be that an 'incarnational' tendency is trying to obliterate the borderline between the life [which is preparation] and the Passion [which is goal]; this calls for renewed attention to be devoted to the Passion's inherent modalities."[122] In virtue of those "modalities", what took place on the Cross "remains a mystery and can never be reduced to a 'system' ";[123] the many theological interpretations found in the Church, beginning with the New Testament, revolve around a "transcendent core".[124] Balthasar finds that Thomas agrees. "All the time [Aquinas] is aware that all the concepts applied to the *mysterium* are more pointers and images than exhaustive definitions, which is why he refers in the same breath to *meritum, satisfactio, sacrificium, redemptio*."[125] These various theories are essentially "open to one another";[126] any unilateralism in deployment will relax the "theo-dramatic tension in the whole", something patent in much modern discussion of the meaning of the death of the Messiah.[127]

---

[121] Ibid., p. 201.
[122] Hans Urs von Balthasar, *Theo-drama: Theological Dramatic Theory*, vol. 4, *The Action*, trans. Graham Harrison (San Francisco: Ignatius Press, 1994), p. 238.
[123] Ibid.
[124] Ibid., p. 237.
[125] Ibid., p. 262, with reference to *ST* IIa, q. 48, arts. 1–4; a. 6 ad 3.
[126] Von Balthasar, *Action*, p. 240.
[127] Ibid., p. 244.

Balthasar thoroughly approves of the "exchange" soteriology of the Fathers, but thinks they did not do full justice to Saint Paul's teaching in his Second Letter to the Corinthians that the Saviour was "made" sin (5:21), rather than simply taking on the burden of its consequences—something also true of Anselm and Aquinas, otherwise admirable figures in orchestrating the pertinent New Testament themes. The nub of Balthasar's Passiology is this: the Sinless One changes places with the sinful, untying in so doing (meritoriously, satisfactorily, sacrificially, redemptively) the knot of sin that held them bound and initiating them into the trinitarian life, for behind the "holy exchange" of the Incarnation there has always been the initiative of the divine Love.

Thomist reactions to Balthasar sometimes include the claim that the way he expresses the "pro nobis"—especially when taken together with his insistence that wrath expresses the divine attribute of righteousness in relation to evil—amounts to treating the death of Christ on the Cross as an act of "penal substitution" by the Father: that is, divine child abuse.[128] But Balthasar warns explicitly how "the atonement wrought by Christ must not be interpreted as a penance imposed on the Son by the divine Father; rather, as we have often repeated, it goes back to that salvific decision made by the Trinity. Jesus Christ sees himself as coming forth from that decision in perfect freedom."[129] Listing major figures who have spoken of "vicarious punishment" (John Chrysostom, Augustine, Denys the Carthusian, the preachers of the seventeenth-century French School, and classic modern Catholic exegetes, including the founder of the Ecole biblique de Jérusalem, Père Lagrange),[130] Balthasar does not wish to join their number. Balthasar's favoured term *Stellvertretung* is best rendered in English as "vicarious representation", for it implies not only substitution (in our place) but also representation (on our behalf). And "vicarious representation", though rejected by many self-consciously modern theologians as anthropologically inconceivable, is not the same as "vicarious punishment". "Subjectively" the Lamb may be

---

[128] An example is Jean-Pierre Torrell, O.P., *Pour nous les hommes et pour notre Salut* (Paris: Cerf, 2014).

[129] Von Balthasar, *Person in Christ*, p. 242.

[130] Von Balthasar, *Action*, pp. 290–92, 296–97.

able to experience the Passion as punishment, but "objectively speaking, in his case it cannot be such."[131]

As to the anger of God at sin, it is an unmistakeable biblical datum, already manifested in the body of the Gospels in the anger of Christ which "flares up wherever there is resistance to his mission and the tasks arising form it, for such resistance offends the Father's love manifest within him, the triune Holy Spirit".[132] That of course describes the passional life of the soul of the humanized Word and is readily accepted by Aquinas.[133] When ascribed to God as God, "anger", in Balthasar's usage, expresses a "free involvement that is controlled by love and righteousness".[134] Though Balthasar uses the language of divine "pathos", introduced by the Jewish theologian Abraham Heschel in his discussion of the prophets, he understands God's anger "non-anthropomorphically",[135] as an attribute of the "ethos" of God—that is, the character of his self-involving activity in Israel and the world.

What is controversial in Balthasar's Atonement theology for Thomists is, rather, the claim that the Lamb went to the "length of vicariously taking on man's God-lessness".[136] The Son-made-man experienced an alienation and distance from the Father made possible by two factors: the relations of opposition (Balthasar may prefer to write "total distinctness") in the immanent Trinity,[137] and the remote ground of possibility for suffering that is constituted by the "vulnerability" or "recklessness" of the Persons in the selflessness of their communion-relations in the divine life.[138] Balthasar's thinking on the "cup of wrath" is prima facie alarming, but its subtlety should not be overlooked. Yes, the Father allows the Son to endure the dereliction of Godlessness (he must experience the human no to the full), but in this "wrathful alienation" which expresses the

[131] Ibid., p. 338.
[132] Ibid., p. 341.
[133] See Paul Gondreau, *The Passions of Christ's Soul in the Theology of St. Thomas Aquinas* (Scranton, PA: University of Scranton Press, 2009).
[134] Von Balthasar, *Action*, p. 344.
[135] Ibid.
[136] Ibid., p. 324.
[137] Ibid., p. 326.
[138] Ibid., p. 329.

"common work of love for the world" of Father and Son, the generating Source and the beloved Only-Begotten are "closer together than ever".[139]

The climactic action has its dramatic context in the "long patience of God". For Balthasar the judicial murder of the Messiah is the final human rejection of the divine solution to the human problem—a problem otherwise insoluble since time and death make man a riddle to himself, experiencing in life, as he must, the "pathos of the world-stage".[140] Man is restless, a paradoxical being, a "synthesis that lacks fulfilment",[141] oriented towards God yet with a "natural desire" for the vision of God that on its own terms must inevitably suffer frustration. God alone can establish the integration broken mankind needs. The Incarnation of the Logos had begun the clearing away of the "pre-Christian impasse".[142] "Man was created with a view to the God-man; in him, the equipoise between the absolute and the relative, which man cannot discover, has been established. True, this equipoise comes from God, since it is his Word that becomes man, but not without the earth giving her noblest fruit [Mary] to cooperate in the Incarnation."[143] Something irreversible happened to human existence when the Absolute came in person onto the world stage, not simply "irradiating" finitude but actually "becoming finite".[144] Through the appearance of the divine-human protagonist finitude has the chance to receive an eternal meaning, one capable of binding up into one all its parts. Inter alia, that must mean dealing with mortality, which is what transpires when God undergoes death as man in a way that cuts deeper than any death ever before (God taking upon himself "without selectivity" the sin of all).[145] It must also mean dealing with evil, which the power of man's ill-aligned freedom has conjured into its own seeming existence. The context of evil, man guiltily implicated in the world's suffering, is where we can witness "the dramatic tension of personal and social existence

---

[139] Ibid., p. 349.
[140] Ibid., p. 131.
[141] Ibid., p. 147.
[142] Ibid., p. 229.
[143] Ibid., p. 110.
[144] Ibid., p. 132.
[145] Ibid., p. 191.

finally explode",[146] as human autonomy affirms itself as absolute, taking the good into its power, thus falsifying its relation both to infinite freedom *and* to its own finitude. In this situation—as Israel's experience, above all in the great prophets, makes plain—the will to evil becomes the more entrenched the greater the counterpower of the divine goodness inviting it to convert.

In the Resurrection, though it is the moment when the humanity of Christ comes to share the eternal glory the Son has always enjoyed with the Father, the wounds he has incurred continue to feature, as in the celebrated meeting with the doubting Thomas in the Gospel of John (20:24–29). The wounds are not only apologetics, to prove the identity of the Risen One with the Crucified. They are there because it is "through his opened body ... and the infinite distribution of his flesh and shedding of his blood"—for he has become "eucharistic", sharing himself out with his disciples in thanksgiving to the Father— that "men can henceforth share in the substantial infinitude of his Divine Person."[147] The drama experienced by the economic Trinity remains "constantly actual", for "what takes place in the 'economic' Trinity is cherished and embraced by the 'immanent Trinity'",[148] so that wherever sin and death reign, the "revolution effected by Christ becomes operative" once more.[149] But there is also another sense in which the drama has not ended.

Presenting the Atonement via the unusual method (probably von Speyr-derived) of an account of the Apocalypse, where "the Lamb is both 'worthy' and 'able' not only to symbolize God's involvement [with the world] but to *be* it,"[150] the consequences of the redeeming death are not the pacification of anti-God powers but, on the contrary, the intensification of their activity. Balthasar terms this the "specifically theological law of proportionate polarization: the more God intervenes, the more he elicits opposition to him".[151] That explains the role of the Johannine Apocalypse in Balthasar's

---

[146] Ibid., p. 160.
[147] Ibid., p. 363.
[148] Ibid., p. 390.
[149] Ibid., p. 363.
[150] Ibid., p. 52. Internal reference is to Rev 5:1–5.
[151] Ibid., p. 51.

soteriology: "Not until John does the core of that negative power emerge—in the post-Easter Church—as the open refusal to accept Jesus Christ as the Word of God who has come in the flesh."[152] "The more I called them, the more they went from me" (Hos 11:2), a prophetic description which, we might think, suited Balthasar's lifetime (from the advent of National Socialism to the flight from the Church in the post-conciliar epoch) far better than it did that of Thomas at a high point of European Christian civilization.

Benefitting from the play

Well before the fourth volume of the dramatics ends, Balthasar has begun to think ahead, about how to present in theo-dramatic terms the benefit that accrues to the audience from this play. What has been described in the Passion of Christ is in one sense exclusive to the protagonist, since *pro nobis* in one of its meanings (the vicarious element) signifies "in our place".[153] Yet in a deeper sense that action is altogether inclusive. "Christ's mission on our behalf is more than a work and a suffering on his part to spare others the punishment they have justly deserved (as is emphasized by the Protestant version of the doctrine); it [also] involves his coworking and cosuffering with those who are estranged from God. In this way, the Second Adam opens up the area of Christian mission in which the latter, *en Christoi*, can be given a share in his salvific work and suffering for the world."[154] The opening up in question comes about in an actor—an actress—whom we have not yet considered in the context of the Cross. Mary's consent, which was the "fruit of Israel's positive history", proving that the ancient covenant was not for nothing, is now renewed in solidarity with the sinners for whom her Child died. Because she is immaculate she is henceforth "in love, infinitely at their disposal, infinitely available".[155] In the "second creation" of the Son's regenerating work, "the Virgin is empowered to new motherhood by the Word

---

[152] Ibid., p. 181.
[153] Ibid., p. 241.
[154] Ibid.
[155] Ibid., p. 355.

who falls silent in death: she is to bring forth redeemed creation's answer to this silenced Word",[156] thus showing herself to be "Mary-Ecclesia", Mary-Church.[157] The Lordship the Lamb acquires at Easter means he can entrust the Holy Spirit to this Church, so that "she can share his Resurrection freedom and communicate the power of the Spirit", notably in the baptismal mysteries by which Christ draws others into his destiny.[158] This "Resurrection freedom" is the liberation of finite freedom from its "self-inclosed servitude", for the finite freedom, the *autoexousion* of John Damascene and Thomas, can be fulfilled only in the context of the infinite freedom of God.[159]

That means *theosis*, divinisation, in the Trinity, and it is the subject of the final volume of the theological dramatics which show a world that is from the Trinity becoming a world in the Trinity—though only through the searing effect of judgment and purification. It also means of course those myriad "missions" of acting persons in Christ. Hidden in this age and incapable of staged exhibition here and now, the "individual's sphere of influence" undergoes an "unimaginable expansion" in the "theatre of action" of the Mystical Body, in what Balthasar calls the "dramatic dimension of the Communion of Saints".[160] Here Balthasar is much indebted to Thomasian texts, notably the commentary on the Apostles' Creed and the second of the *Quodlibetal Questions* as well as the *Summa theologiae*. The communion of saints entails a sharing in all the Church's goods, to the point that while the "mechanism" whereby the members of the Body can act for each other is unknown, there can be a "firm hope that the energies of this 'acting on behalf of others' can affect the innermost regions of others' freedom".[161] Nothing is said in so many words, but this drama of the *communio sanctorum* surely corresponds to Adrienne von Speyr's understanding of her own charism, as well as her explorations of the invisible world of grace in contemplative prayer. Not surprisingly, then, the final volume of *Theo-drama*—as can be seen

---

[156] Ibid., p. 360.
[157] Ibid., p. 361.
[158] Ibid., pp. 364–65.
[159] Ibid., p. 381.
[160] Ibid., pp. 407, 406.
[161] Ibid., p. 412, with reference to Thomas Aquinas, *In Symbolum apostolorum* 10; *Quodlibetum* 2, q. 7, a. 1; and *ST* IIa-IIae, q. 114, a. 6.

from its footnotes—is overwhelmingly indebted to her mystical texts. (No less than thirty-seven of her works appear sufficiently often to warrant at the start of *The Last Act* a list of abbreviations for ease of reference.) In its foreword, Balthasar called its contents, reasonably enough, "our theology", meaning that of Adrienne and himself.

But conscious of the criticisms the previous volumes had elicited from Rahner ("gnostic", complained Rahner, despite Balthasar's sustained polemic against Gnosticism, ancient and modern, and with an excessive "Neo-Chalcedonian"[162] emphasis on the divinity of Christ), Balthasar also invoked the mantle of Thomas to cover both Adrienne and himself. "Following Aquinas, we have tried to erect theology on the articles of faith (and not vice versa): on the Trinity, the Incarnation of the Son, his Cross and Resurrection on our behalf, and his sending of the Spirit to us in the apostolic Church and in the *communio sanctorum*."[163] And he added, "It is only on the basis of such a theology, today and in the future, that men can give witness in their lives and in their deaths to that 'highest gift of God' which is 'irreversible and unsurpassable'."[164] I shall return to the question of how Balthasar saw theology generally in my conclusion.

In what remains of the dramatics, Balthasar is preoccupied with how "earth moves heavenward", the essential claim of a "vertical eschatology" that also gives the historical process its due. This is where "Jewish and pagan ideas of the 'End' are fulfilled and transcended".[165] The challenge to audience belief is mitigated by the range of arguments he deploys for a "Trinitarian ontology". The world is already "from the Trinity", so what is more dramatically plausible than that it may return to where it arose? (The claim that "love alone" is the foundational reality of being—the basis, thanks to what the Trinity is, of *pulchrum*, *bonum*, and *verum*—will be considered in chapter 8 below.)

There can hardly be a comprehensive presentation on stage of the end-time scenario, yet "aspects of the final act" may be exhibited.

---

[162] See Albert Raffl, "Balthasar-Rahner: eine 'Vergegnung'?", in *Logik der Liebe und Herrlichkeit Gottes. Hans Urs von Balthasar im Gespräch*, ed. Walter Kasper (Ostfildern: Matthias-Grünewald Verlag, 2006), pp. 484–505.

[163] Hans Urs von Balthasar, *Theo-drama: Theological Dramatic Theory*, vol. 5, *The Last Act*, trans. Graham Harrison (San Francisco: Ignatius Press, 1998), p. 14.

[164] Ibid.

[165] Ibid., p. 49.

The key difficulty Balthasar faces is the possibility of human rejection of what he terms the "Trinitarian embrace".[166] On this there turns, after all, the answer to the question raised by the opening volume of the theological dramatics. Is the theo-drama a *commedia* where a happy ending can be guaranteed? Is it a tragedy whereby, despite everything, a significant portion of the creation is irredeemably lost? Or is it some kind of tertium quid for which the term that comes inevitably to mind is "tragi-comedy"? The "divine descent" in Incarnation and Atonement indicates the lengths to which the pity of God extends. Here Balthasar raises the question of whether and in what sense God "suffers".[167] Though the Cross of Jesus Christ is "the ultimate historical expression of God's Triune nature", it reveals not a God who is in the same miserable boat as ourselves but One who promises that "by uniting our sufferings to the Cross, we also thereby participate in the inner life of God", the Cross connecting "human suffering to God's Trinitarian essence of self-giving love in a fashion that redeems all human suffering and renders it of salvific value, both to the sufferer and to others"—and hence, finally transforming it into joy.[168] This wondrous prescription does not, though, eliminate the real possibility of man's refusal of the succour of God's love. The love poured out on the Cross may find no response. Indeed, as experience suggests, citing Adrienne von Speyr's commentary on the Gospel of John, "sin will presume to set itself up as the court of judgment vis-à-vis his grace".[169] The descent of Christ into the realm of the dead may suggest a final appeal has been arranged for, where God is vindicated in his "undergirding" of man's salvation, the divine yes trumping the human no. Yet theology can offer no easy guarantee that, in the end, the fire that burns the stubble of creation—the refuse that is sin—will only be purgatorial and therefore transient, not hellish and therefore sempiternal. Theology, or at least Balthasar's theology, can, however, register the hope this may be so.

What theology can more confidently adumbrate, with truly "dramatic" assistance from the mystics, is an account of man gone home

[166] Ibid., p. 191.

[167] Ibid., pp. 212–46.

[168] Jacob H. Friesenhavn, *The Trinity and Theodicy: The Trinitarian Theology of von Balthasar and the Problem of Evil* (Farnham: Ashgate, 2011), p. 2.

[169] Von Balthasar, *Last Act*, p. 289.

to God. When they return to their trinitarian archetype, they will be "breathing with the Spirit" (here Balthasar's source is Saint John of the Cross),[170] because the Son of God is "born" in them (here he appeals to the Rhineland mystics and van Ruysbroeck), in a condition of existence that can only be evoked through a "dialectic of images". In the presence of the Father, that condition is at once "meal and marriage",[171] banquet of rejoicing and nuptial bliss, in a life where love and knowledge of the triune God are augmented without end.

This closing volume of the theological dramatics contains much of what has most disconcerted the "classic" theologians of the Latin Church in Balthasar's writing, as well as a great deal that is clearly based on Scripture, the Fathers, and the witness of the saints (but also Adrienne von Speyr). Several of its constituent themes will thus recur in the chapters of doctrinal discussion that follow my account of the Trilogy as a whole.

---

[170] Ibid., pp. 425–28.
[171] Ibid., pp. 470–75.

4

The Trilogy: Theological Logic

Wahrheit: Wahrheit der Welt[1]—alias, the first volume of the theological logic—might be seen, at its original appearance in the late 1940s, as a response to the contemporaneous Neo-Thomist criticism of the *nouvelle théologie*.[2] The passage of the work most obviously pertinent to that controversy is the section entitled "Truth as Situation",[3] where Balthasar defends himself against the charge of historical relativism in embracing the "dialogical and social nature" of truth.[4] "We cannot grasp the truth of history unless we accompany its immanent process. It is only from within this activity that we can catch the transcendent melody of the whole."[5] That was relevant to a controversy whose first act had been the ecclesiastical censures placed on a manifesto, deemed "semi-Modernist", of the "regent" of the French Dominicans, Marie-Dominique Chenu. Chenu had proposed that Thomas' thought (and Catholic theology generally) should never be studied except in its always time-conditioned historical context.[6] Balthasar too, so I suggested in the first chapter of this study, sought to write a theology that would answer what he considered the legitimate aspirations, as well as healing the wounds, of European modernity— hardly a time-free undertaking. Of course concern with cultural modernity does not equal adhesion to theological Modernism. Actually, Balthasar regarded the condemnation of the latter by Pope Saint

---

[1] Hans Urs von Balthasar, *Wahrheit: Wahrheit der Welt* (Einsiedeln: Benzinger, 1947).

[2] Aidan Nichols, O.P., "Thomism and the *nouvelle théologie*", *The Thomist* 64 (2000): 1–19.

[3] Hans Urs von Balthasar, *Theo-logic: Theological Logical Theory*, vol. 1, *Truth of the World*, trans. Adrian J. Walker (San Francisco: Ignatius Press, 2000), pp. 179–205.

[4] Ibid., p. 202.

[5] Ibid., p. 205.

[6] Marie-Dominique Chenu, O.P., *Une Ecole de théologie: Le Saulchoir* (1937; Paris: Cerf, 1985).

Pius X as "generally justified".[7] Giving due recognition to historical change was not in any case Balthasar's main preoccupation in
Truth of the World. While he counted "intensification and urgency
in temporality and situation" one of the "ingredients in the mystery
of being" (thus neatly giving an ontological character to what might
otherwise be thought an antimetaphysical initiative on the part of
certain historical theologians), this was not an element to which he
gave priority.[8] He wished to show how a more generous and poetic
version of Thomist philosophy was available than that provided
in the manuals, one more readily compatible with appeal to literature,
the phenomenological gaze, and the patristic manner in theology—all
features of the contemporary theological movement of *ressourcement*.
"Generous" and "poetic" are diffuse terms, but Paul Silas Peterson
gives them contour when he writes that, in *Truth of the World*, Balthasar "challenges a view of truth that does not leave room for freedom
[part 2], mystery [part 3] and the supernatural [part 4, on participation
and revelation]".[9]

   In this text, originally from 1947, Balthasar had already asserted his
view of the inseparability of the transcendentals. By 1985, when the
work was not only republished but relocated, that thesis had become
crucial for the Trilogy as a whole. The inseparability theme was
anticipated in Erich Przywara's *Analogia Entis*,[10] of whose Thomism *Wahrheit* is, in this respect, a creative continuation—though
with debts to Goethe on form and its import as well as traces of
Nietzsche's *Lebensphilosophie* and more than a touch of Heidegger on
truth as the "unveiling" of what is otherwise concealed, an emphasis perhaps owed more immediately to Balthasar's highly original
Thomas friend, Gustav Siewerth. And although the source name
is not actually given, Balthasar does not forget the "existentialist"
Thomism of Gilson.

---

   [7] Hans Urs von Balthasar, "Peace in Theology", *Communio* 12 (1985): 402; see pp. 398–
407. Pope Pius X condemned Modernism in 1907 in his encyclical *Pascendi Dominici gregis* and
his syllabus *Lamentabili sane exitu*.
   [8] Von Balthasar, *Truth of the World*, p. 207.
   [9] Paul Silas Peterson, *The Early Hans Urs von Balthasar: Historical Contexts and Intellectual
Formation* (Berlin: De Gruyter, 2015), p. 283.
   [10] Erich Przywara, *Analogia Entis: Metaphysics; Original Structure and Universal Rhythm*
(Grand Rapids, MI: Eerdmans, 2014).

In what had now become the opening volume of the theological logic, some of the Fathers, together with Saint John Henry Newman, and a sprinkling of philosophers (and historians) are awarded an occasional mention. Thomas' name is more often invoked, but even in his case, despite the citation of Thomasian formulae, the presence of the master of Aquino mainly consists in appropriating the spirit of his philosophy as found in the *Disputed Questions on Truth*.

> Aquinas' *de veritate* provides for Balthasar a relatively adequate model of truth, as well as suggesting the negative capability for understanding its co-extensivity with beauty and goodness.... From Balthasar's perspective ... *de veritate* never leaves behind the original well-spring of philosophy which is wonder (*thaumazein*) and the searching that it excites, and never forgets the horizon of mystery that is constitutive of being as excess [the way ontology escapes the control of a set number of theorems and calls out for poetic articulation]. Obviously, Balthasar is complementing or supplementing Aquinas with a significant draft of Neoplatonism which is, arguably, more typical of Pseudo-Dionysius and Bonaventure, nonetheless, he thinks that being as excess can be interpreted as love or agape.[11]

That last claim will be investigated in my final chapter in this study as the key to Balthasar's theological method overall.

The distinctive contribution of the opening volume of the theological logic for a reader coming from such standard works of Thomasian metaphysics as, say, John Wippel's *Metaphysical Thought of Thomas Aquinas*,[12] or Joseph Kockelmans' *Metaphysics of Aquinas*,[13] does not lie along well-trodden paths—though it may be noted that, for example, Balthasar shared the Thomist "moderate realism" for which universals really exist within particulars as particularized and multiplied. In *Wahrheit* he declares, "What the concept first apprehends, what is primarily correlative to it, is the essence in its universality.

[11] Cyril O'Regan, *The Anatomy of Misremembering: Von Balthasar's Response to Philosophical Modernity*, vol. 1, *Hegel* (New York: Crossroad, 2014), pp. 611–12, endnote 2.

[12] John Wippel, *The Metaphysical Thought of Thomas Aquinas: From Finite Being to Uncreated Being* (Washington, DC: Catholic University of America Press, 2000).

[13] Joseph Kockelmans, *The Metaphysics of Aquinas: A Systematic Presentation* (Leuven: Bibliotheek van de Faculteit Godgeleerdheid, 2001).

But the universal contains the particular just as much as the particular contains the universal."[14] Ever since the Gregory of Nyssa book, he had felt the need to do justice both to existence and to essence. He had written there, "It is only, we believe, in emphasizing this twofold character that is at once dramatic and conceptual, 'existential' and 'essential', that we shall succeed in reviving and rethinking the work of Gregory."[15] So, he had no difficulty with the key Thomasian notion of substance, which replicates the idea of essence, while privileging (though not at the expense of substance) *esse*, the act of existence. "From his first writings, Balthasar had been looking for a way to privilege the 'existential' without thereby surrendering (or destroying) conceptual or 'essential' forms."[16] He wrote in *Wahrheit*, the "mysterious dual unity [of essence and existence] is the eternal mystery of every ontology of the created world".[17] But by far the most important thesis in the theological logic as a whole is the claim that the God who "truly and unreservedly ex-posits himself" in the missions of the Son and the Holy Spirit "does not therefore cease to be a mystery".[18] The most important thesis in *Truth of the World*, the logic's opening volume, concerns, then, the possibility of an analogical understanding of this claim about uncreated truth, an understanding that is now to be drawn from exploration of created truth. What Balthasar seeks to show above all is that in worldly truth there is indeed an inherent relation between unveiling and concealing, disclosure and mystery.

Knowing the truth

Appropriately enough, therefore, the relation of subject and object forms the chief topic of the first half of the theological logic's opening volume. In chapter 1, "Introducing Balthasar for Thomists", I

---

[14] Von Balthasar, *Truth of the World*, p. 154.

[15] Hans Urs von Balthasar, *Presence and Thought: Essay on the Religious Philosophy of Gregory of Nyssa* (San Francisco: Ignatius Press, 1995), p. 16.

[16] David C. Schindler, *Hans Urs von Balthasar and the Dramatic Structure of Truth: A Philosophical Investigation* (New York: Fordham University Press, 2004), p. 13.

[17] Von Balthasar, *Truth of the World*, p. 194.

[18] Ibid., p. 22.

have already drawn into the discussion William Norris Clarke, the
Neo-Thomist philosopher who, in the English-speaking world,
comes perhaps the closest to Balthasar's own view of metaphysics.
Like Norris Clarke—and most Thomists before the Louvain school
of the early twentieth century—Balthasar does not, in *Truth of the
World*, spend much time on the "problem of knowledge", in the
sense of seeking to justify a fundamental epistemology of a natural
kind. (Things look different, so we saw in chapter 2, when the theological aesthetics sought to explore supernatural epistemology, the
epistemology of faith.) The relation of subject and object is a mating
of two realities which already find themselves in cognitive union
before the question of how natural knowing might be possible is
even raised. Norris Clarke wrote,

> To function at all as rational beings in a universe we did not make,
> our first move must be at least implicitly to accept with humility and
> gratitude the intellectual nature that has been given to us, with its
> built-in natural correlation with the domain of being as in principle
> open to the light of mind, intelligible in itself. This absolutely fun-
> damental mutual correlation of mind and being, mind for being and
> being for mind, has been beautifully termed by Maritain a "nuptial
> relation", a natural marriage made in heaven, so to speak, where
> each partner completes the other. But notice [Norris Clarke goes
> on] the appropriate roles in this marriage: the human mind is analo-
> gously like the female, the mother; reality is like the father. To know
> truly a reality that it has not itself made, the mind must make itself
> open to receive this reality, to be actively informed by it. The mind,
> fecundated, informed, by reality, then actively responds, pours its
> own spiritual life into what it receives, gestates, then gives birth to
> the mental "word" or concept, which in turns flows over into the
> verbal word expressed to others. Notice [he continues] the deep
> insight encapsulated in this ancient term "concept": for to know is
> for the mind to conceive and give birth to an inner mental word
> expressing the real that has informed it, and bearing the features
> of both parents—reality and the mind. Thus *theoretical* intelligence
> (knowing the world as it already is) is more like a *she*; *practical* intel-
> ligence, on the other hand, as ordered toward guiding some act of
> making or doing on the part of the knower, is more like a *he*, since
> it actively changes or re-creates the world through creative initiative
> and action. It is because of my belief in this "nuptial relationship"

between the mind and reality that I feel such antipathy toward the epistemology of Immanuel Kant.[19]

Despite Balthasar's instrumental employment of such Kantian phrases as the "a priori" and a "transcendental unity of apperception", he uses these terms in a remarkably un-Kantian way, for the "a priori" is divinely originated light and the synthetic unity of the perceiving mind at least as much receptive as performative. So Norris Clarke's attitude is very much Balthasar's mind-set as well. In the introduction to the logic's opening volume, where a comparison is made between engagement with truth and spousal love, Norris Clarke's "nuptial" epistemology comes—for those who have encountered it—spontaneously to mind. And after completing his account of subject and object in the exchange that is truth, Balthasar, looking back, calls that enquiry "an investigation of the masculine and feminine that attends mainly to the functions and inclinations that predispose them for their union".[20] He will revert to the comparison between human love and approach to the mystery of being before he ends.[21]

In the more Heideggerian, rather than Maritainian, idiom Balthasar uses generally for this topic in *Wahrheit der Welt* he describes truth in a preliminary fashion as "unveiledness", since while being (only) *appears* it is nevertheless really *being* that does the appearing.[22] That is so even if the only being of which we are initially aware is the being of consciousness (in German more plainly an experience of being than in English, for the noun *Bewusstsein*, incorporates the very name of "being", *Sein*). That is sufficient to rebut the claims of sceptics who deny the availability of truth. Moreover, that being in its appearing provides a grounding indicates the way truth is "trustworthy", a biblical epithet—and here Balthasar uses the Old Testament Hebrew term to underline this point—to match the Hellenic, and thus extra-revelatory, origin of the notion of unveiledness. In each case, unconcealment and reliability, the appreciation of any truth opens wider

---

[19]W. Norris Clarke, "Metaphysical Reflections", in *The Universe as Journey: Conversations with W. Norris Clarke, S.J.* (New York: Fordham University Press, 1988), pp. 60–61; see pp. 49–92.

[20]Von Balthasar, *Truth of the World*, p. 61.

[21]Ibid., pp. 209–16.

[22]Ibid, p. 37.

perspectives on being, perspectives to which, in the last analysis, no final limit can be set. This is his first and decisive step in making the claim that worldly being is marked by a polarity of knowability and mystery—which can serve then as an analogical starting point for making the same claim about the being of God.

It is a fertile starting point, helping in other ways too. It suggests how truth is always, as Thomists of the strict observance do not fail to remind Idealists of every stripe, an "adequation" of the mind with objective reality, a receptive measuredness by the object to hand. Yet truth is also (and here is where Balthasar has learned from other sources, not least among the poets) an invitation to the subject to engage its creative freedom in the way it actively measures that same object, contextualizing it in a wider whole, evaluating it, pressing on towards that ever-receding horizon—the totality of what is. "We do not, of course, actually know this totality in the way that we know the particular object, but rather potentially, as background capable of being unveiled more and more."[23]

The starting point also furnishes the basis for a kind of argument for the existence of God, drawing on the distinctively Augustinian dimension of Saint Thomas' philosophical inheritance.[24] When the subject "lays hold of itself and, in so doing, learns from the inside what being is", that subject "realizes ... that the truth in whose light it measures the object, and which is nothing other than the illumination of being, is not confined to its own point-like self-consciousness.... Its thinking is embedded in an infinite thinking of being and so can serve as a measuring stick only because it itself is measured by an unmeasured, yet all-measuring, infinite measure."[25] And this is nothing other than "the identity of thinking and being in God".[26] Hence Thomas' statement in the *De veritate* that "all knowing agents implicitly know God in whatever is known".[27] Hence too

---

[23] Ibid., p. 43.

[24] Bernhard Blankenhorn, O.P., "Aquinas as Interpreter of Augustinian Illumination in Light of Albertus Magnus", *Nova et Vetera* 10, no. 3 (2012): 689–713; for the longer story, see Lydia Schumacher, *Divine Illumination: The History and Future of Augustine's Theory of Knowledge* (Oxford: Wiley-Blackwell, 2011).

[25] Von Balthasar, *Truth of the World*, p. 51.

[26] Ibid.

[27] Thomas Aquinas, *De veritate* q. 22, a. 2 ad 1.

Balthasar's assertion that the right form of the "cogito" (Descartes' "I think therefore I am", anticipated by Augustine in his debate with the Academics) runs *cogitor ergo sum*, "I am thought [by God], therefore I am."[28] That also opens the way to the anti–Idealist recognition of the self-standing subjecthood of others, who are in the same boat as me. Or as Balthasar puts it, far more elegantly than I have: "Truth now appears in the world as distributed among countless subjects, which in their original posture of readiness are open to one another and which await from one another the communication of the part of the truth that God has granted them as a share in his own infinite truth. In their mutual openness, in their reciprocal disponibility, finite subjects thus mirror forth the highest measure of what the finiute world can capture of the infinite openness of God's truth."[29] It is a prelude, at the level of metaphysics, to the catholicity of the Church and the communion of saints.

Another way to God, philosophically speaking, arises from the object, rather than the subject, in the experience of truth. Not only does the subject's finite "measuring" depend on infinite divine "measuring". The object's measure does so as well. The divine idea of a thing, "in part given to the object and implanted in it along with its very existence" (the *logoi* inscribed in things by the Logos, as in the Greek patristic tradition most intensively studied by Balthasar in the 1940s), is "the living centre from which the acting, living and sensing being develops, displays its rich multiplicity, and unfolds its historicity".[30] Using the Aristotelean word borrowed by Thomas, creatures have their "entelechies". They have within them a *telos*, or goal, to which they are self-directed. At any given moment, they are likely to be en route. "Things are always more than themselves, and their constantly self-surpassing transcendence opens ultimately on to an idea that is not the things themselves, but God and their measure in God" in an "ever-new meting out of truth."[31] But when, by a further step, we take into account the *context* of such a creature's existence, the network of relations in which it finds itself, we soon

---

[28] Von Balthasar, *Truth of the World*, p. 54.
[29] Ibid., p. 55.
[30] Ibid., p. 57.
[31] Ibid.

see how "creatures fulfil purposes that are not immediately entailed in their essences alone", Balthasar's statement of Aquinas' "fifth way" to God, the "teleological argument".[32] The intricate nexus of such relations indicates a *telos* for (in principle) ever-extendible segments of the universe as a whole. Balthasar considers that, conceivably, higher intelligences are at work in the management of the creation, somewhat along the lines proposed by the co-discoverer of biological evolution Alfred Russel Wallace, an agnostic.[33] But if so, such intelligences would themselves play a part in the "great game of the world" beyond their "fathoming"—and thus "have a part of their truth not in themselves, but in God".[34] Balthasar's combination of a "subjective" way to God through interiority and an "objective" way to God through the cosmos is paralleled exactly (though, so far as I know, without any direct influence) by proposals from Norris Clarke.[35] That the ultimate measure of a *rational* creature, like man, lies in God's hands, awaiting the disclosure over time of the real meaning of its life, suggests already the possibility of that distribution of "missions" in relation to the agency of Christ whereby, for the Balthasar of the theological dramatics, anthropology cannot avoid a final Christological reconfiguration.

In the nuptial union of subject and object, the object finds space in which to be fully itself, something otherwise impossible. Thus, for instance, in a lyrical evocation of a tree—seen, smelt, touched, and even heard (when moved by the wind)—Balthasar concludes: "[The tree] makes use of the space furnished for this purpose just as surely as it makes use of the soil and the ambient air in order to develop. Without the subject's sensory space, it would not be what it is; it would be incapable of fulfilling the raison d'être, the idea that it is supposed to embody."[36] The subject's spontaneous reaction is not subjective in the pejorative sense of arbitrary; rather it is *nature*—and Balthasar says the same of the higher spontaneity involved in forming the concept

---

[32] Ibid.

[33] Michael A. Flannery, *Alfred Russel Wallace's Theory of Intelligent Evolution: How Wallace's World of Life Challenged Darwinism*, rev. ed. (Riesel, TX: Erasmus Press, 2011).

[34] Von Balthasar, *Truth of the World*, pp. 57–58.

[35] W. Norris Clarke, *The Philosophical Approach to God: A Neo-Thomist Perspective*, 2nd ed. (New York: Fordham University Press, 2007), pp. 1–90.

[36] Von Balthasar, *Truth of the World*, p. 63.

of "tree": this too obeys a natural, if intellectual, law. "The fact that the knowing subject is involved in the truth is no argument against truth's objectivity, as long as the subject's attitude remains that of a servant ready to offer his help."[37] Balthasar helps not only to justify his initial starting point, the appearing of being, but the very foundations of his theological aesthetics when he writes, "The appearance of the object is not a pale duplicate of its self-quiescent essence but the necessary unfolding in which its inward plenitude becomes manifest for the first time."[38]

By choosing to deal with the subject before the object, and by emphasizing the interior implications of consciousness, Balthasar might be thought to be departing, at least to this extent, from Thomist realism. And it is true that, in line with the cultural analysis he had offered from his earliest writings, he thought Catholic philosophy and theology in the modern age should give greater thought to what subjectivity—being a personal subject—entails. But, as soon becomes evident when he turns to "the subject in the object", he gives full weight to the typically Thomistic apprehension of being in singular material things. "The subject lays hold of the object on the basis of the images generated by the object in its sensory sphere",[39] an everyday happening to explain which Balthasar brings into play the standard vocabulary of the Aristotelian-Thomist philosophy. But the commentary thereon is altogether his own. "Things enter the subject's space without prior invitation. They place the subject before a fait accompli—we exist!—and the subject awakens to itself from the midst of an already occurring engagement with them.... The subject does not lead a private, withdrawn, aristocratic life in the world, nor is it at liberty to enter into contact with things at its own discretion."[40] This, the "initial onrush of the world", may look like "violation", but just as a couple who wish to have a child must submit to the natural laws that govern conception, so "the intellectual fruit of knowledge can ripen only in a primary, natural constraint that forces them to know."[41] It is a "surrender" that, when recapitulated "at the level of

[37] Ibid., p. 64.
[38] Ibid., p. 65.
[39] Ibid., p. 71.
[40] Ibid., p. 68.
[41] Ibid., p. 71.

conscious freedom", attains the "nobility of love".[42] This is not simply so for sensuous apprehension. The "contents and forms of truth ... offered from outside" enable the subject to accumulate a "treasury of truth from experience and tradition", which he or she can sift, and, by "multiple accentuations and assessments", give the "countenance" they find best.[43] It could be a description of how the twelve writers whose raids on glory were set out in volumes 2 and 3 of the theological aesthetics lived with and refracted the unique form in which the glory of revelation broke through.

The reference above to both "freedom" and "love" in the knowing of being leads Balthasar to conclude the first half of *Truth of the World*. The structure of being and knowledge seems a given of natural existence, and so it is. But it can be taken up and made the instrument of the free spirit in man. That spirit's "openness to the world is already a kind of sketch of the fundamental ways in which it will comport itself in the world: receiving and giving, service and creation, justice and love, which are all just so many definite expressions of loving self-abandonment."[44] With their being, all created things receive their operation (in the Thomist axiom, *agere sequitur esse*), and even at the subrational level they have some power of spontaneity in disclosing what they are—a faint reflection of the infinite freedom of God. Ascending the ladder of being, this capacity for freely exteriorizing what is most intimate increases, finding one sort of climax in the human person who gives witness by the "natural symbolic language of the senses" to what he most interiorly is—a "testimony" to which the appropriate response may be called a kind of natural "faith".[45] Like Saint Thomas in the *Prima Pars* of the *Summa theologiae*, Balthasar finds it desirable to follow the ascending curve of free interiority upwards to a realm known only from revelation, the angelic, the "highest level of freedom attainable within the created world".[46] As to God, "the natural knowledge of God from creation inexorably comes to a halt before the intimacy of God's personal life. And it requires a new revelation of grace in

---

[42] Ibid., p. 78.
[43] Ibid., p. 70.
[44] Ibid., p. 80.
[45] Ibid., pp. 98, 96.
[46] Ibid., p. 99.

order to open man in faith and to communicate to him—in abiding mystery—what God is in his inner being."[47] This insistence on the unavailability to natural reason of the inner communion that belongs to the trihypostatic divine life joins together all Thomist theologians from Aquinas himself to the nineteenth-century Matthias Joseph Scheeben, and does so over against semi-rationalists of all varieties. "There is no access ... to the trinitarian mystery other than its revelation in Jesus Christ and the Holy Spirit."[48] Via the economic manifestations of the Son and the Spirit, it will be the proper topic of the second and third volumes of the theological logic.

Meanwhile Balthasar notes that the matter of interiority already indicates the mysterious character of even worldly being—a vital observation if he is to establish an analogy between worldly and divine being in the specific manner—by reference to the union of disclosure and mystery, in which he wishes so to do. "Volitional disclosure", so far from being irrational, is the "supreme, crowning meaning of all ratio itself".[49] "The existent object's will to disclose itself and the knowing subject's will to open itself in receptive listening are but two forms of a single self-gift," an observation that should trigger the realization that "love is inseparable from truth."[50]

The analogy of being

When in the second part of the theological logic's opening volume Balthasar turns from truth as disclosure to truth as mystery, his enquiry will culminate in his own restatement of the long-pondered analogia entis. Chapter 1 of the present book emphasized how Balthasar and Thomists share an absorbing interest in the "analogy of being". This is an abiding commonality, even when making special allowance for Balthasar's introduction of Christology into analogia entis thinking. The theological aesthetics turn on a creative reapplication of the concept of the analogy of being whereby it becomes instead the "analogy

47 Ibid., p. 102.
48 Hans Urs von Balthasar, Theo-logic: Theological Logical Theory, vol. 2, Truth of God, trans. Adrian J. Walker (San Francisco: Ignatius Press, 2004), p. 125.
49 Von Balthasar, Truth of the World, p. 111.
50 Ibid.

of beauty". The theological dramatics repeated this thought experiment via the notion of an "analogy of liberty" (which at maximal intensity becomes an "analogy of charity"). The matter arises once again in the second half of the theological logic's opening volume. This time it is in terms of the original concept with its roots in the Septuagint, Denys the Areopagite, and Thomas—namely, the analogy between the being of creation and the being of God: pure ontology and *therefore*—at any rate to a writer whose German was affected in this matter by Hegel's usage—"logic". Hegel's *Science of Logic* is his ontology, for Hegel conceives thought and being as a single active unity. For Balthasar, whose primary philosophical commitment is to Christian Scholasticism, there is—so the material we have surveyed so far in this chapter shows—a logic-ontologic identification of a different kind. "Truth is being insofar as it has been unveiled, and in its unveiling grasped."[51] The analogy of being between God and the world can also be called the "analogy of truth".[52]

How to understand the analogy of being has been a divisive issue among modern Thomists, not least when they are trying to settle what Aquinas himself actually taught. "After a number of shifts, not always mutually compatible, [Thomas] finally settled on an analogy of causal participation, which combined the analogy of attribution and the analogy of proper proportionality in a single synthesis."[53] Gerald McCool, the historian of modern Thomism just cited, went on to say: "This analogy did justice both to the proportional similarity of acts of existence diversified by their varied essences and to the intrinsic similitude between finite participants and the Infinite Final and Efficient Cause to which they are dynamically related as their transcendent source and goal."[54] That is exactly Balthasar's view.

By *analogia entis* Balthasar means the participation of creatures in God as the foundation for, but also as illumined by, the community of participation between them. The *analogia entis* is thus for Balthasar a relationship of creature to God such that the former is

---

[51] Ibid., p. 43.
[52] Ibid., p. 244.
[53] Gerald A. McCool, S.J., "An Alert and Independent Thomist: William Norris Clarke, S.J.", in *The Universe as Journey: Conversations with W. Norris Clarke, S.J.* (New York: Fordham University Press, 1988), p. 27; see pp. 13–48.
[54] Ibid.

similar to the latter (both by way of an "analogy of attribution" and an "analogy of proportionality", which are really two sides of the same analogical coin)—but within a greater dissimilarity that clearly underscores the creatureliness of the creature and the free transcendence of the Creator.[55]

Towards the close of *Truth of the World*, Balthasar's account of the "interwovenness" of the transcendentals—which provides a first glimpse of the overall structure of the Trilogy (first, that is, when these writings are read in the order of their production)—is also his way in to the analogous mystery that is God. That truth should not only be good but also beautiful—and therefore disinterested in its utterly nonutilitarian "whylessness"—is a pointer to the mysterious ontology of love which lies at trinitarianism's heart. "For what is more incomprehensible than the fact that the core of being consists in love and that its emergence as essence and existence has no ground other than groundless grace?"[56] On the one hand, and here is the justification of natural metaphysics, "God is ... known as mystery in the form of every creaturely truth, which even in its finitude never ceases to be marvelous, gracious, groundlessly self-opening and self-giving."[57] On the other hand, when truth is realized as participation in the revelation of God as love—and this is only finally possible through the economy of the Son and the Spirit—natural metaphysics is left behind. "Because love is ultimate, the seraphim cover their faces with their wings, for the mystery of eternal love is one whose superluminous night may be glorified only through adoration."[58]

Truth of Son and Spirit

What is different, as volume I of the theological logic gives way to volume 2 where the entire question of *analogia entis* is reviewed from this higher, supernaturally theological standpoint, is the insertion

---

[55] Adrian J. Walker, "Love Alone: Hans Urs von Balthasar as a Master of Theological Renewal", *Communio* 32 (2005): 522–23, footnote 13.

[56] Von Balthasar, *Truth of the World*, p. 225.

[57] Ibid., p. 272.

[58] Ibid.

of Christology and at this very point: "the *analogia entis*, fulfilled in Christ, who is God and man in one person".[59] "Christ, as both God and man, is at once the highest instance and the foundation of this relation [the relation between God and the world]—and in this specific sense can be said to be or embody the *analogia entis* in his own person. By calling Christ the *analogia entis*, then, Balthasar means to underscore how classical Christology implies that Christ is nothing less than the ontological key to all of reality."[60] This is the distinctively Bonaventurian element in Balthasar's presentation of the analogy of being, though perhaps the idea of treating Christ as the cosmic lynchpin would not have occurred to him without the prior example of Saint Maximus.

The remaining two volumes of the theological logic turn on the idea that, in a divine revelation to a created world that from the beginning was meant to be "in" Christ, the Son (who says that he is "the truth" [Jn 14:6]) is the expositor of the truth of the Father who sends him, and the Holy Spirit (whom Jesus calls "the Spirit of truth" [Jn 16:13]), the expositor of the truth of the Son. The "exposition" in question is not just a language event. There are works as well as words in which it takes place in each case, the case of the Son, the case of the Spirit. That might suggest two not only distinct but independent phases of salvation history, or at the least two not only distinct but independent economies for the second and third trinitarian Persons. That is why Balthasar insists at the outset of volume 2, even while explaining his basic proposition of the two "expositors", that "all that [the Son] did and underwent in his coming in the flesh, his Passion, and his Resurrection, he did and underwent in the *Pneuma* whom the Father had sent down upon him without measure", such that a strict "line of demarcation between the works of the Logos and the works of the Spirit is artificial".[61] Though each hypostasis works in his own manner, "the indivisible triune God performs all his saving deeds in unity", a claim we might otherwise more readily associate with Aquinas than with Balthasar.[62]

---

[59] Von Balthasar, *Truth of God*, p. 81.
[60] Walker, "Love Alone", p. 21, footnote 13.
[61] Von Balthasar, *Truth of God*, p. 11.
[62] Ibid.

In these two books, which follow on chronologically from the aesthetics and the dramatics, Balthasar can consciously look back to what preceded in fulfilling his aim. The truth to be expounded is both "glory", as in the aesthetics, and "goodness", as in the dramatics. The sovereign beauty and the benevolent graciousness of the Father are inseparable from the truth declared in the words and works of the Son—and the inexhaustible depth of all three is displayed, thanks to the Spirit. Thus the Trilogy, despite or rather because of its thoroughgoing Christocentrism, proves to have a trinitarian structure in all its parts.

Attempts to find an "image of the Trinity" in the structure of creation are a fragile undertaking, tempting though it may be for one who, on the basis of the opening volume of the logic, hopes to find at the *foyer* of the world the love that, if it is indeed ultimate both protologically and eschatologically, can only be divine—and thus triune in character. There can be no firm truth in this area until the "Logos declares himself",[63] and in so doing comes before man as the invisible Father's interpreter to human senses, on the stage of the world. Balthasar finds depths—both cataphatic and apophatic—in the parabolic mode of utterance selected by the Logos incarnate, which indicate that the situation of combined disclosure and mystery abides even within divine revelation—yet raised now onto a new level.

> As he goes about expositing divine logic in human logic, the Logos does not find the latter unprepared. However disabled and darkened we judge the participation of man's spirit in the truth shining upon the mind from God (Augustine) or in the first principles of truth and goodness (Thomas), natural man knows what ethics and practical reason are, and the man of the Old Testament knows, in addition to that, what the right relation to the living God ought to be. There is a grammar here in which Jesus can encode the divine Word. This is this positive side. There is also a negative aspect: this objective expression—the true intended meaning of the parable—can never be grasped in its otherness without the in-shining of the light of the Spirit of Jesus and the Father, who now begins in earnest to exposit what has already been objectively exposited in itself.[64]

[63] Ibid., p. 65.
[64] Ibid., p. 78.

It is by "generalising" this "law" of the parables that Balthasar presumes to demonstrate in the rest of the theological logic how it is that creaturely logic can sustain the weight of the divine. In so doing he goes quite beyond the linguistic consideration that rhetorical studies of the parabolic mode would entertain. His concern is with the very structures of the creation as possible mediatorial bearers of the missions of Son and Spirit. Once again, this logic is ontologic: *analogia linguae* cedes place to *analogia entis*, speech to being. To Balthasar's mind, shared existence with fellow humans and the multivalent phenomenon of fruitfulness were, among those creaturely structures, especially important registers of communication in the Son's interpretive task.

As to that negative aspect, for Balthasar "negative theology" must always be brought within a larger positive framework: "the Christian certainty of always already having been found by the God of revelation", the true starting point of the specifically Christian "seeking for God".[65] For the Church negative theology does not end in silence, as with the version found in pagan philosophy, but in adoration. Thomas, like many of the Fathers, employed negative theology— and Balthasar does not hesitate to cite his celebrated adage, "We are thus united to him as, so to say, to one unknown";[66] but like them he would always have assumed "both the original affirmation that sustains all negation [the 'via affirmativa'], and its equally original eminence [the 'via eminentiae'], which reaches beyond all negations".[67]

Naturally enough, Balthasar has to make room, in his volume on the *Truth of God*, for discussion of how the divine Son relates to the Father and to the Spirit—in a word, the Son's place in the Trinity. That also meant devoting attention to the delicate issue, in Catholic-Orthodox relations, of the procession of the Spirit from the Father—and from the Son? Balthasar does not think a procession "from the Son" any advance on a procession "through the Son", but directs the interested reader to another theologian of *ressourcement*, the Dominican Yves Congar, for discussion of any practical ecumenical implications this may carry. His account of "the

[65] Ibid., p. 103.
[66] *ST* Ia, q. 12, a. 13 ad 1.
[67] Von Balthasar, *Truth of God*, pp. 98–99.

place of the Logos in God" includes his reasons for giving Saint
Bonaventure the edge over Aquinas on the mode of generation of
the Son,[68] and grateful acknowledgement of the Franciscan Doctor's
ability to write about the "motive of the Incarnation" in a way that
"transcends a priori the Thomist-Scotist controversy".[69] That was
something Balthasar had himself sought to do in the opening chapter of his meditation on the Easter events, Mysterium Paschale.[70] Less
expected, until one recalls the resituating of the analogy of being in
Christ, is the series of reflections on the way in which the Logos,
through becoming incarnate, provides a way of reconciling cosmic
polarities, consummating the arts and sciences, inspiring a theology
of history—all of which serve to introduce Balthasar's account, in
the context of theological logic, of the conception; life; Passion and
death; descent and Resurrection of Jesus (the lengthy discussion of
the descent including some of Adrienne von Speyr's strangest imag-
ery and, accordingly, most taxing claims). For those accustomed to
standard modern theologies, where facts about Jesus of Nazareth are
rehearsed prior to erecting a theological structure upon those facts,
this way of going about things may seem an odd proceeding. But
it mirrors the way Christology is introduced in the Summa theologiae, where Thomas does not venture to comment on the mysteries
of the life of Christ until the student has grasped, by means of an
ontological reflection on the flesh-taking of the eternal Word, the
universal range of significance the particular episodes in the human
biography of the Messiah can possess. Balthasar has already said at
the opening of the second volume of the theological logic that there
is only one way to practice Christology: from above.[71] Throughout, he tries to remember that at this stage in the Trilogy he is no
longer writing an aesthetic or a dramatic Christology but one that
belongs with "theological logical theory"—which means seeking to
highlight the way the course taken by the Word incarnate, as Christ
negotiates resistance to his mission from the side of the sin of the

[68] Ibid., pp. 164–65.

[69] Ibid., p. 168.

[70] Hans Urs von Balthasar, Mysterium Paschale: The Mystery of Easter, trans. Aidan Nichols,
O.P. (2000; repr., San Francisco: Ignatius Press, 2005), p. 11.

[71] Von Balthasar, Truth of God, p. 13.

world, amounts to an assertion of the truth of God over against all lies that falsify its logic.

We come now to the final volume, *The Spirit of Truth*, where Balthasar asks if a theology of the Holy Spirit is "possible"—bearing in mind that he is the hidden enabler of our participation in the Son, and thus of our relation to the Father, rather than a hypostasis whose "face" is disclosed directly in revelation. If in some lesser lights in the Latin tradition there has been inadequate attention to the Spirit, a "pneumatological deficit", this can hardly be said of Thomas, who has a very full doctrine both of the Spirit's role in the Trinity and of his task in the economy.[72] Still, to discover that the volume of the theological logic devoted to the Holy Spirit is by far the longest remains a surprise—and means, obviously, that Balthasar answered his own question about the possibility of pneumatology with a resounding yes. In the context of theologically logical theory the Spirit is, above all, "the indispensable declarer of Trinitarian truth; in all the functions attributed to him he is the final and concluding object of *theo-logic*".[73]

The salience of the Spirit as equally with the Son one of the Father's "two hands" (an image from Saint Irenaeus that Balthasar makes much of in the third volume of the logic) is shown not least through the Spirit's indispensability in making possible the economy of the Son. Balthasar reaffirms what he had already said when writing on the "theo-drama": in the context of the Incarnation, the order of acting of the second and third Persons inverts the order of the trinitarian *taxis* itself—a notion which, it would seem, he took from the Russian Orthodox Sergei Bulgakov's discussion of the Annunciation mystery.[74] Only by virtue of the Spirit's descent, Bulgakov had noted, does the Word come to dwell in the womb of the Mother of God. In Balthasar's view, the Word does not so much "take" (assume) humanity as "entrust himself" to the Spirit who makes

---

[72] Jean-Pierre Torrell, *Saint Thomas Aquinas*, vol. 2, *Spiritual Master*, trans. Robert Royal (Washington, DC: Catholic University of America Press, 2003).

[73] Hans Urs von Balthasar, *Theo-logic: Theological Logical Theory*, vol. 3, *The Spirit of Truth*, trans. Graham Harrison (San Francisco: Ignatius Press, 2005), p. 24.

[74] Balthasar has read the Russian theologian's pneumatology in French: Sergei Bulgakov, *Le Paraclet* (Paris: Aubier, 1946), pp. 167–69.

him man. In this the Spirit fulfils his Old Testament role of inspiring
the prophets to look forward to Immanuel, "God with us".[75] Saint
Thomas, by contrast, had ascribed to the Spirit only the fashioning
of Christ's body (necessary since in the virginal conception there was
no contribution from male seed).[76] Balthasar finds that insufficient. It
does not suffice to form the basis of the "a priori mission-obedience"
of the Son in his entire incarnate economy.[77] And yet the "very
existence" of Jesus "is obedience".[78] Balthasar is sympathetic to the
notion that the eternal Son is, in any case, generated by his Father
"in" the Spirit—though this might seem to call into question that
same *taxis* where the Son is always named before the Spirit in the
Liturgy of the Church, taking its cue, no doubt, from the great missionary command in Saint Matthew's Gospel (28:19).[79] Balthasar felt
reassured by Adrienne von Speyr's insistence that the very fact that
the processions are eternal should in any case deter interpretation of
that sequential order in terms of time.

These reflections might seem to be taking Balthasar beyond the
idiom of a theological logic into dogmatics generally. Not so, however: it is crucial for the logic that the Spirit of truth knows the truth,
knows it intimately "because he is internal to it, that is, internal to
the relationship between the Father (who allows himself to be made
known) and the Son (who makes him known)".[80] And since the
truth in question is ultimately love, the "Spirit's interpretative operation, leading us into 'all the truth', goes beyond all mere theory (even
in the Greek sense of *theoria*)".[81] The truth here is also action—not
so much in the sense of freedom deployed as in the theological dramatics, but in the meaning that the "philosopher of action" Maurice
Blondel gave the word, summed up by Balthasar as "self-realizing
existence".[82] And since existence-as-love, originated from the Father,

---

[75] Von Balthasar, *Spirit of Truth*, p. 48.

[76] *ST* IIIa, q. 32, a. 1.

[77] Von Balthasar, *Spirit of Truth*, p. 48.

[78] Ibid., p. 51.

[79] Mt 28:19: "Go therefore and make disciples of all nations, baptizing them in the name of
the Father and of the Son and of the Holy Spirit."

[80] Ibid., p. 70.

[81] Ibid., p. 76.

[82] Ibid.

was humanly translated by Jesus Christ, the truth the Spirit spreads abroad must also be "discipleship of Christ".[83] That will entail ecclesiology, for the discipleship concerned is that of a people united by faith and love, their life centred on the incarnate Word.

This explanation of the "trinitarian inversion" of "Spirit-Christology" gives a good idea of how what remains of the theological logic will unfold. In the first place, it will describe the growing recognition of the distinct personhood of the Spirit despite, or because of, the meshing of his economy with that of the Son. Here Balthasar wishes to modify that Irenaean metaphor of the "two hands" by insisting that Son and Spirit always work in concert, not "separately in juxtaposition or in sequence".[84] He has now a question for "Neo-Photians" (such upholders of the standard modern Orthodox view of the spiration as Vladimir Lossky) for whom the "reciprocal relations [of Son and Spirit] cannot be put forward convincingly in terms of the 'immanent' Trinity unless one has recourse to 'economic' situations."[85] The question runs, "Can this kind of immanent structure still be given the name 'Love', which the New Testament attributes to the triune God?"[86] The word "love" can hardly be abandoned now, even apart from infidelity to the Johannine tradition, since it has been the central term of ontology since the first volume of the theological logic drew to its close. And in the second place, Balthasar must deal with the unfurling of the Spirit's mission in the life of Christian disciples. In the *ecclesia* the Holy Spirit is at work both "objectively", in Scripture, Tradition, Magisterium, and in the Liturgy of the sacraments as well as in such humdrum media as theology itself, and even canon law,[87] and also "subjectively", in prayer, forgiveness, fruitings in Christian living, and those charismatic gifts Balthasar had considered at length in his commentary on Thomas' texts (see chapter 6 below).[88] All this is with a view to bringing the whole creation, where, even extraecclesially, the

[83] Ibid.
[84] Ibid., p. 185.
[85] Ibid., pp. 216–17.
[86] Ibid., p. 217.
[87] Ibid., pp. 319–67.
[88] Ibid., pp. 369–411.

Spirit, as the universalizing agent in the work of Christ, must be at work, into the mystery of the Father, the true end-that-has-no-ending for the Holy Spirit's truth-bringing work. This is the topic of the last page of the Trilogy, its epilogue aside.[89]

[89] Ibid., p. 448.

5

Doctrine: God, Christ, and Human Salvation

In this chapter, and the chapter that follows, I consider some pre-eminent areas of Christian doctrine as presented by Balthasar (and Thomas). Below, I discuss Balthasar's trinitarian theology as well as his Christology, anthropology, and soteriology.[1]

God the Holy Trinity

Perusal of the presentation of the Trilogy in chapters 2, 3, and 4 above should, I hope, have persuaded the reader already: God the Holy Trinity is the deep centre—as Christ is the centre—of Balthasar's theology. That God's Being and nature are revelationally presented as trihypostatic is the truly ultimate mystery. "This is what is absolutely incomprehensible to us, that in God relation-to-self and relation-to-other, eternal repose-in-self and eternal striving and loving can be identical. And this not at all in the sense that opposite poles, which cannot within the world be reconciled, are here made to be identical in an obscure dialectical or monistic manner. Rather, what occurs is that the incomprehensible mystery—the identity of which we speak—itself appears and becomes visible within God's manner of becoming manifest."[2] That "identity" becomes manifest in salvation history, above all, at the Paschal Mystery when the triper-sonal love exchange—which can also be described as "the indivisible

---

[1] These include but go beyond the Trilogy; for the extra-Trilogy works, much is covered in Aidan Nichols, O.P., *Divine Fruitfulness: Balthasar's Theology beyond the Trilogy* (London: Continuum, 2007).

[2] Hans Urs von Balthasar, *The Glory of the Lord: A Theological Aesthetics*, vol. 1, *Seeing the Form* (San Francisco: Ignatius Press, 1982), pp. 609–10.

essential love of God himself"[3]—appears in all its radiance, and in so
doing throws light on all time, whether at the beginning of creation
or at the end.

At the beginning, Balthasar makes much of the significance of the
Trinity for creation—as does Thomas, whom, along with Bonaventure, he appeals to, notably as the final volume of *Theo-drama* opens.[4]
Yet their manners of evoking the Trinity-creation relation are not the
same. True, in the last volume of the theological dramatics, Balthasar praises both Thomas and Bonaventure for their teaching on the
flowing forth of creatures from God by way of the processions of
the Son and the Spirit. But as in the opening volume of the aesthetics, Balthasar soon develops in this context a distinctly modern
(or postmodern) concern with "the other". The "other" flourishes
best in a creation scenario where the Source is triune. "The otherness of creatures is essentially justified by the otherness that exists
within the identity of God himself",[5] and, since the affirmation of
the "other" is a characteristic of love, Balthasar moves immediately
from this assertion to intimate the wider indebtedness of a contingent
(and temporal) creation to the essential (and eternal) *love* of God—by
which God is three in one. "The creation, which derives from the
freedom of God and can claim no necessity for its own existence, is
nonetheless justified in existence because it is an expression of trinitarian love: it is a gift of the Father to the Son, which the Son then
returns to the Father and which is transfigured by the Holy Spirit
as the love between the Father and the Son."[6] And this implies a
truth about God that also applies analogically to creation: "the fact
that the Other exists is *absolutely good*."[7] This is something the undif-
ferentiated monotheisms of Judaism and Islam are unable to say, a
major motif of Balthasar's *Epilogue* to his Trilogy as a whole,[8] and an
intrinsic part of his attempt to show in that book-length conclusion
that Christian revelation is a totality which can integrate within itself

[3] Ibid., p. 612.
[4] Hans Urs von Balthasar, *Theo-drama: Theological Dramatic Theory*, vol. 5, *The Last Act*,
trans. Graham Harrison (San Francisco: Ignatius Press, 1998), pp. 61–65.
[5] Von Balthasar, *Seeing the Form*, p. 506.
[6] Ibid.
[7] Von Balthasar, *Last Act*, p. 81.
[8] Hans Urs von Balthasar, *Epilogue* (San Francisco: Ignatius Press, 2004), pp. 32–36.

whatever is true and worthwhile in philosophies and other religions, whilst simultaneously going far beyond them.

Thomas' account of the "creative Trinity", especially emphasized in his *Scriptum (Writing)* on the great twelfth-century Parisian theological textbook *Sentences* by Peter Lombard, looks more at the causal impact of each trinitarian Person as inferred from his mode of origination—or, in the Father's case, nonorigination—in the Godhead itself.[9] In the processions of Son and Spirit from the Father, he finds the archetype of which creation bears the *vestigia*, the traces, or, in the case of mankind, the image.[10] Where the divine three are concerned, Thomas' theology is, in its own manner, quite as "personalist" as that of Balthasar. The supposed conflict of "essentialism" with "personalism" is really, for both writers, a straw man. It is impossible to discuss a divine Person to the exclusion of some account of the divinity, the *ousia*, or essence, that is common to each of Father, Son, and Spirit. But Balthasar, unlike Thomas, disapproved of discussing the divine attributes, even the attributes that are predicated exclusively of the divine essence, in total abstraction from the trinitarian processions—including those attributes that already found expression in the Old Testament where the triunity of God was as yet barely glimpsed.[11] Such saturation of the doctrine of God by trinitarianism makes it less surprising that, in reading the Gospel narrative, Balthasar lays more stress on the threeness of the one, Thomas on the unity of the three.[12]

Balthasar's understanding of the Holy Trinity may be described as an amalgam of the Greek and Latin traditions.[13] In the conventional characterization,[14] the *Greek* approach is to begin with the distinct,

[9] Thomas Aquinas, *Scriptum super libros Sententiarum* I, prologue; ibid., dist. 26, q. 2, a. 2 ad 2.

[10] See Gilles Emery, O.P., *La Trinité créatrice: Trinité et création dans les commentaries aux "Sentences" de Thomas d'Aquin et de ses précurseurs Albert le Grand et Bonaventure* (Paris: Vrin, 1995). A summary of this complex study is found in Gilles Emery, O.P., "Trinité et creation", *Revue des sciences philosophiques et théologiques* 79 (1995): 405–30. For further enlightenment on Thomas' triadology, see Gilles Emery, O.P., *Trinity in Aquinas* (Ypsilanti, MI: Sapientia Press, 2003).

[11] Von Balthasar, *Last Act*, pp. 66–67.

[12] See Etienne Vetö, *Du Christ à la Trinité: Penser les mystères du Christ après Thomas d'Aquin et Balthasar* (Paris: Cerf, 2012).

[13] For Thomas' own use of his predecessors, see Aidan Nichols, O.P., *Discovering Aquinas: An Introduction to His Life, Work, and Influence* (London: Darton, Longman and Todd), pp. 60–73.

[14] Typically, in Karl Rahner, *The Trinity* (New York: Crossroad, 1970), pp. 15–21.

yet intrinsically interrelated roles of Father, Son, and Holy Spirit in salvation history (though this is also how the Trinity appears in all the liturgical traditions, Western as well as Eastern), and to think back from there to the one God in himself. On the same customary characterization, the *Latin* approach begins with the eternal issuing within the one God of Son and Spirit from the Father. These are indeed the "processions", to be understood on the analogy of human processes of understanding and love. Albeit not in time—this is but an analogy—these are the two sorts of spiritually productive act, abiding or immanent within the subject, that differences between uncreated and created, nonmaterial and material, eternal and temporal, do not exclude.[15] Unlike the production of a mental word or a loving impulse within the human self, in God these acts are, however, divinely fruitful in generating the Son and spirating the Holy Spirit. And this is the mystery reflected in the creation of things. Prescinding from salvation history does not of course mean that Thomas was unaware of how the Trinity is pertinent to mankind not only as Creator but also as the means of our salvation. So much is apparent from the Scriptures, the Creeds, and the liturgies of the sacraments. In his own words in the *Summa theologiae*'s *Prima Pars*, "The knowledge of the divine persons was necessary to us on two grounds. The first is to enable us to think rightly on the subject of the creation of things.... The second reason, *and the principal one*, is to give us a true notion of the salvation of mankind, a salvation accomplished by the Son who became flesh and by the gift of the Holy Spirit."[16]

For his part, Balthasar appeals to the Greek Fathers in such a way that he can also accommodate the contribution of Augustine and Thomas—with adjustments drawn from other Latin writers, notably Bonaventure and, before him, the Victorine theologians of the twelfth century. This concerns more especially Balthasar's unwillingness to allow the role of love, as a fruitful immanent act in God, to be deferred till the procession of the Spirit. If the Johannine account of the unity of Father and Son is to be credited—and not for nothing did Balthasar name his "community" of laypeople and priests *Johannesgemeinschaft*, after Saint John the Evangelist—the Son too is the

[15] *ST* Ia, q. 27.
[16] *ST* Ia, q. 32, a. 1 ad 3; emphasis added, of course.

fruit of the Father's love. In point of fact, this had also been Thomas' understanding in that early work, the *Writing* on the *Sentences*.[17]

Owing to the influence of the mystically inspired writing of Adrienne von Speyr (but also the philosophical theology of a disciple of Siewerth, Clemens Kaliba[18]), Balthasar reworked the trinitarian "notions" of Aquinas—abstract representations of the distinct character of the divine Persons as these are—so as to propose that the activity of the Person who generates or the Persons who spirate and the corresponding passivity of the Person generated or spirated have in each case a converse. "Passive *actio* is involved in active *actio*",[19] while "passivity" can also be described—and indeed is better described—as active receptivity. "Where absolute love is concerned, conceiving and letting-be are just as essential as giving. In fact, without this receptive letting be and all it involves—gratitude for the gift of oneself and a turning in love toward the Giver—the giving itself is impossible."[20] Allowing for an archetypal link between, on the one hand, activity and masculine symbolism and, on the other hand, receptivity and feminine symbolism (naturally enough, feminists will dislike this—but they are, I suppose, unlikely to be Thomists), that made it possible for Balthasar to apply bi-gendered language in a subsidiary way for all three of the divine Persons, while also maintaining the primacy of the uni-gendered symbolism found in the sources of revelation themselves.

The theological logic in its second and third volumes gives reason for thinking that no single manner of "modelling" the Holy Trinity can do justice to its mystery. In the language of later twentieth-century academic discussion of this topic, two distinct approaches complement each other within Balthasar's overall account. "The interpersonal model cannot attain the substantial unity of God, whereas the intrapersonal model cannot give an adequate picture of the real and abiding face-to-face encounter of the hypostases."[21] A

---

[17] Aquinas, *Scriptum super libros Sententiarum* I, dist. 10, q. 1, a. 1, solutio.
[18] Clemens Kaliba, *Die Welt als Gleichnis des dreieingen Gottes* (Salzburg: Müller, 1952).
[19] Von Balthasar, *Last Act*, p. 86.
[20] Ibid.
[21] Hans Urs von Balthasar, *Theo-logic: Theological Logical Theory*, vol. 2, *Truth of God*, trans. Adrian J. Walker (San Francisco: Ignatius Press, 2004), p. 38.

bi-focal approach is well-placed to overcome these disadvantages. This is not indeed how Saint Thomas thinks about the Holy Trinity, yet a multifocal approach *is* how he thinks about the Passion of Christ.[22] Damage to the coherence of *sacra doctrina* does not seem to follow, then, from nonunifocality as such.

More likely to be controversial, and not just among followers of Saint Thomas, is the extension of the notion of kenosis from the incarnate Son to Father (and to Spirit) by way of the concept of *Urkenosis* (primordial "self-emptying") in the eternal Godhead, the "immanent" or "absolute" Trinity.[23] That is distinct, then, from the "economic" kenosis of the second trinitarian Person affirmed in the Letter to the Philippians, whereby the Son, for the sake of human salvation, so "emptied himself" (Phil 2:7) as to take human flesh and die the death of the Cross. Balthasar's theology of the Trinity is worked out in significant connexion with his theology of the Paschal Mystery, the Easter events—in which regard it belongs to a wider movement in the theological culture of the later twentieth century.[24] But unlike, say, the Lutheran Jürgen Moltmann, with whom he is sometimes compared, Balthasar takes pains to make the reader understand that the Holy Trinity is disclosed in those Easter events, *not* constituted there. While Balthasar treats the immanent Trinity in close union with God's economic manifestation, he does not seek unconditionally to identify them—least of all in the sense that God might need a world to create and save in order to be himself. Here Balthasar is at one with Thomas, and, for that matter, all orthodox theologians who accept "the requirements of Christian doctrine [as] established from the fourth century: the existence and the properties of the divine persons do not depend on creation or on divine action in the world."[25] In the wake of the Russian Orthodox theologian Sergei Bulgakov, Balthasar takes a kenotic view of the eternal Trinity for a good reason, a reason grounded in the most fundamental of all Christian claims— namely, that God is not just loving; God is love.

[22] Aidan Nichols, O.P., "St. Thomas Aquinas on the Passion of Christ: A Reading of *Summa Theologiae* IIIa., q. 46", *Scottish Journal of Theology* 43 (1990): 447–59.

[23] Von Balthasar, *Action*, p. 331.

[24] Anne Hunt, *The Trinity and the Paschal Mystery* (Wilmington, DE: Michael Glazier, 1997).

[25] Gilles Emery, O.P., "The Doctrine of the Trinity in St. Thomas Aquinas", in Thomas Wienandy, O.F.M. Cap., Daniel A. Keating, and John P. Yokum, eds., *Aquinas on Doctrine: A Critical Introduction* (London: T&T Clark, 2004), pp. 45–66, and here at p. 49.

How so? For Balthasar, kenosis begins with the Father, the fount of love in the triune life. The "personal and total surrender of the Father in generating the Son is the ur-kenosis of the triune life and its primal shape. The Son cannot be God in any other way than by following this pattern of self-giving. The kenosis of the Incarnation and of Good Friday and Holy Saturday and the regular pattern of earthly obedience are only new expressions of this triune way of being."[26] For Balthasar, such kenoticism must at all times be interpreted by the axiom that the divine is of itself sheer love-gift. Here Balthasar was helped out by Bonaventure. "Defined ... by scripture and the theological tradition as love, the divine does not give from lack but rather from superabundance."[27] As Cyril O'Regan points out in his great monograph, Balthasar clearly had Hegelian misconstruals of the Trinity in view when he explained that God "does not acquire perfection in and through a process of self-determination and mediation".[28] The second volume of the theological logic makes it especially plain that whereas "while ontologically speaking each of the divine persons has to be considered as unsurpassably full and fulfilled"—in Saint Thomas' terms, each person is really identical with the *actus purus*, the sheer actuality, of the divine essence—nevertheless "the receptivity and openness at the core of each person suggests something like a *coincidentia oppositorum* of emptiness with fullness. In this coincidence of wealth and poverty ... there is no overcoming of the particular emptiness that marks the constitutional receptivity and relativity of divine persons."[29] While the constitution of the Persons in their mutual relation is the basis of this affirmation, it also reflects Balthasar's most basic account of the nature of God. "In the very outpouring of its indigence the soul is an image of the God who ... has poured himself out outside himself through eros, even as Creator, the God who has proved this perfectly in the Incarnation. Hence, at a deeper level, the poverty of Being and of its sensibility reveals the sole treasure Being contains, which is nothing other than—love."[30]

[26] Christopher Steck, S.J., *The Ethical Thought of Hans Urs von Balthasar* (New York: Crossroad, 2001), p. 41.

[27] Cyril O'Regan, *The Anatomy of Misremembering: Von Balthasar's Response to Philosophical Modernity*, vol. 1, *Hegel* (New York: Crossroad, 2014), p. 160.

[28] Ibid.

[29] Ibid., p. 209.

[30] Von Balthasar, *Seeing the Form*, p. 407.

I shall return to this overall philosophical-theological vision in my final chapter, for it furnishes the key to Balthasar's underlying method.

Balthasar's general approach to the changelessness of God is somewhat problematic for classical Latin theology.[31] It is not Balthasar's habit to deny the immutability of the divine nature—or rewrite that concept in moral terms as referring to the reliability of God, the most common escape route recent theologians have taken so as to weaken, if not altogether to evade, its force. But neither is he happy with customary expressions of the doctrine. As the plenitude of *esse*, the divine nature is itself more dynamic than the word "immutable" would normally suggest. More especially, he is concerned to defend the freedom that, on his view, typifies the interrelations of the Persons in their self-involvement with creation, their freedom, in fact, to modulate those relations in that context. In the theological dramatics, by way of a nuanced discussion of some relevant biblical, patristic, and more modern materials, he seeks to find a condition of possibility for the "pain of God"—especially in the Incarnation and Atonement—in the eternal interrelations of the Persons in the immanent Trinity.[32] In *Mysterium Paschale*, that provides a basis for a paradoxical-sounding claim: in principle, there is no mutability here at all. "God, then, has no need to 'change' when he makes a reality of the wonders of his charity, wonders which include the Incarnation and, more particularly, the Passion of Christ, and, before him, the dramatic history of God with Israel and, no doubt, with humanity as a whole. All the contingent 'abasements' of God in the economy of salvation are forever included and outstripped in the eternal event of Love."[33]

In that same context—the God-world relationship—he also holds that divine being, despite its complete actuality, can nevertheless receive accretions from creatures as they respond to God's own gifts to them, on the principle affirmed by the Byzantine Liturgy: "Thine of Thine own we offer to Thee". "What does God gain from the world? An additional gift, given to the Son by the Father, but equally a gift made by the Son to the Father, and by the Spirit to both.

[31] Gerard F. O'Hanlon, S.J., *The Immutability of God in the Theology of Hans Urs von Balthasar* (Cambridge: Cambridge University Press, 1990).

[32] Von Balthasar, *Last Act*, pp. 212–46.

[33] Hans Urs von Balthasar, *Mysterium Paschale: The Mystery of Easter*, trans. Aidan Nichols, O.P. (2000; repr., San Francisco: Ignatius Press, 2005), p. ix.

It is a gift because through the distinct operations of the each of the three Persons, the world acquires an inward share in the divine exchange of life; as a result the world is able to take the divine things it has received from God, together with the gift of being created, and return them to God as a divine gift."[34]

The key to Balthasar's doctrine in both aspects—intratrinitarian and extratrinitarian—lies in the notion of reception as a perfection. William Norris Clarke is a Thomist who, on his own declared principles, would be sympathetic to this aspect of Balthasarianism. Norris Clarke faced the extratrinitarian issue in his own dialogue with process thought—a topic quite distinct from any dialogue of Thomists and Balthasarians, for Balthasar made plain his dislike of that particular twentieth-century movement with its fountain head in the mathematician-cosmologist Alfred North Whitehead. Still there is pertinence to Balthasar—to his theology of the trinitarian relations and not only to his account of the Creator-creature relation—in Norris Clarke's comment that where "the order of the person and inter-personal relations have become the prime analogue for the concepts used in ... metaphysics, ... to give and to receive love is a sign of perfection rather than of imperfection in a personal agent. Thomists' admission of conscious relational change in God, therefore, no longer implies the compromising of any really essential principles. They can even go so far as to admit that such change is temporal, as long as they understand that 'God's time' is of an incomprehensibly different modality from the time of our contingent, moving world."[35]

Norris Clarke's final sentence, in the extract from the overview of his thinking given above, speaks of a mode of duration called "God's time". Balthasar's discussion of a "super-time" in which the divine Being relates to the world, and which he prefers to the more traditional language of "eternity", is, evidently, pertinent to this theme. In the final volume of the theological dramatics, Balthasar speaks in von Speyrian language of the "vitality" and "exuberance" of the trinitarian relations,[36] going so far as to say that the world's becoming (and

---

[34]Von Balthasar, *Last Act*, p. 521.

[35]Gerald A. McCool, S.J., "An Alert and Independent Thomist: William Norris Clarke, S.J.", in *The Universe as Journey: Conversations with W. Norris Clarke, S.J.* (New York: Fordham University Press, 1988), pp. 36–37.

[36]Von Balthasar, *Last Act*, pp. 77–81.

not simply being) "has its origin in the sublime transactions between the Persons of the Trinity".[37] Participation in those transactions by supernaturally elevated creatures means, in the words of one commentator, that "super-time" entails "unthinkable event, absolute emergence, and unanticipable surprise".[38]

One might find in Balthasar's account of time vis-à-vis eternity some affinity with the story told by the "Real-Idealist" thinker Friedrich Wilhelm Joseph Schelling, one of the figures covered in Balthasar's *Apokalypse der deutschen Seele* who towards the end of his life found his way back to a recognisably Christian picture of the world in God.

> Schelling's concept of eternity is something positive, not just a negative concept like the traditional one that says, *aeternum est, quod fine et initio caret* [eternity is what lacks beginning and end]. The positive concept says that God is really the beginning, the middle, and the end, but with God that means, "In God there is no beginning of God's beginning, and no end of God's end." ... So it is easy to find again in this positive concept Boethius' *tota simul et perfecta possession* [the classic description of God's eternity in the Latin tradition], whereby with Schelling, *possessio* speaks of a sovereign lordship and an ability to begin that has power over history.[39]

A Thomist scholar has written, "Responding to the objection that in Scripture verbs with past, present, and future tenses are used for God, Thomas states that God's eternity includes all time. So, eternity is not to be understood as everlasting within time (omnitemporal). Eternity is more than that, although that 'more' is difficult to specify or even impossible to express."[40]

Possibly, Schelling and Balthasar (who respected, without underwriting, the later Schelling's attempts to produce a philosophy of both mythology and the Judaeo-Christian revelation) could help spell out that "more".

---

[37] Ibid., p. 80.

[38] O'Regan, *Hegel*, p. 234.

[39] Walter Kasper, *The Absolute in History: The Philosophy and Theology of History in Schelling's Late Philosophy* (New York; Mahwah, NJ: Paulist, 2018), pp. 316–17.

[40] Herwi Rikhof, "Thomas at Utrecht", in *Contemplating Aquinas: On the Varieties of Interpretation*, ed. Fergus Kerr, O.P. (London: SCM, 2003), p. 120; see pp. 105–36.

In Balthasar's theology "super-time" is matched by "super-space". Referring chiefly to the closing volume of the theological dramatics, Cyril O'Regan remarks that, for Balthasar, "the meta-symbol of 'super-space' at a penultimate level points to the eschatological horizon of action in which the referent is ... an apocalyptic heaven and earth that re-presents the world transformed and transfigured. The ultimate horizon, the horizon of horizons, is defined by the love of the triune God, and more specifically defined by the distance or diastasis between the Father and the Son traversed by the Spirit. There is no beyond with respect to this distance."[41] "Super-space" makes nonsymbolic sense as a description of the renewed creation of the end of ages. Contrastingly, when it has as its referent the trinitarian relations, it surely functions as a symbol or, in O'Regan's term, a "meta-symbol", a word he has coined, no doubt, to indicate some architectonic significance. The symbolism concerned is of homecoming in God, the topic that dominates the last section of the theological dramatics, "The World in God".[42] "Infinite distance is in the end an invitation",[43] an invitation to the world to move "ecstatically"—out of itself—towards God.

Christ, man, salvation

Balthasar's trinitarian theology governs his Christology. For Balthasar, Christ is "the Trinitarian Son", a phrase which has as its background Bonaventure's view that the Word reflects both the Father and the Spirit, the Father whose image the Son is and the Spirit whose procession the Son expresses.[44] Balthasar cannot cope with a separated Christology. The key to the life of Christ is the Son's obedience to the Father in the Spirit. On earth, in a temporal transposition, this is the "intelligible form of his eternal attitude to the Father who

---

[41] O'Regan, *Hegel*, p. 237.

[42] Von Balthasar, *Last Act*, pp. 373–488.

[43] As O'Regan writes, "Distance truly lets otherness be, while being in a sense its embrace." O'Regan, *Hegel*, pp. 237–38.

[44] Bonaventure, *On the Hexaemeron* 9, 2. The same theme is richly orchestrated in Adrienne von Speyr's corpus; see the texts gathered together in von Balthasar, *Last Act*, pp. 121–22.

begets him, namely, that of primal obedience in willing cooperation and gratitude".[45] The question of the self-consciousness of Jesus also belongs here, as the following passage from the introductory volume of the aesthetics makes plain.

> As a man assumed into God, Christ necessarily participates in the self-consciousness of the eternal Son in his procession from the Father and his return to him, and this becomes reflected in the human self-consciousness of Christ to the extent that he possesses this self-consciousness of the Son *interius intimo meo* [more intimate to me than I am to myself] and that he possesses it by opening himself to it. But because ... he is genuine man *only* as assumed man, he understands even his genuinely human experience of God as an expression and function of his divine person; just as, in turn, he becomes conscious of this divine person only in the functional movement of his mission, in such a way that the humility in which he opens himself to the divine is at the same time an expression of the divine will to kenosis.[46]

The "divine will to kenosis" is that will whereby the Father has asked the incarnate Son for sacrificial obedience for the sake of the world's salvation. It is a will that, in any case, the entire Trinity through *Urkenosis* eternally embodies—the peculiar circumstances of a fallen world, which mean for the Son agony of mind and body, alone excluded. The Incarnation, consequently, is both an *assumptio*, and thus a going up, and a *kenosis*, and thus a going down. Hominid assumption and divine kenosis do not represent two Christologies. The affirmation of the "taking of the manhood into God", as the Athanasian Creed has it, does not prevent a confession of the descent of God, in the Logos, into man: "He came down from heaven." On the contrary, the first affirmation calls out for the second.

Furthermore, for Balthasar the "God-Man's experience as creature" reflects the "trinitarian experience".[47] "Experience" is an odd noun to have "trinitarian" as its governing adjective, but the German word *Erlebnis* here denotes what the Trinity lives out in the everlasting communion of the Persons. The "distance" from God that

---

[45] Ibid., p. 123.
[46] Von Balthasar, *Seeing the Form*, p. 328.
[47] Ibid.

Christ now registers as man reflects the "difference" or "distinction" between the Persons in God for evermore—a characteristically Balthasarian observation in which the inner-trinitarian distinctions of Person make possible the vis-à-vis or *gegenüber*—the "over against one another"—of Son and Father on earth, all in the unity, however, of the Holy Spirit, who is not only the fruit of their love (an especially Balthasarian claim) but also its bond (the chief contribution of Augustine to an account of the Spirit's place in the Trinity).

As to mankind, Balthasar does not think a theological anthropology— a treatise on the doctrine of man—can be written without reference to Christology. That does not mean, however, that, for him, no preliminary understanding of created human nature as such can be given. In no way is *homo sapiens* simply a surd, a nonsense or intrinsic absurdity. For both Aquinas and Balthasar the biblical teaching on the divine image in man (Gen 1:26) is of central importance—and in different ways they will go on to relate that image both to Christ and to the Trinity. The supreme image is Christ, the trinitarian Son, and *therefore* the image of the Trinity.[48] Both theologians are too steeped in the thought of the Church Fathers not to regard the divine image-hood as the single most foundational tenet of Christian anthropology. For Thomas, the theme stands guard over the very beginning of the *Secunda Pars* of the *Summa theologiae*: namely, at the passage from the treatment of God—the triune Creator, from whom man issues as his image—to an account of man's return to God through the virtues and Gifts, all mediated by the grace of the Christ who, in the *Tertia Pars*, is shown to be the way to God. In a "circular" sort of movement, then, mankind rejoins its archetype via him. Man the image is a theme of structural importance in the *Summa theologiae*.[49] Thomas gives his own source: John of Damascus, the synthesizer of Greek patristic teaching. "Man being made in the image of God—and by this we must understand ... that he is endowed with intelligence, free will, and power for autonomous action—having dealt with the

---

[48] Michele Schumacher, *A Trinitarian Anthropology: Adrienne von Speyr and Hans Urs von Balthasar in Dialogue with Thomas Aquinas* (Washington, DC: Catholic University of America Press, 2014).

[49] Servais Pinckaers, O.P., "Le thème de l'image de Dieu en l'homme et l'anthropologie", in *Humain à l'image de Dieu*, ed. Pierre Bühler (Geneva: Labor et fides, 1989), pp. 147–63.

Exemplar, who is God ... we must now address what pertains to his image, which is to say man, since he is also the principle for his own acts because he possesses free will and command over his action."[50] This "Damascene"—and Thomasian—affirmation of the individual as *autoexousios* played a major part, so chapter 3 insisted, in Balthasar's theological dramatics. Indeed, a theo-dramatic view of salvation would be impossible were that affirmation not made. And Balthasar, ending his discussion of "infinite and finite freedom" in volume 2 of the dramatics by a lengthy excursus on man made to the "image and likeness" of God, complains that modern theologians, having declared the theme to be central, then go on to ignore it. It is not a mistake he perpetrates. Analysing the condition of the image is a necessary preamble to understanding the "heightening of tension" between heaven and earth when, on the one hand, the archetype of that image is rejected and, on the other, human beings receive the mission which goes with their supernatural vocation in Christ and the Spirit.[51] In the dramatics, Balthasar listed the elements in postlapsarian human nature seemingly incapable of reconciliation. Man is pulled interiorly between cosmic and hypercosmic, spirit and body, male and female, individual and community, the great question mark of death cutting across them all. The rationality and freedom which are the decisive features of the imagehood of God cannot cope from their own resources. But there is a (biblical) promise that suitable agency will come from elsewhere. "This promise comes from a Giver who, far beyond any gift separate from himself, is able actually to give himself. ... However, it is no longer a question of the latter constituting ('natural') subjects; now, in a 'supernatural' way, subsistent Being opens up to them its own life."[52] This supernatural communication both radicalises the human creature's finitude, for it knows it can have no claim to such "initiation",[53] and also incomparably ennobles it, bestowing a "personal call and corresponding endowment".[54]

Balthasar's supernaturalism does not entail indifference to the theological concept of human nature, something that would certainly put

[50] *ST* IIa, prologue.
[51] Hans Urs von Balthasar, *Theo-drama: Theological Dramatic Theory*, vol. 2, *Dramatis Personae: Man in God* (San Francisco: Ignatius Press, 1990), pp. 335–94.
[52] Ibid., p. 398.
[53] Ibid., p. 400.
[54] Ibid., p. 402.

him at odds with the Thomist tradition—and the magisterially adopted body of reflection on the *humanum* that is "natural law" thinking. A good deal that common sense, or philosophical analysis, places under the heading of "nature" may already be affected by the economy of grace—so much he conceded in his dialogue with Barth—and hence require Christological description. Yet a minimum account is available. Formally speaking: "nature is basically *creation* as such", making possible, then, an "ethics of created being as such" likewise. "This natural law will emerge from man's dependence on the Creator, which is itself bound to his specifically human, physical, psychological, sexual and social nature."[55] Admittedly, Balthasar's account of our nature as human animals made "in the image and to the likeness" stresses personhood and thus the uniqueness of individual human beings— and in some contexts at least we define individual person over against common nature. As I noted in the opening chapter of this book, these themes were among his earliest concerns in the context of Catholic apologetics and evangelization from before the Second World War, and they will have a remarkable outcome in the account of vocation and task in the "mature" thought of the theological dramatics. But here "outcome" does not mean reversal.

In the first place, his meditations on theo-drama did not lead him to think that only Christians were really persons. "It is a question of terminology whether we grant the term 'person' to ... every man, who is a spiritual subject ... or only to the man who is called through grace; in the first case, one would have to distinguish between two forms or grades of personhood,"[56] by reference to supernatural vocation or its absence. In any case, "These missions do not, as in Christ's case, constitute an *a priori* synthesis with his person, but are synthesized *a posteriori* along with the created, chosen persons (*Geistpersonen*); sinners only partially accept and fulfil their missions and can even reject them entirely."[57]

And in the second place, the emphasis on—evidently, bivalent— personhood does not suppress an interest in human nature at large.

---

[55] Hans Urs von Balthasar, *The Theology of Karl Barth: Exposition and Interpretation*, trans. Edward T. Oakes, S.J. (San Francisco: Communio Books; Ignatius Press, 1992), p. 291.

[56] Von Balthasar, *Man in God*, p. 403.

[57] Hans Urs von Balthasar, *Theo-drama: Theological Dramatic Theory*, vol. 3, *Dramatis Personae: The Person in Christ*, trans. Graham Harrison (San Francisco: Ignatius Press, 1992), pp. 207–8.

In the early 1960s, at the time of writing *A Theological Anthropology*, Balthasar, by then halfway through the theological aesthetics, had connected personhood and human nature in the created order taken generally.[58] Personal relations are undoubtedly special, notably as one-to-one, in the "dialogical" realm. But they do not render talk of the generalities of human nature superfluous. Balthasar did not grow out of that conviction. In *Love Alone Is Credible*, his report on the theological aesthetics as they neared completion, he wrote: "Two human beings, however different they may be from one another, nevertheless always encounter one another within the same 'nature'; for nature cannot be bracketed out from [what] it means to be a person. While there is no such thing as 'personology', psychology and humanistic studies (*Geisteswissenschaft*) certainly exist, and the reciprocal revelation in love becomes co-extensive with the understanding we can achieve on the basis of nature."[59] Where personhood stands out from human nature—with the latter's powers of intelligence and free will, and capacity for autonomous action—is in its combination of uniqueness and the call to enter into relation with the divine "Thou": the "dialogical" in its most sublime sense. As with the "Damascene" emphasis on natural autonomy (to be seen not as a decoration of heteronomy against God, but as a gift of God's creative generosity), those two elements—uniqueness and the "dialogical" I-thou relation—would soon enter the theological dramatics in a striking way.

Incorporated into the strictly supernatural concept of person as "mission", those elements reemerge there in explicitly Christological form, for each person, so reconceived, constitutes a graced participation in the mission of the divine Son-made-man. It is above all, then, Balthasar's anthropology of the *Christian* human being that is truly incomprehensible without Christology. In volume 2 of the dramatics he wrote, "Anthropology can only attain its full stature within Christology, and so it must adopt its standards from the latter."[60] Even

---

[58] Hans Urs von Balthasar, *A Theological Anthropology* (New York: Sheed and Ward, 1967); the German original is from 1983.

[59] Hans Urs von Balthasar, *Love Alone Is Credible*, trans. D. C. Schindler (San Francisco: Ignatius Press, 2004), p. 47.

[60] Von Balthasar, *Man in God*, p. 202.

in the earliest volume of the theological aesthetics, he had already reached this fundamental conclusion, at any rate so far as ecclesial anthropology—anthropology in the Mystical Body—is concerned.

> The disposition of Christ is the disposition of one who has become expropriated for God and for man: his subjectivity coincides with his mission.... There is in him no unaffected residue of subjectivity which has not been assumed into his task as redeemer: everything down to the foundation of his person has been put at the disposal of his ministry and made available for his work.... This is why a Christian who has been expropriated to become a member of Christ is not even himself in a position to understand his Christian disposition by means of human psychology, much less to explain it to others.... His innermost disposition which until then had seemed to him to be the most private thing a person possesses, can henceforth be conceivable to him only in light of the dogma of God's incarnation.[61]

Cyril O'Regan comments: "In defining human being in terms of 'mission' Balthasar ensures at once that his anthropology is christologically grounded and that it admits, even demands, a Trinitarian horizon for its full and adequate articulation. For in Christ and through the Spirit each human being participates in the mystery of the Trinity, which is a mystery of love and donation."[62]

In his wider Christology, Balthasar's aims include the refuting of modern-day theological challenges to Christological orthodoxy, as well as the elimination of "Platonising currents of Christian spirituality" that seek an "immediate" vision of God, in the sense of one no longer mediated by the Father's incarnate Son.[63] Neo-Nestorian Christologies—for which the personhood of Jesus Christ is not truly the second trinitarian Person, the divine nature united inseparably but without confusion to his humanity—can readily converge with over-Platonised spiritualities, focussed as these are on the ultimately monadic divine Good as the soul returns to its Source. They are spiritualities that in the last analysis can dispense with Christ altogether. Balthasar recalls those tempted by such thinking

[61] Von Balthasar, *Seeing the Form*, p. 254.
[62] O'Regan, *Hegel*, pp. 212–13.
[63] Von Balthasar, *Seeing the Form*, p. 302.

to the teaching of the Church's first systematic theologian, Saint Irenaeus. "The Son is the visibleness of the Invisible One, and ... this paradox, with the simultaneity it expresses, remains the *ne plus ultra* of revelation."[64] Balthasar's disagreements with Rahner turned not least on his insistence that, with the conciliar Christology as it moved on from Chalcedon to Justinian's council, Constantinople II, there is an essential asymmetry in the makeup of the Word incarnate. He is more fundamentally from above, from heaven, than he is from below, from earth.

Balthasar's adherence to the revelation doctrine of Saint Irenaeus suggests a comparison with Saint Thomas' Christology in his commentary on the Gospel of John,[65] the biblical locus behind the Irenaean motif of the Son as "the visible of the Father": *visibile Patris Filius*.[66] Thomas, by his debts to the Christology of Saint Cyril of Alexandria and Saint John Damascene, and his long-lasting research project of acquiring fuller documentation on the councils of Chalcedon and Constantinople II,[67] anticipates Balthasar's patristically informed rejection of a low Christology, while his account of the mysteries of the life of Christ in the *Summa theologiae* makes it plain that only the Saviour Christ, by the efficient and exemplar causality of his life, death, and Resurrection, can be the "way" that takes human beings to the Father's house and keeps them there.[68]

The Latin tradition is sometimes criticized for an inadequate emphasis on the Spirit, but, for his part, O'Regan points out how for Balthasar a worse fate would be the pneumatic displacement of Christ. This anxiety generates a common motif with Thomas— namely, hostility to "Joachimism": the theology of history of the twelfth-century Calabrian abbot Joachim of Fiora (or Flora), for whom the era of the Son was to be replaced by an era of the Holy

---

[64] Ibid.

[65] Michael Dauphinais and Matthew Levering, eds., *Reading John with St. Thomas: Theological Exegesis and Speculative Theology* (Washington, DC: Catholic University of America Press, 1995).

[66] Juan Ochagavia, S.J., *Filius visibile Patris: A Study of St. Irenaeus' Teaching on Revelation and Tradition* (Rome: Pontifical Institute of Oriental Studies, 1964).

[67] Michael Dauphinais, Roger W. Nutt, and Andrew Hofer, O.P., eds., *Thomas Aquinas and the Greek Fathers* (Naples, FL: Sapientia Press, 2018).

[68] Jean Pierre Torrell, O.P., *Le Christ en ses Mystères: La vie et l'oeuvre de Jésus selon saint Thomas d'Aquin*, 2 vols. (Paris: Desclée de Brouwer, 1999).

Spirit. Balthasar's mentor Henri de Lubac had shown how Joachim enjoyed a remarkable posterity: an unexpected posthumous celebrity among speculative philosophers in the postmediaeval epoch.[69] Not the least of them was Hegel.

> In his earliest writings, Hegel reads the Farewell Discourse to mean the concrete individual Jesus must disappear so that his meaning can be realized in the *Gemeinde*, or spiritual community.... In agreement with de Lubac, in *Theo-Drama* and *Theo-Logic* Balthasar suggests that the model for this displacement is supplied ... by Joachim de Fiore.... In terms of content, the critical position Balthasar takes with respect to Joachim recalls rather faithfully the criticisms leveled at Joachim by St Thomas in the *Summa*. Balthasar agrees with Thomas that a Joachimite-style pneumatology thoroughly compromises the finality of Christ, and has the disastrous consequence of downplaying the institutional Church as the mediation of Christ's grace, and correlatively of entertaining too high an estimate of spiritual church which realizes the meaning of the Christological event as an anagogic sign. This, of course, is nothing less than the full realization of freedom and knowledge in the human community. Balthasar has a heightened sense of how Joachimism functions in post-Enlightenment discourses to baptize Enlightenment progressivism in the name of a pneumatological or apocalyptic discourse that upsets the regulative christocentrism of Christian thought.[70]

Balthasar's Bonaventurianism may be even more pertinent in this regard than is the reference to Thomas. From the opening volume of the theological aesthetics on, it is clear that for Balthasar the Spirit is not the "object of regard", but "plays a role in unfolding ... recognition" that the "drama of the crucified Christ" remains eternally pertinent for "understanding of the triune God".[71] This will be the great theme of the concluding volume of the theological logic.

Balthasar has, then, a strongly ontological Christology. How could an admirer of the great Fathers—architects of the Christology of the seven councils—and the high mediaeval Schoolmen not be so? But

---

[69] Henri de Lubac, *La posterité spirituelle de Joachim de Flore* (Paris: Lethellieux & Namur: Culture et Verité, 1979).

[70] O'Regan, *Hegel*, p. 197, with reference to *ST* 1a, q. 39, and Ia-IIae, q. 106, a. 4.

[71] O'Regan, *Hegel*, p. 198.

at the same time, this ontological Christology is always related to his doctrine of salvation. While the Incarnation moment is given its due saving significance (Balthasar rejected the notion that "incarnational" and "staurological" or "Cross-centred" soteriologies are at variance), the emphasis lies on the Paschal Mystery, and hence, in the first place, on the theology of Atonement. Rather, like Thomas, for whom no single concept or image of the meaning of the Passion of Christ can do justice, Balthasar refuses to follow an influential trend in modern theology, initiated by Aulén, for which a classical patristic view of the victory of Christ over sin, death, and the Devil (here Irenaeus would be an obvious representative) is incompatible with the later, high-mediaeval, exclusively Western, "juridical" view of the meritoriously satisfactory work on the Cross (represented most obviously by Anselm). The fourth volume of the theological dramatics, Paschally centred as it is, refused to pit Irenaeus against Anselm, or indeed reject any theological contribution that can appeal to some element in the New Testament's conceptually and imagistically rich orchestration of response to the all-important "Action" of the Logos incarnate in the Cross, descent, and Resurrection.[72]

A vital connexion links Balthasar's anthropology, already considered, to the single most crucial theme of his soteriology, which is *Stellvertretung* or vicarious representation. As noted earlier, Balthasar had included "individual and community" among the elements of human nature that find themselves in tension with each other, not least in the fallen state. It is in any case integral to human nature that the "we" enters into the very constitution of the "I". Balthasar was in agreement with the opening volume of his own theological logic when he wrote of man, "The more spiritual these mutually exclusive centres of self-awareness and freedom become, the greater capacity for the world they possess, the more profound their knowledge of one another grows and the more their communication with one another develops."[73] So "beings existing for themselves simultaneously exist for one another."[74] It is only by another person that the "I" can be awakened to awareness as a free self—typically by

---

[72] Ibid., p. 191.
[73] Von Balthasar, *Man in God*, p. 388.
[74] Ibid.

the mother's smile. That infantine experience which Balthasar regards as the opening to "being in its totality", leading to a recognition of the "gift-quality" of human nature and its "response-character", now appears as at the same time admission into the "appropriate community", the free subject realizing that he is "for himself with others".[75] *Gottunmittelbarkeit*, a "nonmediate presence before God", is inseparable in each individual from "shared humanity", *Mitmenschlichkeit*.[76] The importance of this for Balthasar's soteriology can hardly be overstated. "Since we share a world with others, there is in every human subject a formal *inclusion* of all the other subjects (who are materially excluded because each one is 'for himself'). The a priori of the 'we' is the anthropological point of departure for Christological representation, although the latter is something totally new and qualitatively different from it."[77] That means, then, that "when, in the presence of God, [mankind's] guilt is borne by another on their behalf, something in them is changed, without their knowledge; something that they alone—one would have thought—are authorized to change by making a free decision with regard to God."[78] In this way, atoning acts, made by vicarious representation, are possible, and if such an act was carried out by one who was himself divine while simultaneously self-identified with "all that is anti-God in the world, ... with the second chaos, brought about by man in his freedom"—one who was God "made him to be sin" for us (2 Cor 5:21),[79] then such a vicariously representative atoning act would be utterly universal in its purchase, a matter of salvation for all the world. That such an act has taken place in the death of the Messiah is declared with full efficacy in the Resurrection. "Not only are sinners inwardly liberated from the inability to turn to God and given the grace of faith, hope and love for the God who forgives them and makes them sharers in his life; the internal complex of problems associated with the 'Old Adam', who was hindered at all points from attaining his own fulfillment, is transcended in the 'New Adam'.... The resurrection

---

[75] Ibid., pp. 389–90.
[76] Ibid., p. 391.
[77] Ibid., p. 408.
[78] Ibid.
[79] Ibid., p. 409.

not only guarantees redemption: it enables the natural man to be whole."[80] So much for the claim that "vicarious representation" cannot be conceivable for "modern men".

The redemption is thus achieved by the Incarnation and the Paschal Mystery, within which totality of interrelating mysteries the descent is an especially neuralgic point for non-Balthasarian students of Balthasar.[81] Were we to follow the linguistic cue of Adrienne von Speyr, we should regard the descent into hell not as a separate mystery from that of the Crucifixion but the Crucifixion's own obverse. The descent is certainly crucial (in both the plain and the punning sense of that word) for Balthasar's theology of the Paschal Mystery, axle of the world's salvation. The Argentinian scholar Juan Sara usefully places the descent in terms of the Trilogy as a whole.[82] It will, I think, be helpful to preface an account of Sara's reading by pointing out Balthasar's view of the Son-made-man's "immediate vision" of the Father, which Sara presumes. This has been, inevitably, a point of criticism by Thomists, since Thomas' affirmation of the permanency of the beatific vision in the human soul of the Word incarnate seems incompatible with Balthasar's language of the "abandonment" of the Son on the Cross, with as its obverse, the "Godforsakenness" of Christ in the tomb. Despite speaking of the *"fides Christi"*,[83] a phrase which might seem to eliminate the beatific, or as Balthasar prefers to write, "immediate" vision (actually, it denotes rather the maximal "covenant-fidelity" of Jesus than an epistemic lacuna), the Swiss theologian does in fact affirm that, throughout his human life, Christ enjoyed a unique vision of God—albeit in more than one mode. "The *visio immediata* which Christ has of the Father (that is, of God)

---

[80] Ibid.

[81] Alyssa Lyra Pitstick, *Light in Darkness: Hans Urs von Balthasar and the Catholic Doctrine of Christ's Descent into Hell* (Grand Rapids, MI: Eerdmans, 2007); Alyssa Lyra Pitstick, *Christ's Descent into Hell: John Paul II, Joseph Ratzinger and Hans Urs von Balthasar on the Theology of Holy Saturday* (Grand Rapids, MI: Eerdmans, 2016). It is not clear that there is a Catholic "doctrine" of the descent in the sense of an elaborated theological construction of the credal tenet of an authoritative kind; see Paul Griffiths, "Is There a Doctrine of the Descent into Hell?", *Pro Ecclesia* 17, no. 3 (2008): 257–68.

[82] Juan M. Sara, "*Descensus ad inferos*, Dawn of Hope: Aspects of the Theology of Holy Saturday in the Trilogy of Hans Urs von Balthasar", *Communio* 32 (2005): 541–72.

[83] Hans Urs von Balthasar, "Fides Christi", in *Explorations in Theology*, vol. 2, *Spouse of the Word* (San Francisco: Ignatius Press, 1991), pp. 43–79.

may fluctuate between the mode of manifestness (which befits the Son as his 'glory') and the mode of 'concealment' which befits the servant of YHWH in the hiddenness of his Passion."[84] That the vision may for periods not be specifically beatifying—that is, creative of joyful bliss—Balthasar does concede.[85] What appears to be the outright denial of the possession of the vision *in any sense* by the human mind of the Logos in the "events" of Holy Saturday is often the main reason why Thomists resile from Balthasar's theology of the descent. But this is a misunderstanding, as may be shown when the motif of *Gottesverlassenheit* is reached in Sara's account which takes each of the three parts of the Trilogy in turn. In any case, in the last volume of the dramatics, Balthasar makes it plain that it is perfectly possible for Jesus not to have faith in Thomas' sense of "faith", but to have it in Balthasar's which, claims the latter, is also at least in First Corinthians that of Saint Paul. When Paul tells the Church in Corinth that these three abide—that is, "faith, hope, [and] love" (1 Cor 13:13)—he has in mind the model of Abraham, where faith means total surrender to God, hope finding security in God. With faith (and hope) so understood, this theological virtue is, like that of charity, for *comprehensores* as well as *viatores*; it is for those who have arrived at the vision of God as well as those on their way to that vision.[86]

Let us turn, then, to Sara's presentation of the descent in the three parts of the Trilogy. First, the theological aesthetics presents Christ's descent as the culminatory movement in the mysteries of his humiliation—and thus of the Incarnation when the latter is seen as the kenosis of the eternal Son. Giving everything on the Cross, Jesus enters the condition of having given everything. He is "dead with the dead".[87] Relying on the visionary materials of Adrienne von Speyr (a proceeding only possible, of course, on the supposition of their authenticity and the correctness of her—presumably Balthasar-assisted—interpretation), Balthasar contemplates with her how the

---

[84] Von Balthasar, *Seeing the Form*, p. 329. Note, though, that in the dramatics Balthasar describes this *visio immediata* as not only "inseparable from the intuition of his mission-consciousness" but also "defined and limited by this same mission-consciousness". Von Balthasar, *Person in Christ*, p. 166.

[85] Ibid., p. 195.

[86] Von Balthasar, *Last Act*, pp. 408–10.

[87] Sara, "Dawn of Hope", p. 547.

Christ of the descent perceives the sin of the entire world in its separation from sinners—a separation that is the fruit of the Passion. In so perceiving—in a dreadful counterpart to that movement of rapture which follows from perception of the beautiful—Christ is "drawn, 'enrapt', through the horror of hell by and towards the Father in a total, chaotic, and incomprehensible abandonment."[88] Balthasar interprets the texts from First Peter about Christ's preaching to the departed (3:18–20) as a passive, but no less real, "preaching" *with his actual being.* "The Son's obedience of love offers the splendour of the Father's love a right and adequate form from the heart of which it can irradiate precisely in and through the amorphous horror of hell—and so conquer it as a moment of the glory of the mutual love of the Father and the Son in the Holy Spirit.... The obscure limit that remained in the Old Testament and prevented its consummation falls away from within. There opens once and for all ... the New and Eternal Covenant between heaven and earth, God and the world."[89]

In the theological dramatics, where Christ acts as the covenant in person, the reciprocal penetration of infinite and finite freedom,[90] he elects to "undergird" mankind's negative response to the loving kindness of God by opening out that "No" into a "Yes" from within. "This embrace of our being from underneath ... must embrace not only our death but also the refusal, the 'No', which concretely conditions and shapes our death. And not only that. Christ, embracing death from below, must also take upon himself the solitude of having been separated and cut off from God that is the result and essence of this 'No'."[91] This is the *Gottverlassenheit,* "God-forsakenness", where the *visio immediata,* though still entertained, is concealed in accord with the fact that, as the sin-bearer who has entered into the distance from God of what is antidivine, the Son's relation to the Father no longer bears the mark of unitive joy. In the aesthetics, Balthasar has warned in advance about a misconstrual of this moment

---

[88] Ibid., p. 548.

[89] Ibid., pp. 548–49.

[90] Already in the aesthetics, "the covenant between God and creature as a covenant of free partners is forever surpassed and indissolubly established, in anticipation, upon the hypostatic union." Von Balthasar, *Seeing the Form,* p. 480.

[91] Sara, "Dawn of Hope", p. 552.

when, in Chesterton's words about the Passion, "God was forsaken of God."[92] It is not "God's 'self-alienation' ... but ... the appearance, conditioned by the world's guilt, of the God who in himself is incomprehensible in his love for the world."[93] It is the moment of unsurpassable expression of covenant fidelity, the perfect correspondence of God and man. Where Thomas thinks of levels of the soul pertinent to maintenance of the vision (notably, in the soul's "apex"), Balthasar speaks in terms of modalities; and though in the dramatics the modality of the Passion is dark indeed, the claim is made that in and through its obscurity—accepted in obedience to the Holy Spirit—the Son-made-man is united more than ever to the Father. It may be objected to this account that a "vision" that is entirely "concealed" can hardly be called a vision at all. The counter to this objection is presumably to point out that the term "vision" is itself based on metaphor: "seeing" expresses the intimacy of co-presence, and the latter is what Balthasar affirms albeit in mind-bogglingly paradoxical language, "separation as a mode of union".[94]

In this work, the redeeming Word "breaks open from within our ownmost 'No', but without any heteronomy. His entrance into the immobility of death on Holy Saturday is the seal of his objective victory over sin, a victory that has already occurred subjectively on the Cross."[95] His Resurrection portends that the act of *Unterfassung* has displayed the triune Love in its full extent and efficacy, that the Spirit was never uniting Father and Son more closely than in that moment when their distinction appeared to take the form of utter distance, the one from the other.

Finally, for the theological logic, that no of the theological dramatics is interpreted as a contradiction in the logic of love. On the Cross, the trinitarian Persons turn sin-borne distance into the means of manifesting—triumphantly so—the logic of love that their relations eternally embody. The incarnate Logos "undergirds" the "gratuity" (understood as "futility" or "perverse folly") of sin with the ever-greater "gratuity" (the mad or "super-positive" folly) of

[92] G. K. Chesterton, *Orthodoxy* (London: John Lane, 1909), p. 255.
[93] Von Balthasar, *Seeing the Form*, p. 462.
[94] Von Balthasar, *Last Act*, pp. 256–64.
[95] Sara, "Dawn of Hope", p. 553.

the Father's love.[96] The Logos demonstrates himself to be the unveiling of the "groundless ground" that is the Father's love: the "logical form par excellence".[97] Sara's conclusion runs, "The silence of Holy Saturday is at the center of the transcendental *verum*."[98] The power—and also strangeness—of Balthasar's treatment of this theme explains, of course, the resistance it has aroused—and also the impressive apologias mounted to defend it.[99]

The ascent of man to God in salvation and deification is only made possible by the descent of God to man, and on Balthasar's understanding, that

> descent goes from the act of incarnation right down to the "obedience unto death, death on a cross" (Philippians 2:8), and continues downward in the "descent into hell" in solidarity with those who are lost to time. It goes farther: from the obedience of the Cross to the atomizing of his bodily being, shared out in the Eucharist. None of these forms of descent is revoked in the Resurrection on the third day and in the Ascension. Bodily resurrection and Ascension are not disincarnation but a transformation of the entire human form, spirit and body, into the pneumatic mode of existence. The divine Pneuma is the power behind this transformation, making sure that the definitive descent of the Word becomes sacramental, for all time.[100]

This catena of extraordinary yet credally based statements brings us—conveniently enough for a chapter's ending—to the topic of eschatology.

---

[96] Ibid., p. 561.

[97] Ibid., p. 562.

[98] Ibid.

[99] Edward T. Oakes, S.J., "The Internal Logic of Holy Saturday in the Theology of Hans Urs von Balthasar", *International Journal of Systematic Theology* 9, no. 2 (2007): 184–99; Edward T. Oakes, S.J., "Descensus and Development: A Response to Recent Rejoinders", *International Journal of Systematic Theology* 13, no. 1 (2011): 3–24.

[100] Von Balthasar, *Man in God*, p. 412.

6

Doctrine: Eschatology, Ecclesiology, and Ethics

There remain to be considered in fact three major areas of doctrine: eschatology, ecclesiology, and ethics—for doctrine, on the Catholic understanding, concerns faith *and morals*. Balthasar's eschatology has been the object of much-bruited negative criticism; his ecclesiology has largely been of interest to Mariologists; his ethics have been little investigated—perhaps because it is fundamental and dogmatic theologians rather than moral theologians who have been stimulated to read him by the principal themes of his Trilogy.

Eschatology

Eschatology is of huge importance to Balthasar—as it is indeed for Aquinas, for whom human beings, at their creation, have by natural desire an initial orientation to the vision of God that is rendered an existential possibility for them by the "second gift" of grace and in whose theology the act of faith is the *inchoatio gloriae*, the first sketch of that participation in glory in which beatitude, the goal of all moral and spiritual striving, consists. Balthasar's motivation is, however, rather different from Thomas' as an eschatologically minded writer. For in the first place, he wants to combat non-Christian or sub-Christian accounts of hope in history, a preoccupation of the last volume of the theological dramatics in particular. Though the high mediaevals had some sense of the theology of history—analysis of the overall thrust of the historical process in the light of revelation[1]—it was by no means as important for them as it became with the advent of historically minded philosophies, and the advance of historical research in

[1] Beryl Smalley, *Historians in the Middle Ages* (New York: Charles Scribner, 1975).

all areas: in sum, in Idealist, Romantic, Marxist, and other "historicis-
ing" styles of thought. For Balthasar, every attempt to accommodate
Church thinking to an ideology of progress misses the point. "Horizontal hope" can hardly be at home in a world where "earth moves
heavenward", the title of a substantial section of the dramatics.[2] Christian time, as eschatological, is entirely vertical. In the opening volume
of the aesthetics, with a reiteration of that adjective, he declares, "Salvation has descended vertically from God and, through the Resurrection and Ascension of the head of mankind, it has opened up to man
in a new way the vertical path into eternity. This alone counts, and in
keeping with the logic of revelation, the extension of the history
of the Church is but the patient expectation of the manifestation ... of
what is already a hidden presence."[3] And Balthasar points out that, in
that sentence, the words "manifestation" and "presence", were they
to be expressed in New Testament Greek, would be (parousia) exactly
the same. Balthasar does not, though, exclude all reference to the
"horizontal" dimension of hope, which has its theological basis in
the Old Testament, as confirmed by later Judaism. In the closing volume of the dramatics, he explains that while "Christian hope changes
this one-sided movement toward the future into a hope for something
that is present and final, although it still waits for its fulfilment",[4] theological hope can integrate with itself the notion of taking-the-world-
with-the-Church to a single supernatural goal—something best done,
in Balthasar's opinion, via his own notion of multiple "missions" for
actors in theo-drama, missions which bring with them multivalent
responsibilities. The obvious concern here is to avoid a "theology
of progress" on an evolutionist or Marxian model; Balthasar will not
tolerate any "immanentising" of the life eternal.

There is an eschatological promise of "eternal life" in Paul and John
that is betrayed by ... every revisionist who insists that "eternal life" is
a metaphor for the full realization of an ethical or cognitive virtue in
the here and now. "Eternal life" is for Balthasar, a symbol of unbroken

[2] Hans Urs von Balthasar, Theo-drama: Theological Dramatic Theory, vol. 5, The Last Act,
trans. Graham Harrison (San Francisco: Ignatius Press, 1998), pp. 111–88.
[3] Hans Urs von Balthasar, The Glory of the Lord: A Theological Aesthetics, vol. 1, Seeing the
Form (San Francisco: Ignatius Press, 1976), p. 644.
[4] Von Balthasar, Last Act, p. 152.

participation with the triune God, in whom we live and have our being. And if death is the breach, the hiatus that would stamp itself as absolute, "eternal life" is the promise of death's powerlessness, that the breach has itself been breached by love, overcome in the descent of Christ into Hades, in his giving of sight and voice to the ones forgotten in history.[5]

Though Thomas' premature death prevented his writing the section on the last things (i.e., death, judgment, heaven, and hell) in the *Summa theologiae*, we might suppose that his mature reflections on the age to come would have anticipated Balthasar's second objective in eschatology: the enlivening of the Christian sense of "heaven", the world's intended goal. Like Gregory of Nyssa, for whom our "stretching out", *epektasis*, towards God does not end with death but pervades the life everlasting, Balthasar, while appealing (surprisingly enough) not to Nyssa but to Augustine, proposes a "'dynamic becoming' of ecstatic knowing apparently indifferent to the distinction between the pre-eschatological and eschatological state".[6] In other words, even in heaven there will be a learning curve in delight in God which will have its own mode of duration in a time without end. The notion corresponds well enough to the thesis of the contribution to the Trilogy that was the first to be written—the opening volume of the theological logic—for which "the human subject [is] constitutively erotic and ecstatic."[7] Cyril O'Regan's use of those adjectives is not of course taken from the idiom of the street where they would signify, respectively, sexually aroused and "over the moon". Recycled though they are in the idiolect of postmodernism, they occur in Balthasar's corpus by courtesy of Saint Gregory of Nyssa, who wrote in his treatise on the Beatitudes, "We are permitted a happiness that surpasses our desire, a gift that surpasses our hope, a grace that surpasses our nature."[8] That is how human

---

[5] Cyril O'Regan, *The Anatomy of Misremembering: Von Balthasar's Response to Philosophical Modernity*, vol. 1, *Hegel* (New York: Crossroad, 2014), p. 246.

[6] Ibid., p. 141. The text in question is Augustine, *Enarrationes in Psalmos* 118, 26, 6, on which Balthasar writes in *Prayer* (1961; San Francisco: Ignatius Press, 1986), p. 25.

[7] O'Regan, *Hegel*, p. 142.

[8] Gregory of Nyssa, *De beatitudinibus* 7, 1, cited in Hans Urs von Balthasar, *Presence and Thought: Essay on the Religious Philosophy of Gregory of Nyssa* (San Francisco: Ignatius Press, 1995), p. 161.

beings are, prospectively now, in reality in heaven, tending ever-more towards God.

In effect, heaven is "the world in God", and, after an exposition of the contents of the Trilogy, it will not surprise the reader to learn that Balthasar conceives it from a Christological viewpoint. "We find this vantage point in the Resurrection of the Crucified One. For through his Trinitarian existence he has made it possible for us to believe that this finite, historical world can be enfolded in the life of the infinite, eternal God: in his 'forty days' and his sending of the Spirit, he has given us a kind of foretaste of what man's ultimate salvation will be."[9] The Holy Spirit will be the "executive of Son's prodigal self-giving, not only on earth but in heaven", when "beholding and inwardly participating in the Son in his eucharistic self-giving" during the time of purification, Liturgy, and discipleship on earth turns into a "beholding and participating in the life of the Trinity" in supertime—the life of heaven.[10] (Balthasar has already warned that the preliminary "purification" in question is typically not just earthly. It will be "characteristic of purgatory" really to open one's eyes to "what the Lord has done on the Cross".[11]) Balthasar synthesizes references to the late mediaeval Flemish mystic Jan van Ruysbroeck with citations from von Speyr as he seeks not to imagine but to conceive the outcome. "We cannot imagine how our earthly existence is embedded in God. This is because the mode of this embedding is given us from above, on the basis of its Trinitarian original. This does not destroy our creaturely modes (which are copies and likenesses) but causes them to transcend themselves. Thus they attain their real destination (*gratia non destruit naturam, elevat, perficit naturam*). Since in God there is eternal life and hence 'eternal surprise' we too shall experience this surprise."[12] The incorporation there in partial paraphrase of one of Thomas' best-known maxims is almost too obvious to point out.

So much for heaven, though I cannot resist adding one minor but telling difference from Aquinas. Balthasar finds it a "cruel verdict"

---

[9] Von Balthasar, *Last Act*, p. 373.

[10] Ibid., p. 384.

[11] Adrienne von Speyr, *Das Wort und die Mystik, II: Objektive Mystik* (Einsiedeln: Johannes-verlag, 1970), p. 368, cited in Von Balthasar, *Last Act*, p. 367.

[12] Von Balthasar, *Last Act*, p. 400.

that Thomas allows into the world of the resurrection only humans and minerals, while the "world of plants and animals simply falls into oblivion".[13] Balthasar understands how it is that in ancient cosmology this might be thought to result (the "movement of the heavens", a condition of organic life, would be stilled), even if the incapacity of subhuman creatures for the vision of God is a more specifically theological consideration in Thomas' mind. But for the Swiss theologian, not the Old Testament sense of solidary of the botanical and animal orders with the human realm, nor the Christian sense of the affinity of the saints with the beasts (the life of Saint Cuthbert is specifically mentioned), nor (again) the evidence of iconography favour in the least the Thomist position.

As to hell, on which his writings are the more celebrated (or notorious), Balthasar was ill-served by the English title of his little treatise on the extent of salvation, *Dare We Hope "That All Men Be Saved"?* The German original is "What Are We Allowed to Hope?" The two questions are patently distinct: the second is detached; the first might be thought tendentious. Elsewhere, Balthasar wrote evenhandedly (one might even say neutrally): "In the place of systematic elucidations which purport to *know* that in the cosmological context a number of people are condemned to hell, and a number called to heaven, or to *know* from an anthropological system that hell can only be a pedagogical threat, and that 'everything' will turn out for the best—the Christian is entrusted with something of incomparably greater value: Christian hope."[14] And again: "A love that contemplated the majesty of God's love on the Cross and was not filled with awe would have every reason to mistrust itself; and the same would be true of a love from which all fear of judgment had been banished."[15] Adrienne von Speyr cannot be entirely acquitted of responsibility for Balthasar's openness to—not assertion of—an ultimately universal salvation. Yet his study of Barth's dogmatics, not to mention his explorations of Greek patristics (Origen before Nyssa), had already given him the idea. But von Speyr's mysticism is certainly pertinent.

---

[13] Ibid., pp. 421, 420. Thomas' view is stated in *Disputed Questions on the Power of God*, q. 5, a. 4, corpus.

[14] Hans Urs von Balthasar, *Love Alone Is Credible*, trans. D. C. Schindler (San Francisco: Ignatius Press, 2004), p. 77; emphasis in original.

[15] Ibid., p. 78.

As has been pointed out, her mystical theology has its closest anticipation in the *Showings* of the fourteenth-century English mystic Julian of Norwich,[16] whom Balthasar does not fail to mention in his discussion of what it is legitimate to hope for, salvationally speaking, in the last volume of the dramatics.[17] "Like Julian, von Speyr raises the prospect of universal salvation as an element or at least an implication of vision and the logic of divine love in Christ, but without asserting it and contravening church teaching, and not without leaving open the prospect of an incorrigible decision taken by the creature against God."[18] But like Julian, Balthasar will not adjudicate when the only judge is divine. Both in the closing volume of the aesthetics and in the last two volumes of the dramatics, Balthasar "insists that the 'all in all' of Christ does not exclude the prospect of waste, of elements of reality that are not reconciled to God's will".[19] O'Regan claims the authority of Balthasar (and Joseph Ratzinger) when he writes, "It is simply not possible to exclude personal sin from consideration, to pass over in silence individual judgment, and to turn a blind eye to the hope that the kingdom is not simply a human kingdom in the future, but the kingdom of God in which not only the ills of history are transcended, but also the frailty of desire and the fragility of human beings marked by physical and psychological vulnerability and mutability."[20]

This reminds us that not all eschatology is individual eschatology, concerned with the destiny of the unique person or soul. There is corporate eschatology too. Here the Johannine Apocalypse commands Balthasar's view, with its "unfolding of the hyperbolic escalation of resistance to the victory of the Lamb".[21] The latter was the ultimate divine love gift; yet, it also focussed the struggle of pro-Christ and anti-Christ attitudes and acting. Balthasar's analysis of the apocalyptic materials furnished by the New Testament gives him reason to think that hatred of God—but also commitment to

---

[16] See Denys Turner, *Julian of Norwich, Theologian* (New Haven, CT; London: Yale University Press, 2011), and especially for the issue of universalism, see pp. 103–9.

[17] Von Balthasar, *Last Act*, p. 317.

[18] O'Regan, *Hegel*, p. 619, endnote 23.

[19] Ibid., p. 391.

[20] Ibid., p. 442.

[21] Ibid., p. 388.

the divine Love—will escalate in the world. Yet there can hardly be a convincing eschatology whose conclusion is simply agonistic— ongoing conflict would meet nobody's description of an "end". Moreover, the question arises as to the dispersion, in such a scenario, of the elements of beauty, goodness, and truth that, historically speaking, culture has comprised (along with their ugly, wicked, and false counterparts, of course). Balthasar's metaphysical—but ultimately trinitarian—concept of the positivity of the finite in its otherness from God (which is also its embedding in God through the Word) gives him the basis of this wider hope. "It is futile to assume that history will go into eternity only in the form it will have at its final (and possibly most grim) stage. Whatever positive elements the world has known, at any stage of its development, will be worthy to participate in God's eternally new event."[22]

This provides the nucleus at least of an eschatology considerate of more subjects than simply the individual human soul, another version of the fulfilled "City of God" of the Augustinian tradition (conventionally exploited by Thomists in the absence of any specifically Thomasian equivalent), but avoiding the hubris of developmental schemes whether Liberationist or Teilhardian in character. As Balthasar remarks, it may be that "what seemed primitive and undeveloped" will turn out to have the "greater latency and potency"; "Jesus's praise of the little child, who is more receptive and docile than the adult, is relevant here."[23] And so it is, he adds, to the development of the Church, a comment which brings us to the topic of his ecclesiology.

Ecclesiology: The Church and her sacraments

Ecclesiology plays a more obvious part in Balthasar's theology than in that of Aquinas'—for the former was living after (or, better, in the midst of) the ecclesiological awakening of the twentieth century, when, as Romano Guardini once put it, the Church was coming to life again in the souls of men.[24] Guardini was referring to the

---

[22] Ibid., p. 418.
[23] Ibid.
[24] Romano Guardini, *The Church and the Catholic* (New York: Sheed and Ward, 1935).

Church as a focussed subject of reflection within the totality of Christian belief—with a gesture towards the notion of the Church's own subjectivity or "personality" as both Balthasar and such Thomists as Maritain conceived it (or "her").[25] Thomas discusses the mystery of the Church in a concise manner in his scriptural commentaries, in passages where he is considering the topic of grace, and, not least, in his little commentary on the Apostles' Creed where he considers the four "notes" (or, in his term, "conditions") of the Church as one, holy, catholic, and apostolic—even though only two of those notes are explicitly mentioned in the short baptismal Creed used by Latins.[26] For the Thomas of *Expositio in Symbolum Apostolorum*, the Church is essentially the "congregation of the faithful", and as such it is a body, animated by the Holy Spirit. (Thomas thinks this is why the clause on the Church comes immediately after that on the third trinitarian Person.) The Dutch ecclesiologist Herwi Rikhof concluded from Thomas' account of the sanctification of the Church's members in terms of washing, anointing, and trinitarian indwelling that while "Thomas neither calls the Church a sacrament as later theologians have done, nor compares the Church to a sacrament as *Lumen gentium* [the Dogmatic Constitution on the Church of the Second Vatican Council] does,... his reflections on the holiness of the Church exhibit sensitivity toward this deep structure of the Church."[27] And yet in general, Thomas' account of the Church is so modest, confining itself as it largely does to a rehearsal of the pertinent biblical texts, that—despite the place he gives to consecrated religious, monastics, and the like, in the *Secunda Pars* of the *Summa theologiae* and his acknowledgement of the Roman bishop as adjudicator of doctrinal disputes (both obvious reflections of the Church situation of Latin Christendom in his time)—his ecclesiology, one

---

[25] Hans Urs von Balthasar, "Who Is the Church?", in *Explorations in Theology*, vol. 2, *Spouse of the Word* (San Francisco: Ignatius Press, 1991), pp. 143–91; Jacques Maritain, *On the Church of Christ: The Person of the Church and Her Personnel* (Notre Dame, IN: University of Notre Dame Press, 1973).

[26] Herwi Rikhof, "Thomas on the Church: Reflections on a Sermon", in *Aquinas on Doctrine: A Critical Introduction*, ed. Thomas Weinandy, Daniel Keating, and John Yocum (London and New York: T&T Clark, 2004), pp. 199–223. The "sermon" of Rikhof's subtitle is in fact Thomas' *Expositio in Symbolum Apostolorum*, i.e., his minicommentary on the Creed.

[27] Ibid., p. 205.

might venture to say, has no especially distinctive Catholic qualities. It is not so surprising that a modern student (George Sabra) has subtitled a fairly comprehensive overview of Thomas' "vision" of the Church *Fundamentals of an Ecumenical Ecclesiology*.[28] That is not to say that Thomasian principles cannot lead later Thomists to construct a highly wrought ecclesiology that could hardly be anything but a product of Latin Catholicism.[29]

From Sabra's perspective, the contrast with Balthasar could hardly be clearer, owing principally to the uncompromisingly "Marian" nature of Balthasar's corresponding "vision".[30] For Balthasar, the Church is above all feminine, the Bride and Mother, just because she inheres in the person of Mary.

> In spite of the highly privileged character of Mary's figure and mission, she remains the archetype of the Church precisely as hearer of the Word, whom her Son declared blessed (Matthew 11:28), the hearer who also knows how to keep and guard, nourish and bear the Word, and even after she has given it birth, continues to ponder it in her heart (Luke 2:19, 51). Precisely as the feminine womb of God's Word, Mary is the believing and remembering womb of the Church, who as the "Bride" of Christ receives not only the seed of Christ, but in an absolute sense the "seed who is Christ".[31]

Consonant with his high doctrine of divine revelation, he sees the Church as, under these titles, enabling the individual believer's reception of the Word. "In so far as the word of Scripture belongs to the Church, the Bride of Christ (because she puts into words what has been 'done unto her'), the Church, the archetype of faith,

---

[28] George Sabra, *Thomas Aquinas' Vision of the Church: Fundamentals of an Ecumenical Ecclesiology* (Mainz: Matthias-Grünewald Verlag, 1987).

[29] A good example is Charles Journet, who, according to Balthasar himself, combined the view of the late fifteenth-century Thomist Cajetan that Christ is the "personalising hypostasis of the Church" with the notion that the Church is the Bride of the Spirit, such that "the dialogue between Christ and the Church, at its highest level, is a dialogue between Logos and Pneuma." Hans Urs von Balthasar, *Theo-drama: Theological Dramatic Theory*, vol. 3, *Dramatis Personae: The Person in Christ* (San Francisco: Ignatius Press, 1992), pp. 345–46.

[30] Brendan Leahy, *The Marian Profile in the Ecclesiology of Hans Urs von Balthasar* (London: New City, 2000).

[31] Von Balthasar, *Seeing the Form*, p. 538.

the bride and mother, must present the word to the individual as the living preaching of the word, a function (a holy serving office) which, like the Church itself and the word of Scripture, must have been implanted by revelation, into the answer to revelation."[32] Man can give that answer only by grace—that is, "because he was given the power to make an adequately loving response to the love of God. He can only answer under the 'protective mantle' of the fiat spoken archetypally for him and all men by the bride and mother, Maria-Ecclesia."[33] When at the Cross, in the Gospel of Saint John (19:26–27), the Son "places Mary in the care of one of the apostles and thus inserts her into the apostolic Church", he "gives the Church her centre or apex: an inimitable yet ever-to-be-striven-for embodiment of the new community's faith, a spotless unrestricted Yes to the whole of God's plan for the salvation of the world. In this centre and apex the Church is the bride 'without spot or wrinkle', the *immaculata*, as Paul expressly calls her not only in the eternity to come but already now."[34]

That does not mean, however, that the Church is not also Christologically described in Balthasar's theology. In the aesthetics, he insists that the Church has no separate "form" from that of Christ: she exists to point to his form as impressed by Son and Spirit in the power of divine revelation—something perfectly possible so long as no anti-Christ factor ("a sinful power of opposition, whether human or diabolical") intervenes.[35] That possibility is verified in—once again—the Mother of the Lord, the Church's preeminent member as well as matrix. "To the extent that the church is Marian, she is a pure form which is immediately legible and comprehensible."[36]

More widely, Balthasar sees the Church as patterned by archetypal missions that themselves reflect the "Christological constellation"— the grouping of key figures around Jesus that help constitute the meaning of his life and ministry. These include Peter as type of

---

[32] Von Balthasar, *Love Alone Is Credible*, p. 64.

[33] Ibid., p. 65.

[34] Hans Urs von Balthasar, with Joseph Ratzinger, *Mary—the Church at the Source* (San Francisco: Ignatius Press, 2005), p. 110, with an internal citation of Ephesians 5:27.

[35] Von Balthasar, *Seeing the Form*, p. 562.

[36] Ibid.

the Church of office and sacrament (a theme thoroughly explored in *The Office of Peter and the Structure of the Church*);[37] Paul as entrusted with the apostolate to the Gentiles, the *Ecclesia ex gentibus*; James, who represents for Balthasar the principle of Tradition; and John, who embodies the "personal"—the intimate and contemplative—principle in the Church. All these missions are, however, embraced in the mission of Mary, a mission that overshadows two further female missions in the constellation—that of Mary Magdalene, "the redeemed sinner at the foot of the Cross who will proclaim the Easter message to the Church's office-holders",[38] and Mary of Bethany, who represents the contemplative principle in its feminine mode as John the Divine does in its masculine. The interrelating of "states of life" in the Church, a concern of Thomas' in the *Secunda Pars* of the *Summa theologiae* (to be considered in connexion with Balthasar's commentary thereon in chapter 7 below), forms a major part of his book-length study, *The Christian State of Life*.[39] The term "state of life" is a complex one in Balthasar since it also denotes the diverse conditions of humanity at major stages of salvation history (original state, fallen state, redeemed state, ultimate state). Exactly the same ambivalence attaches to Thomas' use of the term "status" (of which Balthasar's *Stand* is the translation). The ambivalence is explicable, and theologically suggestive: "status" for Thomas concerns a use of freedom. That is helpful for a Balthasarian ecclesiology, constructed at least in part in a "theo-dramatic" form.

For the theological dramatics themselves, where the multiple missions of diverse Christian actors come to the fore, the Christological constellation turns out to expand exponentially. This is one of the points in the Balthasarian corpus where the influence of Saint Ignatius and his *Exercises* may surely be detected. "Reading John particularly through the eyes of Ignatius, there exists an infinite variety of calls and thus an infinite variety of personal identities."[40] Insofar as this interlacing of these identities constitutes the Church, it makes

[37] Hans Urs von Balthasar, *The Office of Peter and the Structure of the Church* (San Francisco: Ignatius Press, 1986).

[38] Von Balthasar, *Person in Christ*, p. 279.

[39] Hans Urs von Balthasar, *The Christian State of Life* (San Francisco: Ignatius Press, 1983).

[40] O'Regan, *Hegel*, p. 213.

her communion an image of the Holy Trinity. The *perichoresis* of the Persons in the trinitarian communion of life is also defined by gift-giving and gift-receiving.

Ecclesiology might well be considered the correct locus for discussion of the Church's sacraments. Balthasar's account in the theological aesthetics considers them not under the twin rubrics of "sign" and "cause", which are Saint Thomas' preferred explanatory concepts in sacramental theology, but under that of "form", ubiquitous as that notion is in *The Glory of the Lord*. (In Thomas, the sacraments of the New Covenant are both signs and causes, while the rites—also termed by him *sacramenta*—of the Old Covenant are simply signs without causal power.) The idea of "form" lends itself more readily to aesthetics in particular than does that of sign—not that the latter is without aesthetic possibilities, as the work of the artist, poet, and lay theologian David Jones had been showing Anglophone contemporaries.[41] Balthasar also deemed it more generous in its capacity to give an overview of the pertinent data; for this reason, he dispensed with "sign" in his account of the materiality of the Incarnation epiphanies in their overall unity, except in a subsidiary way when discussion of the *semeia* (signs) of the Gospel tradition, notably in Saint John's Gospel, made reference unavoidable. As to the metaphysically denser term "cause", he evidently hoped that the notion of a form's impact would suffice to indicate causality, without the obligation to enter into an explicit discussion of causation, whether effective ("efficient"), exemplary ("formal"), or goal-producing ("final"). "The order of this form, imposing itself ever more inexorably, passes judgment on my formless disorder."[42] That is said of the Christ-form, but the same is true of the sacraments when considered as mediations of that same form. In any case, these concepts, as building blocks of ontology, belong on the whole more naturally with a theological logic. Balthasar's option for form governs what he has to say about the sacramental realm in the theological aesthetics where the sacraments appear (along with Scripture

---

[41]David Jones, "Art and Sacrament", in *Epoch and Artist* (London: Faber and Faber, 1959), pp. 143–79.

[42]Von Balthasar, *Seeing the Form*, p. 485; on the "inherent power of the form [of Christ]", cf. pp. 490–95.

and the Church) as "mediations of the form": the form, that is, of Jesus Christ, the trinitarian Son. "In the sacraments, the Christ-form itself in turn appears before us and impresses its shape upon us in a valid form which is free of all subjective ambiguities."[43] There is a parallelism here with the presentation of the sacraments (interrupted by Thomas' demise) in the *Tertia Pars* of the *Summa theologiae*. Having dealt compendiously with the chief events in the life of Christ, Thomas announces: "After considering those things that concern the mystery of the incarnate Word, we must consider the sacraments of the Church which derive their efficacy from the Word incarnate himself."[44] Balthasar's "mediation" idea makes the link between Christology and sacramentology even closer than in Aquinas. This explains his concern that a view of the sacraments as "separated instruments" may lead to ascribing to them "an independent meaning and a form of their own".[45]

Balthasar departs from the Thomist school in his account of the internal differentiation of the seven signs within the "sacramental system". Saint Thomas had seen the seven as so many ways of applying the Passion of Christ, either to key moments or to stages of the individual human living (Baptism, corresponding to biological birth; eucharistic Communion, to physical nourishment—with similar natural analogues for Confirmation, Penance, and the Anointing of the Sick) or to key institutions of human society (Holy Orders and Matrimony, corresponding to social structures that enable the spiritual and physical continuance of the race). But for Balthasar, "if we regard the sacraments as defined and differentiated not from within themselves but by various basic situations in human life and the life of the Church", then "we are not allowing the archetypal, formative power of the life of the God-man its full validity."[46] Thus, for instance, Matrimony is not a supernatural blessing on a natural institution so much as the drawing of a man and a woman into the relation between Christ and his Bride.

[43] Ibid., p. 582.
[44] *ST* IIIa, q. 60, prologus.
[45] Von Balthasar, *Seeing the Form*, pp. 582–83.
[46] Hans Urs von Balthasar, *A Theology of History* (1963; San Francisco: Ignatius Press, 1994), p. 96.

For Saint Thomas, the Holy Eucharist is the consummation of all the sacraments.[47] It is the "central sacramental act" embodying the "whole of the sacramental economy", for in the first place, it is "an act of sacrificial worship, in which the mystical body of Christ offers, in union with its Head, the one perfect offering of his life", while in the second place, it aims at the "unity of the Body of Christ, and the preservation of its bonds of mutual charity".[48] Enabling our sharing in Christ's saving act of worship of the Father, and strengthening the common life of charity, the eucharistic rite orders the faithful towards heaven, the happiness of the blessed in God and with each other to which the Liturgy points.[49] In Thomas' words, "The whole mystery of salvation is comprised in this sacrifice."[50]

Balthasar likewise affirms the preeminent status of the Eucharist in the sacramental order. When writing of the "mediated form" in the theological aesthetics, he treats the "Eucharistic Cult" *before* he writes of the "Sacramental Figure". That was possible since by the time he reaches the discussion of sacraments towards the close of the opening volume of the aesthetics, he has had occasion already to speak of the Holy Eucharist in particular, making his own the patristic and mediaeval concept of the *corpus triforme* of the Lord: the Lord's physical body, assumed at the Incarnation, has other modes of its existence: both scriptural and ecclesial—which must also mean eucharistic.[51] The Eucharist remains for Balthasar a dominant theme whenever the self-communication of Christ as Lord of the Church in the post-Ascension era is in question. The "Forty Days" between Easter and Ascension constitute for Balthasar the inauguration of a new mode of time that is "sacramental and most especially eucharistic".[52]

In the post-conciliar period (and it may be recalled that the opening work of the Trilogy, the aesthetics, was not completed until 1969), the issue of the relation between the ecclesial body and the

---

[47] *ST* IIIa, q. 63, a. 6.

[48] John P. Yocum, "Sacraments in Aquinas", in Weinandy, Keating, and Yocum, *Aquinas on Doctrine*, p. 168; see pp. 159–82.

[49] For an overview of Thomas' "liturgiology", see David Berger, *Thomas Aquinas and the Liturgy* (Naples, FL: Sapientia Press, 2004).

[50] *ST* IIIa., q. 83, a. 4.

[51] Von Balthasar, *Seeing the Form*, pp. 529–31.

[52] Von Balthasar, *Theology of History*, p. 98.

eucharistic Body of the Lord had become, owing not least to de Lubac's *Corpus mysticum*,[53] an area requiring delicate management. The American Jesuit theologian Avery Dulles would point out how it was supposed by some that "because the purpose of the Eucharist is to form the Church as the body of Christ, his ecclesial presence is more intense and more important than that in the consecrated elements."[54] Dulles went on to explain that "the error in this logic can be exposed if one thinks of the Incarnation. Jesus became man and died on the Cross for the sake of our redemption, but it does not follow that God is more intensely present in the community of the redeemed than in the Incarnate Son, or that our devotion should focus more on our fellow Christians than on Christ the Lord."[55] Balthasar's notion of the "Eucharistizing" of the substance of the God-Man in his continued post-Easter outpouring made any such inappropriate inversion impossible.[56]

In his theological dramatics as elsewhere, Balthasar made up for the rather weak account of the sacrificial nature of the eucharistic cultus in the aesthetics, where the "eucharistic surrender" of the Son is made more "to the world" than it is to the Father—the consequence of an emphasis on eucharistic Presence and Communion rather than the eucharistic sacrifice. In the dramatics, Balthasar's notion of the eucharistic sacrifice is expounded more fully, yet still in relation to the Real Presence of the Person rather than for its own sake. Owing to the Cross, Christ's "whole existence can be understood as a perpetual, eternal self-offering to the Father on behalf of mankind; thus the Church's Eucharistic sacrifice would refer to this eternal gesture of his."[57] Is the "referring" in question rhetorical or real? That Balthasar understands it as fully real emerges from his discussion in the short but pivotal study *A Theology of History*, where he speaks of the sacramental sacrifice as already anticipated

---

[53] Henri de Lubac, *Corpus mysticum: Essai sur l'Eucharistie et l'Eglise au moyen âge* (Paris: Aubier, 1944).

[54] Avery Dulles, S.J., *Church and Society: The Laurence J. McGinley Lectures, 1988–2007* (New York: Fordham University Press, 2008), p. 462.

[55] Ibid.

[56] Von Balthasar, *Last Act*, p. 382.

[57] Hans Urs von Balthasar, *Theo-drama: Theological Dramatic Theory*, vol. 4, *The Action*, trans. Graham Harrison (San Francisco: Ignatius Press, 1994), p. 392.

in the bloody sacrifice of the Cross. "Insofar as the new and eternal marriage between Godhead and manhood was sealed in blood on the Cross by the loving sacrifice of that one individual whose dual nature was itself the centre and source of the Covenant, to that extent his *one* sacrifice to the Father contains, from the very start, a duality within itself: it is the sacrifice of the Head and of the Body, of the Bridegroom and of the Bride."[58]

Theological ethics

Balthasar wrote very little about theological ethics (or moral theology) simply as such.[59] His "Nine Propositions in Christian Ethics", originally written as a position paper designed to influence the Pontifical International Theological Commission to take a more Christocentric view of moral theology, does not represent his view in its entirety.[60] To flesh out the skeleton fully it would be necessary to scan the Trilogy, and other writings, in search of a fuller if implicit theory—with the inevitable risk of producing a construction which may not entirely reflect his mind. The aesthetics and dramatics have been quarried in this fashion by, for instance, the American student of Balthasar's work Christopher Steck—often with great insight, though the overall conclusion that the two first parts of the Trilogy furnish "an 'Ignatian configuration' of divine command ethics" seems rather too tributary to the Jesuit loyalties of the author.[61] There are, however, some brief but lucid doctrinal statements on the moral life—and the moral law—in the shorter works where "eisegesis" is less of a danger. From them it emerges that, as in his ontology, Balthasar sought to combine a universally reasonable account of the human good with the specific truth claims of doctrinal

[58]Von Balthasar, *Theology of History*, pp. 97–98.

[59]Hans Urs von Balthasar, "Nine Propositions in Christian Ethics", in *Principles of Christian Morality*, by Heinz Schürmann, Joseph Ratzinger, and Hans Urs von Balthasar (San Francisco: Ignatius Press, 1986), pp. 77–104.

[60]This is rather too quickly assumed in Marc Ouellet, "The Foundation of Christian Ethics according to Hans Urs von Balthasar", *Communio* 16 (1990): 379–401.

[61]Christopher Steck, S.J., *The Ethical Thought of Hans Urs von Balthasar* (New York: Crossroad, 2001), p. 5.

Christianity—as the latter may be understood in the light of the glory and drama of revelation as its climax in Jesus Christ. In other words, he wished to bring together the "natural law" tradition of ethical reflection with a moral inspiration based on Christological—and ultimately trinitarian—foundations.

In the first instance, like all orthodox Catholic theologians, Balthasar was concerned to uphold an objective system of moral values that holds good for man at large. That entails, then—in the words of a North American moralist, Jean Porter—the recognition of "values which are independent of our perception of them or our stance towards them, and therefore a cognitivist view for which ethical sentences express propositions and as a result are truth-apt: able to be true or false".[62] Congruently, but in the far warmer language of Saint Thomas' Augustinian sources, the Flemish Dominican Servais Pinckaers remarks: "Love is not a purely subjective outpouring.... It poses objective demands. It can be authentic only when it is rightly related to the goods it seeks. Love calls for order and uprightness; these make it true and a thing of beauty. St Augustine defines it in two words: 'Here is a brief, true definition of virtue, I think: [it is] ordered love'. This definition expresses the very essence of Augustinian morality: love and truth embrace, as we read in the psalm."[63]

For her part, Porter goes on to explain how in Latin Scholasticism the natural law tradition is already *to a certain extent* synthesized with Scripture, furnishing as it does "a particular orientation toward the moral teachings of Scripture, on the basis of which some norms are taken as strictly binding commands, others are taken as indications of what is permissible or ideal, and still others are considered to be ceremonial or judicial prescriptions that bind only in a particular time and place".[64] At the very least, then, "the scholastic concept of the natural law implies a selective privileging of the tendencies inherent in human nature, in accordance with which some are given normative

---

[62] Jean Porter, *Natural and Divine Law: Reclaiming the Tradition for Christian Ethics* (Ottawa: Novalis, 1999), p. 53.

[63] Servais Pinckaers, O.P., *The Sources of Christian Ethics* (Washington, DC: Catholic University of America Press, 1995), p. 209; the internal quote is from Augustine, *The City of God* 15.22.

[64] Porter, *Natural and Divine Law*, pp. 166–67.

priority and others are de-emphasized or discouraged".[65] "Ordered love" might exemplify that happy selection.

Yet this by no means conveys the whole story. So much can be inferred from the fact that, in the tradition of Thomas, charity, a *supernatural* virtue (surpassing then the "love"—*amor*—of that Augustinian "definition"), and inseparable from its "sisters", theological faith and hope, inherits the place given to prudence by the pagan Greeks as the principle of coherence among the virtues in coordinating the moral life as a whole. Pinckaers provides an admirable short account of Saint Thomas' ethics, which combines reasonableness, and its attendant natural virtues, with those supernatural virtues and the "Gifts of the Holy Spirit": Messianic endowments of the regenerated person (listed in Isaiah and profiled in the Western rite of Confirmation) that enable the graciously virtuous life to proceed with facility and ease.

> Moral theory is governed by practical reason, which is in turn perfected by the infused and acquired virtues. The reference to reason constitutes the principal criterion for forming a moral judgment. Yet this reason is rooted in faith and receives from faith, as well as from the Gifts of wisdom and counsel, a higher light. It is also closely linked with the concrete experience produced by the will and sensibility, and their inclinations and desires, rectified and strengthened by the moral virtues and their corresponding Gifts. For St Thomas, therefore, practical reason functions in coordination and harmony, in synergy with the world of faith and the integrated human person. When, later on, reason became increasingly separated from faith on the one hand and from the will and sensibility on the other, scholasticism was in danger of turning into rationalism and intellectualism.... Scholastic moral theory was greatly impoverished by its loss of contact with human and spiritual experience.[66]

Here it is not simply a matter of reviewing the norms suggested by natural law reflection in the light of biblical teaching. Rather, the reasonable natural virtues and norms are to be married with divinely originated, supernatural dispositions and rules for acting (including "rule" by the Holy Spirit, who can never inspire any act that runs contrary to charity). It does not seem excessive to interpret Pinckaers'

[65] Ibid., p. 216.
[66] Pinckaers, *Sources of Christian Ethics*, p. 234.

recommendation to consult "human and spiritual experience" as a call to hearken to the voices of Christian poets and novelists, on the one hand, and, on the other, the mystics and saints (a highly Balthasarian mode of proceeding).

This does not mean that human flourishing ceases to be the goal of ethics, but that the flourishing in question is both immeasurably enhanced in itself and also furnished with new resources for its achievement. In Thomas' moral anthropology, true freedom had always consisted in the power to act in truth, in quest of the highest good. Now, with the grace of Christ, mediated by the Holy Spirit, it reached its supreme perfection in those who could no longer sin—namely, the *beati* or saints, those who have attained true happiness, beatitude.[67]

There is nothing in the Thomist account of ethics that Balthasar does not accept. Thus he writes of how natural ethics—summed up in the four fundamental virtues acknowledged in Greek and Roman paganism—are simultaneously, in Christianity, confirmed yet surpassed.

> The highest sphere gives order to the complex life of the community, the family, and the individual; the doctrine of the four cardinal virtues—the "prudence" that risks and discriminates, the "fortitude" that vanquishes in confidence, the modest hierarchical ordering ("temperance"), and the "justice" that strives for cosmic reason and providence—do not need to be violated by Christianity, but rather elevated and perfected. But they must be perfected in such a way that all four dimensions of virtue, and the higher modes of the God-relationship along with them, are measured by a standard of judgment that lies beyond what can be achieved or even understood on the basis of the virtues themselves, and so which must appear "foolish". When they are so judged, their deepest meaning must first become meaningless in order to receive a superabundance of meaning in faith, beyond what philosophy can see.[68]

The "foolishness" in question is cruciform charity, and Balthasar makes his own the Thomasian principle that, in the New Covenant, such sacrificial love becomes the "*forma virtutum* [form of the virtues]" and consequently the "fundamental principle of all Christian

[67] Compare the account in ibid., pp. 354–99.
[68] Von Balthasar, *Love Alone Is Credible*, pp. 132–33.

ethics".[69] If Balthasar often speaks here of the *obedience* of charity-love, this is to give an Ignatian touch to a theology shared by the Johannine school, the great Fathers and the High Scholastics, not to replace such a theology by an ethics of simple command or context-free obligation. That Ignatius "touch" is certainly justified, for there are in the word "obedience" profound biblical resonances of hearing the divine Word (etymologically, *obaudire* links "obeying" to "hearing", *audire*). Such charity goes well beyond natural ethics, for "Christian action is above all a secondary reaction to the primary action of God toward man",[70] action whose supreme expression is the Cross where a humanly measureless love was enacted for the world. "The standard that God lays down becomes the standard that I must lay down and thus the standard by which I myself am measured", by the "logic", that is, of "absolute love",[71] "Christ's form of love".[72] In these phrases from Balthasar's *Love Alone Is Credible*, the message of the theological aesthetics is summarised, and that of the theological dramatics anticipated. True, within the natural realm there are "inchoate forms and ways of love", but these "threaten to stray into trackless thickets" unless and until "worldly being" is seen in the "light of the Cross"—that is, by reference to their "true transcendental ground".[73] This accentuated Christological—and Cross-centred, "staurological"—formulation does not lead, then, to a replacement of a universal ethic addressed to all men of good will by an alternative that is both more limited in its outreach and distinctly esoteric in that it is dogmatically derived. There are two reasons for saying so. First, the synergy of natural and supernatural ethics strengthens *all* moral practice by treating ethical existence as a response to the manifestation (compare the theological aesthetics) and the action (compare the theological dramatics) of God in salvation history, adding fresh motives of admiration, gratitude, and self-commitment. And secondly, and in more quintessentially Balthasarian terms (drawn ultimately, however, from Saint Bonaventure), it simply is the case that "all creatures have a *conatus*

[69] Ibid., p. 110.
[70] Ibid., p. 112.
[71] Ibid., p. 113.
[72] Ibid., p. 130.
[73] Ibid., p. 142.

toward becoming imitative of the Son, that is, becoming expressive words of the Father."[74] On a Bonaventurian understanding of the world's being—and consequently of its "value"—"the Father always intended creation to have its exemplar and goal in the Son",[75] and therefore in the Son's glorious Cross. As Balthasar puts it in the theological dramatics, "Prior to revealed Christology, man the agent can establish certain 'general' norms of action, abstracted from human existence, and these may be relatively correct. But once the absolute norm [i.e., Christ] has appeared on the scene ... they must be understood as rays emitted from it or approaches toward it."[76] The freedom that, by dint of man's original constitution, has always had the task of acting in truth by ordination to the good turns out, in the light of revelation, to take the form of a "Christomorphic task".[77] In his short study *Theology of History*, written in 1950 and revised in 1958, he wrote,

> We are therefore driven to say that insofar as Jesus Christ is true man, the universal validity of those normative laws which are grounded in human nature has, with him and *in him*, been assumed into union with the person of the divine Word. This elevation means neither that the universal validity of these laws is destroyed (for after all human nature is to be redeemed, not annihilated), nor that it is merely preserved, side by side with, but unaffected by, the concrete norm which is Jesus Christ: it is rather that, without being nullified, the abstract laws are, in him, integrated and subordinated within his christological uniqueness, and formed and governed by it.[78]

And since Christ, as the trinitarian Son, can never be thought, or approached, without reference to Father and to Spirit, we can go further and say that "through the work of the Spirit, human action is incorporated into the very tripersonal dynamics of the Trinity."[79] In this manner, Balthasar sought to meet the request of the Second

[74] Steck, *Ethical Thought*, p. 17.

[75] Ibid., p. 12.

[76] Hans Urs von Balthasar, *Theo-drama: Theological Dramatic Theory*, vol. 2, *Dramatis Personae: Man in God* (San Francisco: Ignatius Press, 1990), p. 61.

[77] Steck, *Ethical Thought*, p. 35.

[78] Von Balthasar, *Theology of History*, p. 18.

[79] Steck, *Ethical Thought*, p. 36.

Vatican Council for a moral theology that was explicitly centred in the "Mystery of Christ".[80]

If Saint Thomas found the eudaimonistic "flourishing" to which Aristotelian ethics had directed him only truly realized in the "eternal life" of the Gospel of Saint John, so likewise for Balthasar there is in such "trans-natural" ethical activity an eschatological dimension.[81] Actually, Balthasar prefers here the word "parousial" (in German, *parusial*), since the believer, he says, acts in view of "this essential tenet of Christian faith": "Christ will come again in the 'glory' of the revealed love that judges and rectifies all things at the (timeless) end of the chain of all temporal events."[82] Putting that message of theological aesthetics and dramatics into the language of naked philosophy, he writes: "Action that arises from the Absolute proceeds toward the absolute future, which lies within and beyond the relative history of the world."[83] The same could be said, of course, of "eternal life" in the Gospel according to John: already, and not yet (5:24; 17:2–3).

These further dimensions make it more understandable that Balthasar's teaching on ethical action is closely connected with his theology of the saints. The "sole credibility of the Church Christ founded lies, as he himself says, in the saints, as those who sought to set all things on the love of Christ alone".[84] "The people who live entirely for love are not merely 'moral examples' of Christian action, but, because they have handed themselves over to the fruitful love of the Redeemer, they are also our intercessors and chosen helpers. In the place that has been designated for them, however, they do no more than point to the total reciprocal integration of the deeds of all those who love; in the infinite, their lives and deeds open up to one another and mutually interpenetrate (the 'communion of saints')."[85] The saints enter into morals not simply as exemplars of both the goal and the way to the goal, but as provisioners of the wherewithal to follow

[80]Second Vatican Council, *Optatam totius* (October 28, 1965), no. 16.

[81]In Russell Hittinger's words, "For both Aquinas and Balthasar the activity of moral theorizing is meant to serve the goal of moral perfection." Russell Hittinger, "Theology and Natural Law Theory", *Communio* 17 (1990): 403; see pp. 402–8.

[82]Von Balthasar, *Love Alone Is Credible*, p. 113.

[83]Ibid.

[84]Ibid., p. 122.

[85]Ibid., p. 119.

the way—a claim that turns on Balthasar's account of the interlocking character of the missions of all those who come theo-dramatically "on stage". In a Balthasarian coining, they are "transethical": "There are saints who are hidden not only from themselves—like all saints—but also from the world and who, without being aware of it, had effects of great magnitude on world history by simple acts of prayer and self-surrender that, assessed 'psychologically' seem to be 'nothing special' ".[86] Though God's distribution of the fruit of Christ's sacrifice is the defining instance as well as the causal principle of this phenomenon, considering Balthasar's spirituality will throw some light on how, by grace, it comes about.

---

[86] Von Balthasar, *Person in Christ*, p. 29.

7

Spirituality

Like Thomas, who uses the word rather sparingly (and when he does the overlap with our contemporary usage is comparatively narrow),[1] Balthasar is not a proponent of a "separated spirituality". By that phrase is conventionally meant a pious, or, at any rate, theologically undemanding, discipline suitable for those who wish to add a touch (or even a showerful) of religion to everyday life. Thus, for instance, an excellent place to look for Balthasar's account of what is now termed "spirituality" would be the section of the theological aesthetics devoted to the "subjective evidence" for the impact of the form of God in Jesus Christ.[2] The reader will find nothing that is merely pious or theologically loose in those pages. In Balthasar's usage, the term "subjective" in no way implies a purely affective (and, in the worst scenario, sentimental) approach to the Christian life as lived. While, in that discussion, his concept of faith—the gateway to Christian spiritual life—includes such dimensions as obedience, surrender, hoping, and trusting, and these, taken by themselves, might suggest a distaste for the strongly intellectual doctrine of the *actus fidei* held by Thomas, faith for Balthasar is absolutely inseparable from the *knowledge* of God, and hence from the mind's initial, but also ongoing, assent to the divine Word. As to Thomas, in the words of Jean-Pierre Torrell introducing the second volume of his magnum opus on Aquinas, the Dominican master's intellectualism is by no means at the expense of a

---

[1] Jean-Pierre Torrell, O.P., "*Spiritualitas* chez S. Thomas d'Aquin: Contribution à l'histoire d'un mot", *Revue des sciences philosophiques at théologiques* 73 (1989): 575–84; Jean-Pierre Torrell, O.P., *Saint Thomas Aquinas*, vol. 2, *Spiritual Master*, trans. Robert Royal (Washington, DC: Catholic University of America Press, 2003), pp. 18–21. The denotation of *spiritualis* is either noncorporeal or under the impact of the Holy Spirit.

[2] Hans Urs von Balthasar, *The Glory of the Lord: A Theological Aesthetics*, vol. 1, *Seeing the Form* (San Francisco: Ignatius Press, 1976), pp. 129–427.

holistic account of "sacred doctrine" that integrates the mystical with
the speculative (and the historical).

> Before all else, theology is an expression of a God-informed life, an
> activity in which the virtues of faith, hope, and charity are given full
> scope. If we speak primarily of faith in the following pages, it is to keep
> things brief and to emphasize the explanatory core of certain aspects
> of theology. But it should be clear that this faith is not a pure intellec-
> tual adhesion to the collection of truths that occupy the theologian.
> It is, rather, in Saint Thomas as in the Bible, the living attachment of
> the whole person to the divine reality to which the person is united
> through faith by means of the formulas that convey that Reality to us.[3]

Thomas' holism here has its mirror in Balthasar, for whom, in the act
of faith, all human powers—intelligence prominent among them—
are drawn into play.

So little is Balthasar a prey to anti-intellectualism that, despite his
profound antagonism to ancient Gnosticism and its later reincarna-
tions (Joachimism, Hegelianism), he seeks to wrest the term *gnosis*
(knowledge) from the heretics, and re-employ it (in the way the
early Alexandrian theologians did) for the Christian experience of
faith.[4] This is because he wishes to see faith not as pious consciousness, which could perfectly well be humanly self-generated, but as a
sharing in the self-revelation of God. God gives himself so as to be
recognized—which, on the believer's part, implies knowledge. That
recognition, in grace-augmented intimacy, unfolding over a lifetime,
is, for Balthasar, the essence of Christian spiritual existence.

It is also a sign that the Messianic era has come, that in Christ
the prophecies have been fulfilled.[5] There is a great deal of "realized eschatology" in Balthasar's presentation of spiritual living. Faith
does not just *seek* understanding. That Anselmian (and Augustinian) maxim requires a complement. Of its nature, and not merely
in some hypothetical future contingency, faith *finds* understanding.
It is not only *quaerens*; it is *inveniens*.[6] It does not acknowledge its

---

[3] Torrell, *Spiritual Master*, p. 4.
[4] Von Balthasar, *Seeing the Form*, pp. 136–41.
[5] Ibid., pp. 131–33.
[6] Ibid., p. 136.

Object *in absentia*; it contemplates its presence now. "Both in John and Paul as well as in Clement and Origen, the gnosis of faith can be clarified by the concept of *theoria*, meaning steadfast, illuminating contemplation—provided *theoria* is taken along with its theological prerequisites: incorporation into Christ through faith and sacraments; participation in the Holy Spirit, who introduces us to the fullness of truth; revelatory will of the heavenly Father, who through Word and Spirit already now, within the veil of faith, wants to grant us a share in his own triune truth."[7] If someone objects to the word "gnostic", Balthasar offers an alternative term: "philo-sophianic", meaning "wisdom-loving", or, yet again, in a Latinate English equivalent to the adjectival form of *theoria*, "contemplative".[8]

That is useful background for Balthasar's book *Das betrachtende Gebet*, which, inexplicably, lost the German equivalent of "contemplative" from its title when translated into English as *Prayer*, first in 1961 and then again in 1986.[9] On any Christian account, prayer is the heart of spirituality. For spirituality, whatever else we may say about it, concerns the foundations and the context of personal relation with God. And personal relation with God means prayer. But in Balthasar, reflection on prayer will be "philo-sophianic", wishing to open up all the theological riches implicit in the act of faith. *Prayer* is almost a compendium of Balthasarian theology, dealing as it does with the Holy Trinity, Christology, soteriology, the Church and her worship, and eschatology—all seen in the prism of the "act", "object", and "tensions" of contemplation. Saint Thomas did not leave a treatise *De oratione* and wrote only the briefest of commentaries on the Lord's Prayer (which is how the Fathers of the Church would have proceeded in the matter). A zealous German scholar, Lydia Maidl, has brought together Aquinas' numerous scattered references to praying into a single whole.[10] But to compare even the totality of Thomas'

---

[7] Ibid., p. 139.

[8] Ibid., p. 146.

[9] Hans Urs von Balthasar, *Prayer* (1961; San Francisco: Ignatius Press, 1986).

[10] See, e.g., Lydia Maidl, *Desiderii interpres: Genese und Grundstruktur des Gebetstheologie des Thomas von Aquin* (Paderborn: Schöningh, 1994). Her singling out the theme of the "interpretation of desire" fits well with the wider assessment in Torrell, *Spiritual Master*, pp. 330–36. Torrell points out that it is reading Thomas' biblical commentaries, far more than the *Summa theologiae*, which enables the student to ascertain the primacy of this motif in Thomas on (hope and) prayer.

comments with Balthasar's would not be adequate, precisely because
of the wide-ranging character of Balthasar's approach—in the sense
just explained. A more helpful plan might be to compare Balthasar's *Prayer* with the synthesis of Thomas' spiritual theology found
in Jean-Pierre Torrell's study of a "spiritual master", which ranges
through all the principal themes of Aquinas' understanding of the life
of faith.[11] A preliminary scan would suggest Balthasar has more on
heaven; Aquinas, more on the creation—justifying (to that extent)
Joseph Ratzinger's whimsical yet profound suggestion that if, like
certain Carmelite nuns and friars, Thomas were to be given a "title of
devotion" it should be "Thomas of the Creator".[12]

Thomas and the Charismatics

The importance of Balthasar's debt to Thomas on the matter of spiritual doctrine has already been noted in the introduction, a propos
of his contribution to the German-Latin edition of the *Summa theologiae*. In the early 1950s, Balthasar was invited to contribute a volume
(no. 23) to the new bilingual (Latin-German) edition of Thomas'
Summa theologiae, then emerging from the Dominican study house
at Walberberg, located between Bonn and Cologne. The book saw
the light of day in 1954 and reappeared from Balthasar's own publishing house at Einsiedeln under the new title "Thomas and the
Charismatics" in 1996.[13] Balthasar had taken care of questions 171
to 182 of the *Secunda Secundae*, which deal with special graces (the
gratiae gratis datae) as well as the two basic lifeways in the Church—
the "contemplative" and the "active" lives, an ancient contrast in the
Latin Fathers and, before them, in Aristotle. He had much less to

---

[11] "If we assume that there is a reflexive level for theology where it brings forward the basic
laws that command human action and Christian life in this world and before God—as Saint
Thomas does—then we shall quickly discover that this reflection is pregnant with a spiritual
doctrine." Torrell, *Spiritual Master*, p. 21.

[12] Joseph Ratzinger, "'Consecrate Them in the Truth': A Homily for St. Thomas' Day",
New Blackfriars 68, no. 803 (1987): 112–15. Ratzinger had borrowed this fancy from G.K.
Chesterton, *St. Thomas Aquinas* (1933; London: Hodder and Stoughton, 1943), p. 95.

[13] Hans Urs von Balthasar, *Thomas und die Charismatiker: Kommentar zu Thomas von Aquin,
Summa Theologica Quaestiones II II 171–182: Besondere Gnadenlehre und die zwei Wege menschlichen Lebens* (1954; Einsiedeln: Johannes, 1996).

say about the "lives" than he had about the "gratuitous graces"—
probably owing to the way that Adrienne von Speyr's mystical experience had focussed his mind on "special graces", and dramatically
so. Consequently, the title given to the republication ("Thomas and
the Charismatics") fits the final product well. Surprisingly, Balthasar
was not asked to comment on the "Questions" immediately following those on the "two lives". Here the topic is the office and "state"
of the pastoral clergy (notably bishops) and "Religious" (monastics of
different kinds), and would have been a natural continuation of his
commission. Perhaps the Dominican editors found in Balthasar's status as a former religious (he was now only a *Welt*-priest or "secular"
priest) a reason for caution.

Be that as it may, Balthasar's treatment was thorough, both historically and theologically, even though he claimed not to be offering a
"systematic-theological discussion".[14] Where appropriate, it moved
beyond the *Summa*, citing from other parts of Thomas' corpus of
which Balthasar shows an enviable grasp. In "Thomas and the Charismatics", Balthasar adjusts Thomas' teaching while accepting it in its
main outlines. Thomas had distinguished between what is *substantially*
beyond human nature and what is beyond human nature simply *in
its mode*. Despite the impression the language gives, it is the "modally
supernatural" that, for the Dominican Doctor, is the more important
feature of engraced humanity. Knowing and loving God in himself is what is modally supernatural, for it requires sanctifying grace
and in an intrinsically habitual form. Performing some extraordinary
action on a "one-off" basis, such as working a miracle or coming to
learn some secret hidden in the divine wisdom, might sound more
impressive (indeed, "substantially" so), but the help human capacities
require here is sufficiently supplied by transient acts—the "special"
graces to which the bulk of *Thomas und die Charismatiker* is devoted.

Thomas' evaluation, so Balthasar explains, turns on his view of
grace in its relation to nature: that "hot potato" of the Church con-
troversies of the 1940s and '50s. "The manner of natural understanding, to know God through creatures, is not so closed on itself that it
cannot be opened to another [manner of understanding, that is itself]
supernatural and divinely freely afforded: to know God in himself.

---

[14]Ibid., p. 252.

To this degree whatever in the supernatural order 'substantially' transcends human capacity is embraced by and related to [this] modal supernaturality."[15] So, charismatic actions are substantially supernatural if transient when compared with acts that are modally supernatural but abiding—such as the acts made habitually possible by the virtues of faith, hope, and charity.

For his part, Balthasar would prefer to put all this somewhat differently. He thinks it should be enough to say that the charismatic order remains within the grace order of holiness. Why does he want to rewrite Thomas (and other Scholastic theologians) in this fashion? In the first place, it is because he wishes to give the charism of prophecy, understood as covering the case of Christian mysticism, greater connectivity to sanctification—as in the lives of the mystical saints. And in the second place, it is because he considers the ethical and spiritual preconditions of the reception of singular charisms to be more demanding than Thomas was prepared to say. Balthasar approved of the way the sixteenth-century Spanish Jesuit Scholastic Francisco Suárez had framed his treatise on charisms as an appendix to a tractate on faith: the essential act of the Christian life (*pace* the opening chapter of "Balthasar for Thomists", here is an example of the continuing influence of historic Jesuit Scholasticism). But Balthasar recognizes that Thomas draws a sharper distinction than some others between prophecy and the regions of Christian experience covered by the "Gifts" (with a capitalized "g") of the Holy Spirit—the latter are, for Thomists, the foundation of the consciously mystical life. This would help to explain the relatively tenuous connexion between the biblical prophets and the Christian mystics in Aquinas' text.

Prophecy was, however, uppermost in Thomas' mind (as in Balthasar's) where extraordinary charisms are concerned. As Balthasar reads him, prophecy is the superordinate concept governing Thomas' "take" on all charisms that are concerned in some way with knowledge (and these are the chief ones that interest Thomas—as is also true for Balthasar).[16] Saint Paul himself had led the way by placing

---

[15] Ibid., p. 243. On Balthasar's reading of Thomas' texts, "it lies in the essence of human nature to long for the vision of God without being able, of this essence's own capacities, to strive after and reach that perception." Ibid.

[16] Ibid., p. 286.

the prophets on the very next step to the apostles (cf. 1 Cor 12:28). In Aquinas,

> the teaching on the charisms ... was changed almost entirely into a treatise on prophecy, or, more accurately, the complex of questions about prophecy already to hand in the pre-Thomasian tradition was artfully gathered up and, together with the likewise much discussed question of rapture, and some fragmentary effusions about individual gifts of grace, so erected as to fill the need for a tractate on ecclesial charisms. In order to judge it aright, one must always have before one's eyes the meaning of the *Summa* as a whole ... [one of] ordering, clarifying and simplifying questions already discussed by contemporaries rather than throwing up new questions or contributing viewpoints otherwise lacking.[17]

Balthasar did something to make good the possible "lacks" in Thomas' account. On the basis of New Testament philology, he points out that "grace" (*charis*) and "charism" (*charisma*) just have to be related terms. The Pentecostal outpouring of the Holy Spirit was an effusion of *charis* that included certain "signs" that can suitably be termed *charismata*. How are we to understand the relation between the two? Balthasar's answer was as wide-ranging as it was profound. "The descent of the Holy Spirit onto the visible-invisible Church bears a sort of analogy to the Incarnation of the Son. But in the latter case, the stress lies on the becoming visible in the flesh of the spiritual God who remains invisible, whereas now the stress lies on the spirituality—indeed invisibility—of 'sanctifying grace', as on its essentially gift-character as a 'sharing the divine nature'." Yet because the Church is "visible and, indeed should be visibly animated by the Spirit, this includes a visible aspect in the order of 'sign' and 'expression', and also of 'function', in the visible-invisible total body of the Church."[18] So *charismata* and *charis* are truly related—at Pentecost but also beyond. Balthasar agrees with Thomas, however, that grace and the charisms do not have an "unproblematic unity"—as can readily be seen from the life of the Church at Corinth in Paul's epistles to

[17] Ibid., pp. 254–55.
[18] Ibid., pp. 256–57.

the same.[19] The charisms are, since Pentecost, a sign of sanctifying grace at work, and yet they are, up to a point, detachable from the essential order of grace—something Balthasar explains by saying that the Church's visible order is "dialectically" related to her invisible essence.[20] "The whole charismatic thing in the primitive Church is, from the salvation-historical perspective, a very delicate phenomenon", transitional yet unavoidable, spanning the distance between the prophetic movement in the Old Testament and mysticism in the Church.[21] Paul certainly wanted for the Corinthians the higher gifts of prophecy and gnosis, which latter term Balthasar takes to mean, for Paul, an "understanding of the eschatological goods of salvation".[22]

Modern (i.e., mid-twentieth century) practitioners of mystical theology, so Balthasar claims, tend to revise upwards the previous estimate of the charismatic. True, the *charismata* are, in Paul's language, gifts (with a lower case "g"), rather than fruits, of the Spirit. That implies they are to be distinguished from *personal* holiness—but not necessarily, warns Balthasar, from *ecclesial* holiness, the holiness of the Church. With the exception of the gift of tongues, they imply a task—and therefore, one could say, some sort of office in the Church. Among the early Fathers, Saint Irenaeus and Saint Justin thought the Old Testament prophetic charisms had found their fulfillment in Christ and the Church. Certainly Hermas, author of *The Shepherd*, that monument of the earliest Roman Christianity, was aware of his mission as the Christian equivalent of a prophet, as was the German Benedictine abbess Hildegard of Bingen a millennium later. Unfortunately, the Montanist crisis of the late second and early third centuries, with its abusive exaggeration of prophetic gifts, triggered a negative reaction. The idea of the Christian prophet was increasingly absorbed into a generalized ascetical and mystical ideal of the contemplative saint.

The Scholastic tractate which Thomas inherited combined this patristic-era programme of contemplative mysticism with a debt to

[19] Ibid., p. 257.
[20] Ibid.
[21] Ibid., p. 258.
[22] Ibid., p. 260.

later Jewish and Arabic texts (Maimonides, Avicenna) on the nature
of prophecy, generating in so doing a theology of the Gifts (capital-
ised initial letter, once again) of the Holy Spirit. On those "Gifts of
the Holy Spirit", Balthasar points out that, leaving aside a few rather
slight references in the Fathers, this is essentially a high-mediaeval
topos, starting in a major way with Bonaventure and continuing
in the German mystics of the later Middle Ages. The Gifts are for
Thomas very much an entailment of sanctifying grace in its development in the individual soul. The Scholastics had not always been
either entirely clear or in agreement with each other on various
aspects of the economy of grace ancillary to its central reality: sanctifying grace which itself is uncreated grace communicated to the
soul as the engracing of its powers. Here Thomas could clarify matters. He distinguished "helping grace", *auxilium Dei moventis* (later
called "actual grace"), from, on the one side, spiritual inclinations in
human nature that serve as a midpoint between our given rational
nature and the prospective good of virtue at which that nature aims
(and to this degree are a preparation for sanctifying grace), and, on
the other, the charismata, defined as supernatural gifts which have
as their purpose the justification of other people rather than their
immediate recipients.

Balthasar was not keen on that "of other people", at any rate in the
perspective of Mystical Body ecclesiology. It is, he thought, mon-
strous to suppose that someone "holds through grace a function in
this forward movement of love [*Liebesvorgang*] without himself being
in the love of God".[23] And looking at the same matter—whom do
charismata benefit?—from the other end, that of the seven "messianic" Gifts, surely such Gifts of the Holy Spirit as wisdom, knowledge, and counsel ought to be regarded as *social* in character, just
like the charisms, and not simply personal acquisitions. Can those
Gifts be exclusively intended as personal possessions if the Church
is the essentially corporate Body of the Lord, the *communio sanctorum*? Balthasar did not favour contrasting the personal with the social
in the Mystical Body. The more personal an inner life with God,
the more personal the resultant commission in the Church—a social
phenomenon—is likely to be.

[23] Ibid., p. 283.

If Balthasar wants to expand Thomas' treatise, it is because he thinks that, after Thomas, Scholastics concerned for "essential forms" had little if anything to say about the "concrete embedding of these essences (*Wesen*) into the existential and historical-dynamic order of being (*Dasein*)",[24] a comment where we can hear echoes of his reading of Gilson, Guardini, Heidegger, sundry poets, and such Greek Fathers as Maximus and Gregory of Nyssa—discussed in the opening chapter of the present study. In consequence, the analogy between, on the one hand, the charismatic workings of grace, and, on the other, the fruitfulness (a favourite Balthasarian term) of personal grace and graced "missions", went largely unnoticed. Yet Thomas himself—elsewhere in the *Summa theologiae*—had recognized that if, on some occasion, *gratiae gratis datae* manage to produce in another what someone would desire for himself by way of sanctifying grace, then, in such a case, the charismatic graces should actually be regarded as the higher gift. In Thomas' metaphor, the illuminating sun is more sublime than the illuminated body.[25]

Prophecy and the mystics

On prophecy, Balthasar goes through numerous texts from the Fathers and the early mediaevals with the aim of showing how they "read" prophecy in a dual manner: foretelling the future and interpreting Scripture by the spiritual sense. For Thomas, the prophet is essentially a mediator of divine knowledge—a term that can cover both of these activities. That concept enabled Aquinas to grade in a systematic way the bearers of prophecy: Christ in his prophetic office, the apostles, the prophets, the Church teachers. This, thought Balthasar, is rather neat, but it somewhat obscures the connexion of prophecy to other charisms.

Balthasar's general account of the nature of the mystically charismatic dimension was indebted to the Dominican Réginald Garrigou-Lagrange, a well-known representative of "Commentatorial Thomism" on the eve of the Second Vatican Council, as well as to the German Benedictine Anselm Stolz, for many years a professor

---

[24] Ibid., p. 284.
[25] *ST* Ia-IIae, q. 111, a. 5 ad 2.

at the Anselmianum, the Roman college of the Benedictine abbot-primate, and, nowadays, a distinctly underrated figure who deserves a rediscovery.[26] Thomas himself, Balthasar pointed out, has no treatise on mysticism. To arrive at such, one would have to put together his account of the missions of the Son and the Spirit, his teaching on the Gifts, and what he has to say about contemplation as well as the charisms. Thomas had conceded that archetypal prophets had figured in the tradition as models of contemplative holiness: Moses and Elijah are obvious examples. Balthasar was inclined to agree with Stolz in calling Adam in Paradise the real *Vorbild* and *Urtyp*—image and archetype—of all prophetical-mystical knowledge of God.[27] Thomas too had treated Adam as enjoying a grace-elevated vision that lay midway between a knowledge of God through creatures and the knowledge of God through glory. In his *Writing on the Sentences*, Aquinas speaks of the way that, after the Fall, contemplative men continued to receive heavenly disclosures. Pursuing that train of thought might have helped Thomas overcome a certain dualism between the charismata and the Gifts of the Holy Spirit in the doctrine he inherited and passed on.

Thomas was well-placed to rediscover the social nature of the contemplative mysticism of the New Testament precisely because he placed contemplation within the prophetic and placed the prophetic close to the mystical. That gave the right direction for treating of Christian prophets and mystics. But, said Balthasar, all this needs to be rethought Christologically and ecclesiologically if it is not to remain restricted within a fundamentally Old Testament frame of reference. "What in the New Covenant can be called prophecy will henceforth have to come from the obedience and the vision of the Son and the life of his Church."[28] When that rethinking takes place, it will be realized that the gap between the prophetic and the mystical is slight.

> The vital and personally developing life of faith in the soul is, thanks to the Gifts of the Holy Ghost, not at all the contemplation of a naked, abstract truth, but encounter with the incarnate, personal truth of God

---

[26] An excellent start is made in Fabio Angelo Bressan, *Lo sfondo mistico della teologia: La lezione breve di Anselm Stolz* (Padua: Edizione Messagero, 2004).

[27] Anselm Stolz, O.S.B., *The Doctrine of Spiritual Perfection* (St. Louis, MO: Herder, 1948).

[28] Von Balthasar, *Thomas und die Charismatiker*, p. 314.

in Christ, an exchange of life not only in the realm of ontic grace but also in that of spiritual actions, a being led by the Spirit into highly interior and unnoticeable impulses and stimuli, a reception of divine wishes, commands, illuminations, of the most personal kind. So this entire mystery-filled life withdraws ever more completely from a univocal reckoning as belonging to the category of "mystical" on the one side, "prophetic" on the other.[29]

Even Garrigou-Lagrange, who came close to excluding extraordinary charismata from mysticism, had to admit there could be "illuminations" that "approach the order of sanctifying grace" and indeed of "infused contemplation".[30] Looking back at these issues from the time of writing the first volume of the theological aesthetics, Balthasar saw matters especially clearly. Where there is "retained only the mysticism of the *dona* [Gifts] of the Holy Spirit ... this mysticism wholly loses the ecclesial dimension of mission; it becomes essentially a mysticism of the individual.... This, however, yields a paradox: it is precisely the charisms (which, supposedly, can 'function' even without sanctifying grace and love) that require and maintain their basis in a love serving selflessly, whereas a mysticism without 'function' and aiming solely at theological love stands in danger of degenerating into a private affair."[31] A subtradition to this supra-functional effect, stemming from Augustine and John of the Cross, could play into the hands of those who spurn mysticism in the Church altogether.

Looking in closer detail at Thomas' account of prophecy, Balthasar picked out some key themes from question 171. The most important is the identification of the prophetic act itself. It is, Balthasar insists, at its heart a *Vernunftakt*, an act of reason, by which he means in this context an "act of the self-conscious and responsible intellectual (*geistig*) person", over against a pagan or a sectarian-Christian concept of prophecy (compare the Montanists), where prophecy becomes a kind of mania.[32] Among the Fathers, Augustine in particular stresses how prophecy belongs to *mens*, which Balthasar

---

[29] Ibid.
[30] Réginald Garrigou-Lagrange, O.P., *Perfection chrétienne et contemplation selon S. Thomas d'Aquin et S. Jean de la Croix* (Saint-Maximin: Editions de la Vie spirituelle, 1923), 2:541, 547.
[31] Von Balthasar, *Seeing the Form*, p. 411.
[32] Von Balthasar, *Thomas und die Charismatiker*, p. 320.

translates *Geistgrund*.[33] This influences his own German vocabulary when he comes to explain Thomas' view. For Thomas there are, within the act of prophetically communicated knowledge, two constitutive moments: "inspiration" and "revelation". These Balthasar understands as the directing of the *Geist* to God (*inspiratio*) and God's disclosure to the *Geist* (*revelatio*). Thomas' preoccupation in regard to the first is with its act-character—as against any notion of a prophetic habit, a cognitive "light" permanently at the prophet's disposal. There is indeed such a thing as the *lumen propheticum*, a more intense participation in the divine light than is the *lumen naturale* of our ordinary knowing, but it is given *akthaft*—that is, precisely not in such a way that it is the prophet's to command.[34] Thomas' discussion of *revelatio* stresses that the content of prophecy does not necessarily consist of contingent future events. "Revelation" can take for its subject matter objects of many kinds, a conclusion rather forced upon him by the Bible's diversity of topic (the biblical writers—the hagiographs—were, by definition, engaged in producing such *revelatio*). For Balthasar, the economy of salvation is always the *proper* object of prophetic knowledge—and feminists may be pleased to hear that, on this basis, he was inclined to call Hildegard of Bingen "perhaps the greatest ... prophetess of the New Covenant".[35] For Balthasar, specifically Old Testament prophecy does not aim in any way to be comprehensive, to explore the depths of the wisdom of God—unlike the believing Christian's contemplation which may well have that character. "One can ... draw one essential distinction between the prophetic and the generally contemplative vision of faith. In the latter, an at least unconscious and implicit process of deduction, in the light of the Gift of Wisdom, is not only permitted but seems positively commanded—the one contemplating moving forward into the depths of divine truth through the intrication of the hidden in the already known. But in the former, the act of prophetic revelation, a circumscribed content is fixed and, as such, has to be transmitted to those outside as adequately as possible."[36] A mystical

[33] Ibid., p. 321.
[34] Ibid., p. 324.
[35] Ibid., p. 331.
[36] Ibid., p. 334.

vision might be more like prophetic revelation, so described. A mystic with a short and sweet message for the Church, such as Bernadette at Lourdes, would evidently fit this category. Alternatively, a mystical vision may more closely resemble contemplative faith as such—which Balthasar considers equivalent to "gnosis" (in the Alexandrian not Irenaean sense of the word) in its scanning of the heights and depths of the kerygma. No doubt Adrienne von Speyr's visionary experiences, which were prolonged and elaborate and gave themselves to speculative theological elucidation, exemplified for Balthasar this second kind of case.

Subjacent to Balthasar's entire discussion, one might hazard, is the status of Adrienne's visionary material, not an issue he explicitly raised in his *Summa* commentary, understandably enough, for it was neither the time nor the place, not least because the visionary was still alive. Twenty years later, in 1974, by which date she was dead, he returned to the theme, and, without—once again—mentioning her name, spoke more strongly for a high doctrine of the possible significance of mystical—charismatic—visions. Here his tone is distinctly polemical.

> It is hard to gainsay the suspicion that behind Thomas' denigration of these special charismatic visions stands, more or less consciously, the Neoplatonic (and Buddhist) denigration of all sensory and imaginative visions that—allegedly still bound to the material world—should be transcended by the seer and perhaps even rejected outright.... But if this is true, then logically all of the images in the Book of Revelation must be categorized as but the expression of a lower level of mysticism. Indeed, perhaps this holds true even of the whole order of the Incarnation itself: the Gospel with its popular parables, narratives and events must then be valued only as a propaedeutic introduction into the purely spiritual. But that would of course be Gnosticism pure and simple and no longer Christianity.[37]

One ought not to "argue the case of charismatic phenomena from borderline cases"—as with Thomas' discussion of the pagan Balaam, but "recognise that these graces, which according to Paul are given

---

[37] Hans Urs von Balthasar, "Understanding Christian Mysticism", in *Explorations in Theology*, vol. 4, *Spirit and Institution* (San Francisco: Ignatius Press, 1995), pp. 328–29; see pp. 309–36.

for the benefit of the Church's *communio*, must also be accepted in the Church's living spirit, that is, in faith, hope, love and obedient readiness".[38] Perhaps if Thomas had encountered a mystic with so rich a theological programme as von Speyr's he would have modified his view of the matter. If so, it would doubtless be because he considered such a mystic to have furnished forms of *convenientia* in Christian discourse that served well the overall coherence and beauty of sacred theology, to have contributed highlights to what the First Vatican Council would call *connexio mysteriorum*, the connectedness of the mysteries.

Balthasar also addressed some further themes raised by the issue of the prophetic. The first of these, at the end of question 171, was the *truth* of prophecy where he thinks in tandem with Thomas about the problem of future-oriented prophecies that go unfulfilled.[39] God may simply communicate to the prophet the divine knowledge of events in their primordial causes, rather than God's own knowledge of them, as through human freedom they can be realized diversely. Furthermore, the *Wirkung* of the *Wirkende* (the activity of the agent) may not always be at full throttle—here Thomas leaves the door open to the possibility of some defect in the reception or interpretation of prophetic disclosure. Balthasar finds this relevant to the case of Christian mystics as well—which suggests he recognized there might be grounds for caution in utilizing their material in dogmatic construction. "What Thomas says here of prophetic knowledge and expression is correspondingly valid for genuine mystical vision and its articulation."[40] Yet Balthasar also wants to rule out the inference that any inadequacies of mystical apprehension and expression demonstrate the pointlessness of relying on the mystics for testimony. Thomas is not arguing that "everything human and created is deficient in regard to the divine".[41]

Another theme is the role of the cosmic powers.[42] In the first place, in Thomas' text, this introduces a discussion of natural, as distinct from supernatural, prophecy. In such situations as sleep, ecstasy,

---

[38] Ibid., p. 329.
[39] *ST* Ia-IIae, q. 171, a. 6.
[40] Von Balthasar, *Thomas und die Charismatiker*, p. 340.
[41] Ibid.
[42] *ST* Ia-IIae, q. 172, a. 2.

or near-death experiences, the soul can be more receptive, awaking as it does to spiritual spontaneity (though Balthasar would not want to say this follows from de-corporealisation, exactly—he is anxious that Thomas might be making too many concessions to Platonism here).[43] Citing the twelfth of the *Disputed Questions on Truth*, "Through both kinds of prophecy the human spirit is so far raised up that, in some way made like the heavenly spirits, it understands what, as to grounds so to consequences, they see in a simple comprehensive view, without deduction of the one from the other, in perfect assurance."[44] For Balthasar, this makes room for "all forms of artistic, philosophical and mystical intuition, but also for the different possibilities of cosmic religiosity, which, with whatever world-powers it is in contact, can include certain genuine experiences which, however, are not supernatural".[45] Perhaps he thought that "covered" many of his less conventional theological sources, or, better said (for there is no suggestion that they rank with Scripture and Tradition) *Hilfsmittel*, instrumental aids in theological thinking.

As to "world-powers", Balthasar was thinking especially (with Thomas) of the angels, who are pertinent to supernatural prophecy as well. The role of the angels, remarked Balthasar, is too embedded in the revelation process of salvation history ever to be removed. But theological accounts of the angels have tended to synthesize biblical and nonbiblical sources in a way that calls for some unravelling, a task where Karl Barth (he reports) did sterling work in the *Church Dogmatics*. In the *De veritate*, Thomas sees the *lumen propheticum* as issuing directly from God, yet grants the angels the power to shape the imaginative species in which the divine communication is clothed.[46] Insofar as the angels belong to the cosmic order they have a part in natural prophecy; insofar as they are servants of revelation they take their share in supernatural prophecy. Balthasar notes a lacuna where secondary causes of prophecy are concerned. Really, Aquinas' account of the role of mediatorial figures is based on the

---

[43] When discussing streams of spiritual interpretation of the "experience of faith" in the aesthetics, he is always on the watch for symptoms of an "anti-incarnational element". Von Balthasar, *Seeing the Form*, p. 315.

[44] Thomas Aquinas, *Quaestiones disputatae de veritate*, q. 12, a. 3.

[45] Von Balthasar, *Thomas und die Charismatiker*, p. 340.

[46] Aquinas, *Quaestiones disputatae de veritate*, q. 12, a. 8.

Old Testament theophanies. How it comes about that in the New Covenant prophecy and mysticism are mediated by the "humanized Son and perhaps through the heavenly Church remains undiscussed by Thomas".[47]

Balthasar's discussion of the theme of the relation between prophecy and the state of grace (and moral goodness) harks back to his preliminary introduction of Thomas' treatise.[48] For Old Testament prophecy it may suffice to say that only the intellect is affected, but the New Testament has a less "external" sense of divine instrumentality, and in that context, it is difficult, not to say impossible, to separate illumination or vision from the obedience of faith. The Johannine Apocalypse and the Letter to the Ephesians call the prophets "holy",[49] which implies at the very least worthiness in the moral realm. Writing to the Magnesians, Ignatius of Antioch speaks of the "God-enlightened prophets who lived by following Jesus Christ".[50] Of course there can be exceptions, as for the Hebrew Bible (here the example is Thomas' own) Balaam, and for mediaeval Christians, Merlin. The High Scholastics had varied in their attitude to this issue as can be seen from their musings as to whether prophecy entails spiritual delight. If Thomas had answered the general question differently, he would not have risked speaking of the evil angels as possible mediators of prophecy, a response that "leads, practically speaking, into the darkest and most dangerous zones, setting the ecclesial discernment of spirits the most difficult of tasks".[51] Yet Balthasar does not sound as though he regrets Thomas' opening up this question,[52] writing of how demonic possession can at times include the letting through of a genuine divine light, while, conversely, it is not impossible that God possession may permit an accidental demonic possession.

A further theme—by now Balthasar has reached question 173—concerns prophecy as knowledge. The High Scholastics spoke of the prophets as looking into the "Mirror of Wisdom", Albert the Great explaining this as a "verbum magistrale": not a term from the Fathers

---

[47] Von Balthasar, *Thomas und die Charismatiker*, p. 354.
[48] *ST* Ia-IIae, q. 172, a. 4.
[49] Eph 2:20 and Rev 18:20.
[50] Ignatius, *Ad Magnesios* 8.
[51] Von Balthasar, *Thomas und die Charismatiker*, p. 363.
[52] *ST* Ia-IIae, q. 172, arts. 5–6.

but deriving from recent masters in the schools, cathedral or university as may be. For Thomas the "mirror" in question is the eidetic images the prophets see in the *lumen propheticum*. These images reflect the divine vision by which God knows future things as present. Certainly, for Thomas, comments Balthasar robustly, God cannot be the mirror. In the Thomasian philosophy and theology, things mirror God, not the other way round. The relation of the prophetic light, the formal principle of judgment, to some material content—concept or image—stimulates Thomas to write what is, in Balthasar's view, the most important article of them all.[53] Thomas asserts the primacy of *noesis* over the *noema*, the light of judgment, vis-à-vis the concept (which may be generated by the light) or the image (which, by contrast, may itself be entertained by someone other than the prophet, as in Joseph's deciphering of Pharaoh's dream or Daniel decoding the writing on the wall at Belshazzar's feast). In this article Thomas has also established an important aporetic principle: prophetic knowledge aims at the intuitive without ever being able to abandon the discursive.

There is in prophecy the possibility of a certain "alienation from the senses". Thomas' concern here is with the psychological conditions under which illumination and the acceptance of images or concepts takes place.[54] In the *Summa* text, over against the *De veritate*, Thomas admits that, as well as psychological-physiological causation, ecstasy may have behind it the *virtus divina rapiens*, and so a strictly supernatural cause.[55] In accepting a prophetic or mystical message or commission (*Botschaft*), an ecstatic condition may be highly relevant. Christian mysticism provides examples, claims Balthasar, of a divine enlargement of the consciousness of the charismatic, such that the exterior world and the vision world lie near each other—or even inside each other—though without confusing or disrupting those distinct orders of the real. (This sounds very much like a report on Adrienne.) Furthermore, there can be degrees of ecstasy since the Spirit blows where he wills. If the one charged with prophetic-mystical knowledge can obscure the content, that is entirely bearable since

---

[53] *ST* IIa-IIae, q. 173, a. 2.
[54] *ST* IIa-IIae, q. 173, a. 3.
[55] Von Balthasar, *Thomas und die Charismatiker*, p. 394.

the divine intention of the communication is always the superordinate criterion for what is spoken. And as to that, the best earthly interpreter is the "consciousness of the Church as Bride of Christ to whose consciousness the individual believer can [only] more or less approximate".[56] Evidently, that solution to the problem of a visionary who has not got the proper bearings of his own message belongs with Balthasar's "nuptial" ecclesiology as outlined in chapter 5 of this study.

Lastly, Balthasar looks with Thomas in question 174 to the "kinds and levels of prophecy", *divisio prophetiae*. On *kinds*, Balthasar doubts that ranking prophecy (something Aquinas attempts in article 3) is of much help. God gives diverse commissions, and he gives them in an overall unity. Within that unity, the burden of the message, the *officium* given the recipient, may be more important than the elevation of the charism, the gracious means of the giving. God works "ever new and other" and can alter the levels of prophecy as he wills; there is "no detectible rule".[57] Relevantly to the controversial small book on universal salvation, written towards the end of his life,[58] Balthasar suggests that all threats of punishment in prophecy are conditional, whereas all divine promises are unconditional, citing for this purpose Paul's Letter to the Romans: "For the gifts and the call of God are irrevocable" (11:29). On the sort of prophecy involved in biblical inspiration, where he draws into play a number of moderns, Balthasar considers that while the Thomist stress on the transcendentally operating divine cause for the whole process is the best founded view both philosophically and theologically, the "Jesuit" opinion for which the biblical authors are passive and unfree in the reception of spiritual ideas and the preparation of a plan of work, yet totally free to choose in matters of verbal composition and stylistic redaction, is the easier view for contemporary biblical criticism to work with. Balthasar proposed combining features of each, depending on the particular problem involved.

On *levels* of prophecy, Thomas' discussion of the "process of time", *temporis processus*, in article 6 of question 174, elicited from Balthasar a

---

[56] Ibid., p. 399.

[57] Ibid., p. 418.

[58] Hans Urs von Balthasar, *Dare We Hope "That All Men Be Saved"? With a Short Discourse on Hell*, trans. David Kipp and Lothar Krauth (San Francisco: Ignatius Press, 1988).

thumb-nail "theology of history", on which he would write a brief but important book.[59] Where levels of prophecy are concerned, Thomas has four viewpoints: linear progress; periodisation, with a stress on a certain sort of fulness at the start of each epoch; the Incarnation, considered as the midpoint of time; perfection (meaning, absence of progress) in each salvation-historical situation so far as the "steering" (*Lenkung*) of human acts is concerned. Balthasar agreed that "the growth of revelation is no mechanical straight line growth within a quantitatively progressing time-medium but an organic growth within a qualitative time that has its mid-point and plenitude in Christ."[60] Development towards the coming Incarnation cannot be continued in the same manner after it. Yet nothing forbids prophecy under the New Covenant from serving to explicitate more fully the revelation in Christ. Gifts of the Holy Spirit could be the means that the Paraclete has used, uses, and will use to lead the Church into the whole truth. No prizes for guessing who Balthasar may have had in mind.

Rapture

When, with question 175, Balthasar moves on to Thomas' treatment of *raptus*, he is entering a realm especially important to him since "enrapture" (*Entrückung*) is going to play a major role in his theological aesthetics. Balthasar commends Thomas for abandoning in this context his normal assumption that *charismata*—and *raptus* is the highest grade of the prophetic *charisma*—are disconnected from sanctifying (habitual) grace.

The most celebrated instance of rapture was Saint Paul's, as described, allusively, in his Letters to Corinth (2 Cor 12:1–50). The authority in the West of Saint Augustine, who discussed the matter, was such that no one questioned that Paul had seen God *in some sense*. The Scholastics were of two minds as to whether he had really seen God's essence, or simply God in a creaturely medium, which might even be just some mediating concept. Balthasar himself took the view

---

[59] In the foreword to the second edition, he would call it, modestly but not inaccurately, the "nucleus" (only) of a theology of history: Hans Urs von Balthasar, *A Theology of History* (1963; San Francisco: Ignatius Press, 1994), p. 7.

[60] Von Balthasar, *Thomas und die Charismatiker*, p. 426.

set out by a Louvain New Testament scholar, Jacques Dupont, in the late 1940s. The "third heaven" (out of seven!) to which Paul says a "certain man" was taken up is not in fact the vision of God.[61] In that case, of course—and Balthasar does not hesitate to draw this conclusion—the entire Augustinian-Thomasian conception is misplaced, and with it the "whole patristic-scholastic theology of rapture" insofar as it turns on the Corinthian text. Paul was speaking "economically": he had glimpsed eschatological truths that cannot be brought into the knowledge frame of this age.[62]

The necessity of rapture had been discussed by Scholastics in connexion with a variety of themes: how the risen see God; how Christ saw God on earth, and others too. In Thomas' view, the absolute transcendence of God makes it impossible for any created intellectual or spiritual image to be the medium in which to see him. Images come from the sensuous. That objection has behind it a Platonic argument about the need to transcend the corporeal. Yet this time Balthasar does not bridle at "Platonism". The claim, he says, finds support in empirical psychology. Attention cannot be given at one and the same time to the sensuous realm and to the all-absorbing God. This is why rapture can be necessary: in certain situations of approach to God there must be a "ligature" of the senses.[63] "In fact, the thought that, with the exception of Christ, a man on earth might share in the unveiled vision of God, without seeing his everyday world affected, is not supportable from a Christian view—not just from Platonic prejudice. The eschatological moment in Christian mysticism raises here a very serious barrier. And this eschatological moment is precisely what Augustine and Thomas in their Platonising arguments wished to validate."[64]

And the rest

As to the remaining charisms, Balthasar had the impression that Thomas was not especially interested, even when compared with

[61] Jacques Dupont, *Gnosis: La connaissance religieuse dans les épitres de saint Paul* (Louvain: Nauwaelerts, 1949).

[62] Von Balthasar, *Thomas und die Charismatiker*, p. 481.

[63] Ibid., p. 486.

[64] Ibid., p. 490.

other High Scholastics who occasionally made intriguing suggestions on this or that gift. Speaking in tongues, for instance, the subject of question 176: Thomas could have rallied to the intriguing speculation that "tongues" denoted a heavenly language, which at Jerusalem on Pentecost day was both spoken and understood whereas in the Church at Corinth in Paul's day it was only deficiently practised and required hermeneuts. Thomas took a less esoteric (but otherwise more difficult) view: Pentecost was not a miracle wrought in the hearers, who heard celestial utterance but imagined they were listening to their own native tongues. Rather, it was a miracle worked in the apostolic speakers who were given supernaturally—charismatically—the ability to speak for a short but decisive interval these various entirely telluric tongues.[65] Otherwise, thought Thomas, there would be about the first Pentecost an element of mendacity quite unbefitting the first manifestation of the Church. Considered as a linguistic event Pentecost is comparable to the wonderful pouring of language into the soul of the first man, as Thomas had described that in his theological anthropology in the *Prima Pars* of the *Summa theologiae*.[66] Thomas also agreed with Augustine that the miracle of multilingual speech foreshadowed the future quantitative catholicity of the Church.

Balthasar has no difficulty with any of this. Seen as a charism, speaking in tongues in the later community cannot possibly be placed higher than the visions found in prophecy. It is a sign of some supernatural truth—but not in the soul in its totality, only in an organ of communication. This is why the gift of interpreting tongues is higher, and indeed leads back to prophecy. For Saint Thomas, Balthasar takes the opportunity to comment that the Fathers of the Church and, after them, her recognized Doctors are the *real* bearers of the prophetic charism in the Church.[67] That is a view Balthasar can accommodate so long as it is not held so exclusively as to bar the mystics from any role as successors to the prophets. As to the gift of "speech" (question 177) described by Paul as a charism of wisdom or knowledge, the *sermo gratiosus* of the High Scholastics (especially commonly discussed among the Dominicans) implies charismatically

---

[65] Ibid., p. 509.
[66] *ST* Ia, q. 93, a. 3.
[67] Thomas Aquinas, *In I ad Corinthios* 14, lect. 6.

supported speech, a charism thus achieving in a higher way what human art seeks to perform in a lower. In the postapostolic epoch the gift of *miracles* (question 178) tended to become, in general estimation, the principal charism, whereas for Thomas it serves to confirm a prophetic charism: another indication of the preeminence of "prophecy" among these diverse gifts.

The two lives

In *Thomas und die Charismatiker*, Balthasar found less to say about the contemplative and active lives, reflecting his Thomasian source. It was, says Balthasar, an uncontroversial topic for the Fathers and the Scholastics alike. (In his *Writing on the Sentences*, Thomas had thought it sufficiently treated between two of the Gifts of the Holy Spirit!) If there is any tension in the background, it lies between two distinct streams of mystical endeavour feeding the contemplative life. One was the "more intellectualist mysticism and contemplation of the vision of truth as it comes from the Greeks and Augustine, and holds good in the Benedictine tradition where Butler calls it 'Western mysticism' till the time of Thomas"; the other, "a stronger affective direction, as initiated by Bernard and William of Saint Thierry, and taken up by Bonaventure, without however denying the intellectual point of departure".[68] In this context, Thomas sees ethical purity as a precondition of intellectual purity in soul: the possession of the moral virtues, joined together by *caritas*, is, for him, a prerequisite of loving contemplation. Thus the two streams join, but not seamlessly.

On the manifold yet unitary character of contemplative activity, Thomas seeks to bring his authorities together. They range from Aristotle on *eudaimonia* and (an unrecognized) Evagrius on "natural" and "theological"—that is, supernatural—contemplation to Denys the Areopagite (and therefore Plato), Augustine on "fruition", the enjoyment of the divine, and Benedict insofar as his God experience

---

[68] Von Balthasar, *Thomas und die Charismatiker*, p. 546. The reference is to Cuthbert Butler, O.S.B., *Western Mysticism: The Teaching of SS Augustine, Gregory and Bernard on the Contemplative Life; Neglected Chapters in the History of Religion*, 2nd ed. (London: Constable, 1927).

was reported in the life by Gregory the Great. The overall result, notably in article 7 of question 180, is new—and, thinks Balthasar, quite brilliant. In the Thomasian synthesis, there is both an immanent and a transcendent aspect to the contemplative act. As immanent, that act can furnish more delight than any sensuous experience, because the understanding can reflect its own act more fully than the sensibility can. As transcendent, delight is elicited in an entirely different fashion—by love for the beloved Object. "Thomas is not intending to give up the immanent first aspect of the delight in favour of the transcendent second dimension (as Bonaventure appears to do); instead, he raises both aspects at the same time into the supernatural sphere: the immanent through the gifts of the Holy Ghost (*habitus sapientiae et scientiae* should be taken thus), the transcendent through *Personliebe*, personal loving."[69] An intenser movement of transcendence towards the beloved God means an intenser immanent presence of God in the one loving. As to the duration of such acts, dealt with in article 8, Thomas follows Augustine and Gregory in thinking they can only be *blitzhaft* (like lightning strikes) on earth—despite what Aristotle had to say on the enduringness of *theoria* and Saint Luke about the "better part which will not be taken away from her" in the episode of the contemplative Mary of Bethany in the house of Lazarus and his sisters (Lk 10:38–42).

On the active life, discussed in question 181, Thomas teaches that while all the moral virtues are directed thereto, that life may itself be directed "dispositively" to a life of contemplation. The principle of the active life is *ratio*, so the practical reason (prudence), though an intellectual virtue, can be ordered to the acquisition of moral virtues—and in that way to the "peace" (the overtones are those of the biblical "Sabbath" and the *hesychia* of the Fathers) that belongs with the contemplative life. Thomas treats prudence as "a kind of place of exchange between theory and praxis, between eternal and temporal considerations".[70] Every Christian who, living in the midst of the world, apprehends and evaluates what is temporal by reference to the eternal needs that "mysterious [prudential] virtue", simultaneously both "special" and "general", even more than does someone

---

[69] Von Balthasar, *Thomas und die Charismatiker*, p. 560.
[70] Ibid., p. 566.

living either the "purely contemplative" or the "purely active" life.[71] Balthasar is undoubtedly thinking of the members of the *Johannes-gemeinschaft*, that secular institute for consecrated laypeople, founded by himself and Adrienne von Speyr—and no doubt of others who, more informally, parallel that calling.

Thomas' view that the duration of the active life is limited to earthly existence might seem self-evidently correct.[72] But Balthasar shows some dissatisfaction. He mentions how for the thirteenth-century Franciscan Scholastic Alexander of Hales (in the "Golden Summa", now believed to have been a composite Franciscan pro-duction), the angels live both lives, but only in an analogous way, for they can carry out the acts of both at the same time, something impossible for human beings. But even Alexander says this spiritual dexterity of the angels will come to an end with the present age of the world. The Schoolmen are influenced here, comments Balthasar, by Hellenic antiquity and the "Egyptian monastic theology" for which the human ideal is eternal *vacatio*, even if contemplation is described as some sort of *operatio*. Balthasar prefers the use of complementary descriptions for the life of heaven—the last volume of the theological dramatics will make this plain—and not simply "the beatific vision", a name which denotes contemplation to the seeming exclusion of action. Not that he slights Thomas' account of that vision. Indeed, he holds Thomas to be less intellectualist than he appears, for "he based *visio* on *connaturalitas*, this latter was ordered more to the *donum sapientiae* (which presupposes love), rather than to the *donum scientiae*."[73] There is in heaven loving activity, and not just elevated cognition.

On comparing the two lives, which he does in question 182, the last Balthasar must deal with, Thomas has no ambition to say any-thing new.[74] Balthasar finds problematic Thomas' tacit assumption that contemplation is about love of God, the active life about love of

---

[71] Ibid.

[72] *ST* Ia-IIae, q. 181, a. 4.

[73] Hans Urs von Balthasar, *Love Alone Is Credible*, trans. D. C. Schindler (San Francisco: Ignatius Press, 2004), p. 146, footnote 1. Here Balthasar relies on an essay on the "principle of supernatural contemplation" in an early number of the *Revue Thomiste*: Raymond Martin, O.P., "Le principe formel immédiate de la contemplation surnaturelle", *Revue Thomiste* 17 (1909): 587–608.

[74] Von Balthasar, *Thomas und die Charismatiker*, p. 571.

neighbour. The two loves cannot be distinguished quite so readily. Another difficulty: the Fathers, meditating on the contrasting Old Testament figures of Leah and Rachel (a reference to Gregory the Great's *Morals on Job*), find the active life to be fruitful, the contemplative life to be one of insight. Balthasar will not agree that there is no fruit for others in the contemplative life. The history of the fruitfulness of the contemplative life, he says, "has not yet been written"; the "power of irradiation, efficacy, transformation which unconditionally attaches to it as the highest form of prayer", has not found its chronicler.[75]

On the superiority of contemplation over action, Balthasar is not fully convinced either. The close links Thomas makes between Aristotelian contemplation and the Gospel need to be at some points loosened if not dissolved. Sensibility, imagination, interpersonal dialogue may be key elements in knowledge; turning to the neighbour and intellectual, cultural, and even technical construction may be as humanly valuable as contemplative insight; the laws and demands that flow from love may be superordinate when compared with solitary contemplation. True, Thomas seeks to do justice to this issue later, beyond the questions that Balthasar was invited to treat, when in question 188 of the *Secunda Pars* we hear that passing on to others the fruits of contemplation, *contemplata aliis tradere*, is better than simply contemplation by itself—a covert apologia for the Dominicans over against more traditional monastics.[76] The addition struck Balthasar as rather extrinsic. As he wrote elsewhere, "Action and contemplation are indissolubly linked to each other in a variety of ways. They are not two moments in life that can be adequately separated from each other in the Christian dispensation. For the hearkening, reception and open readiness for God is the ground of all action; and action must itself want to transcend itself in a deeper accomplishment that, as a passion, is the allowing of God's action to overburden man. So Christian life is to this extent always something that already lies beyond both moments, fulfilling them, not externally, but permeating both."[77]

[75] Ibid., p. 573.
[76] *ST* IIa-IIae, q. 188, a. 6.
[77] Hans Urs von Balthasar, "Beyond Contemplation and Action?", in *Spirit and Institution*, p. 307; see pp. 299–308.

"As a passion": that curious phrase is illuminated by the commentary on Thomas' text where Balthasar opines that until John of the Cross the spiritual tradition lacked a doctrine of a *vita passiva*. But with John of the Cross, the night of contemplation presses on towards the night of the Cross, which means, on Balthasar's distinctive construal of the Crucifixion mystery, to a condition of *stellvertretende Gottverlassenheit*, "vicariously representative God-abandonedness".[78] It is then that the end point of the *vita activa*—and not just the *vita contemplativa*—is also reached, in a climax where everything that is one's own is surrendered for the brethren in a triumph of *Hingabe*: "self-surrender", that quintessentially Balthasarian word.[79] Don't necessarily trust the Spanish Carmelite's own interpretation of his experience, says Balthasar, but do build a better account of the relations of action and contemplation upon it. "God can, yes, rob the contemplative of his sweetness and do so much more than he does the active man, who, in praying and contemplating, experiences relatively more consolation than the one whose real 'work' is contemplation in dryness and comfortlessness. But this 'work' too is apostolate [and hence action] together with the crucified Lord."[80] The emphasis on apostolically fruitful self-surrendering identification with Christ in his Passion (and descent?) suggests yet again that Balthasar is thinking of Adrienne, whose visionary material was, in his judgment, forged in such a crucible of love that it cannot be without truth to offer that can profit the present and future consciousness of the Church.

[78] Von Balthasar, *Thomas und die Charismatiker*, p. 576.
[79] Ibid.
[80] Ibid., p. 581.

8

The Underlying Principle of Balthasar's Theology

"Is it not possible [asked Balthasar] to perceive Christianity in such a way that, avoiding both the 'blind faith' of the simple (*haplousteroi*) and the gnostic pretensions of those who understand (*gnostikoi*), we could perceive the genuine evidence of the light that breaks forth from revelation without at the same time reducing that light to the measure and laws of human perception?"[1] The most obvious thing to say about Balthasar's fundamental approach to theology is that it seeks to do justice to divine revelation in all its glorious objectivity—to which revelation's similarly wonderful power to transform human subjectivity, including intersubjectivity, takes second place. Like Thomas' theology, then, it lies at the antipode from the theological liberalism which would find in human experience (usually contextually interpreted, as in liberation theology, feminist theology, and so forth) the central and all-absorbing theme for reflection to which all else in Scripture and Tradition should be subordinate. "What has to be seen is the fact that divine revelation has been received into the womb of human faith, a faith *effected by the grace of revelation itself.*"[2]

The trouble with modern theology

The distinguished Balthasar translator Adrian Walker wrote:

> The great tradition of Catholic theology has always known that faith is not just assent to propositions (while also insisting that it is not

---

[1] Hans Urs von Balthasar, *Love Alone Is Credible*, trans. D. C. Schindler (San Francisco: Ignatius Press, 2004), pp. 51–52.

[2] Hans Urs von Balthasar, *The Glory of the Lord: A Theological Aesthetics*, vol. 1, *Seeing the Form* (San Francisco: Ignatius Press, 1976), p. 536; emphasis added.

less than that), but includes a lived conformation to the theological realities which the propositions assented to are about. The current appeal to experience departs from this venerable tradition, though, in that it tends to make untutored experience an a priori measure of all truth-claims purporting to be drawn from divine revelation. However much contextual theologians might thunder against "Enlightenment rationalism", their own appeal to experience in truth continues the Enlightenment project of confining "religion within the limits of reason alone". The only difference is that they have replaced the objective "reason alone" of Kant with a subjective "experience alone".[3]

But this is a metaphysical disaster if the God of revelation is the Really Real. "The classical transcendental properties of Being—unity, truth, goodness, and beauty—must no longer be conceived as *properties* of Being, but as characteristics *attributed* to Being from the side of universal subjectivity. All postmodernity has to do to achieve nihilism, it would seem, is to deny any universal subjectivity. Postmodernism is not so much an alternative to modernism as its *reductio*."[4]

At Balthasar's hands—as in those of the recent Thomistic renaissance in North America and Francophone Europe—theology has recovered its own identity. A decadent—because effectively nominal—theological culture has regained the confidence whose loss was draining it of life, for in Balthasar's own words, theology can "never be anything other than an explication of the revelation of the Old and New Covenants, their presuppositions (the created world) and purposes (infusion with divine life)".[5] Extraordinary as, in the light of Church tradition, it may seem, by the end of the twentieth century this statement needed making. Yet by itself the reaffirmation does not suffice. As Walker explains, "Theology must not only have a distinctive principle that sets it apart from other forms of knowing, but this principle must also be capable of illumining all of reality. Without abandoning the platform of its unique, non-negotiable commitment to

---

[3] Adrian J. Walker, "Love Alone: Hans Urs von Balthasar as a Master of Theological Renewal", *Communio* 32 (2005): 518–19.

[4] Rodney Howsare, "What You Need to Know about Hans Urs von Balthasar", *Front Porch Republic*, August 19, 2013, https://www.frontporchrepublic.com/2013/08/what-you-need-to-know-about-hans-urs-von-balthasar/; emphasis in original.

[5] Hans Urs von Balthasar, *Theo-drama: Theological Dramatic Theory*, vol. 1, *Prolegomena*, trans. Graham Harrison (San Francisco: Ignatius Press, 1988), p. 125.

the Creed, theology must also be universally relevant—and not just an in-house 'grammar' by which the Christian community 'parses' what happens to be its peculiar world-view."[6] A "tendentiously historicist valorization of the peculiarity of Christian tradition"—this is Walker's characterization of "post-Liberal" theology—will not do, unless it is matched by a "corresponding emphasis on how this peculiarity vehicles a universal revelation addressed to all men by a God who wants them to be saved and to come to a knowledge of the truth."[7] That means, then, an integrated philosophical-theological vision—which is what Balthasar was ascribing to Aquinas as early as the opening volume of the theological aesthetics in 1961. "For [Thomas Aquinas, too,] the normative tradition of thought remains the integrated philosophical and theological method common to both the Platonic-Aristotelian and the Augustinian-Dionysian streams."[8]

An integrated philosophical-theological vision

In any of its "streams" that constitutes, of course, an ambitious programme, and few theologies achieve it. By general consent, Thomas' is one. As the Dutch Thomist Rudi te Velde explains, "Aquinas places himself within the particular tradition of Christian faith, not simply by identifying himself with the particularity of its 'truth', but by arguing for the intelligibility of the Christian self-understanding. In this way he opens a universal perspective of truth, from within the particular tradition of Christianity, in so far as he aims to show that the notion of revelation has an intelligible sense."[9] And again, "Being a *scientia*, sacred doctrine cannot be restricted to factual revelation in Scripture; rather, it considers the whole of reality under the aspect of the intelligibility which things have when seen in the light of God's revelation."[10] Balthasar's theology is, surely, yet another example

[6] Walker, "Love Alone", p. 520.

[7] Ibid.

[8] Von Balthasar, *Seeing the Form*, p. 72.

[9] Rudi A. te Velde, "Understanding the *Scientia* of Faith: Reason and Faith in Aquinas's *Summa theologiae*", in *Contemplating Aquinas: On the Varieties of Interpretation*, ed. Fergus Kerr, O.P. (London: SCM, 2003), p. 60; see pp. 55–74.

[10] Ibid., p. 68. This is his construal of Thomas' statement that sacred doctrine extends to all things "revealable of God".

of integrated universality. That is why, in the last analysis, Balthasarianism and Thomism are worthy to be compared one to the other.

Without abandoning the claim of theology to speak to universal human reason, Balthasar takes as his starting point something
uniquely Christian—namely, that in theology all things are to be seen
in relation to the revelation of the triune love of God in Jesus Christ.
That would amount, then, to Balthasar's equivalent of Thomas' statement in the first question of the *Summa theologiae*—namely, that in
sacra doctrina everything is treated *sub ratione Dei*, in the perspective
of God and the relations of all things to God.[11] The most "Balthasarian" statement in Torrell's great study of Saint Thomas is when he
glosses Aquinas' statement that God is the true "subject" of theology
with the words, "In everything that concerns him, the theologian is
constantly referred to the primary origin, which is Love flowing from
its Trinitarian source."[12]

In Thomas' theology, that exploration of reality *sub ratione Dei*
is especially focussed on *ens* and *verum*, and thus on the truth of
being. In comparison, the Balthasarian commitment to "love
alone" might sound at best biblicist, and at worst sentimental—
not least when it is linked to *pulchrum*, the beautiful. But, explains
Walker, the manifesto of "love alone" is anything but the statement
of an unphilosophical—or antiphilosophical—theological positiv-
ism decked out in gorgeous raiment. Especially in the Trilogy, but
not only there, Balthasar maintains "christological love as the first
principle of theology, while simultaneously developing a philosophy of a 'truly metaphysical range' whose intrinsic openness to that
love secures the connection between the uniqueness of Jesus Christ
and universal human reason in its quest for first principles."[13]

Thus, in the closing volume of the dramatics, Balthasar expresses
his agreement with the philosopher of religion Klaus Hemmerle
(whose work he had published), to the effect that "while Christian
theology's adoption and adaptation of secular (Greek) philosophy
did make significant advances toward an understanding of being in

---

[11] *ST* Ia, q. 1, a. 7, corpus.

[12] Jean-Pierre Torrell, O.P., *Saint Thomas Aquinas*, vol. 2, *Spiritual Master*, trans. Robert
Royal (Washington, DC: Catholic University of America Press, 2003), p. 11.

[13] Walker, "Love Alone", p. 521, citing John Paul II, *Fides et ratio* (September 14, 1998),
no. 83.

its totality, nevertheless there remained a certain 'historical deficit of Christian ontology'." If to the question, what is the foundation of this ontology? "the New Testament answer had been given, 'what abides is love', this would surely have resulted in the expansion of philosophy's world-bound ontology. For love 'abides' only by giving itself, right from its very first source."[14]

In this context it is telling that, when Balthasar seeks to justify an appeal to specifically Christian experience, he lays the foundations by reference not only to the theological account of the effects of grace in Aquinas but also, *and first of all*, to Thomas' metaphysics. Glossing a text from the *Summa theologiae*'s *Prima Secundae*, Balthasar finds Thomas affirming an "ontological concordance" which gives the sentient and rational creature an "inclination" towards the real, an "intimate kinship" and "experiential contact" that entails an "attunement to Being", the "Being which in its totality points to God as its ground".[15] All proportions guarded, as the French say, the creature is "ontologically resonant to God" by a "primal attunement" to him, simply because "Being as such and everything it entails, continually directs us to the inaccessible Fount."[16] Only with this philosophical foundation established will Balthasar go on to claim for "the theological principle of *sapientia*" an "attunement" to the self-revealing God of salvation that permits the "experience of the *sapor divinus*", that "tasting of God" in spiritual experience described in their homilies, biblical commentaries, and theological treatises by the Fathers of West and East as well as by the high-mediaeval Scholastics, including Aquinas—notably, in the latter case, in what Thomas has to say about the Gifts of the Holy Spirit.[17] For Balthasar, the concord between God and man at that level is achieved in the transformative power that impresses itself on the believer in the experience of faith,[18] the trinitarian love revealed in glorious fashion in Jesus Christ.

[14] Hans Urs von Balthasar, *Theo-drama: Theological Dramatic Theory*, vol. 5, *The Last Act*, trans. Graham Harrison (San Francisco: Ignatius Press, 1998), pp. 73–74, with an internal citation of Klaus Hemmerle, *Thesen zu einer trinitarischen Ontologie* (Einsiedeln: Johannes Verlag, 1976), p. 79.

[15] Von Balthasar, *Seeing the Form*, pp. 244, 245, citing *ST* IIa-Iae, q. 15, a. 1, corpus and ad 3.

[16] Von Balthasar, *Seeing the Form*, p. 245.

[17] Ibid., pp. 249–51.

[18] Ibid., pp. 241–42.

So here metaphysical reflection and the Christian experience of faith would seem to be on convergent trajectories. It looks as if, in Adrian Walker's words, the "love revealed in Christ has to do with the very logos of being."[19]

This would be a truly audacious claim. It goes far beyond the thesis that the trinitarian love makes sense of *Jesus'* being—a statement which any orthodox Chalcedonian who has read the First Letter of Saint John would be minded to support. "The only *logos*, the only principle of intelligibility, which makes Jesus' figure cohere into that single, compelling *Gestalt* [the 'form' that so entranced the saints] ... is a love that comes uniquely from the Trinitarian God."[20] That such "Trinitarian love" explains the Christ of the Paschal Mystery is one thing; regarding it as the key to all being whatsoever is quite another. Admittedly, one could point to the message of Christian soteriology and its expected outcome in eschatology, drawing attention to how the saving work of Christ enjoys an unlimitedly transformative significance, for that holds out a hope that one day trinitarian love will come to reign in cosmic fashion. No doubt, the triune love made known in the Paschal Mystery offers in that way a vantage point for interpreting the world and its future. But more than this is required for "love alone" to have the status of universal logos of all that is. The saving work and its final outcome can only be relevant to the logos of *universal* being if it confirms, albeit in innovatory fashion, what has all along been the case with being—with the real—ever since the foundation of the world.

Ontology and the Incarnation

To pursue this claim calls for tough-minded metaphysics. In *Love Alone Is Credible*, Balthasar brought into play the ontology he had learned from his select masters in the school of Thomas. "Beyond existence in general and beyond the composition of essence a light breaks on the constitution of being itself, insofar as it subsists in no other way than in the 'refusal-to-cling-to-itself', in the emptying of

---

[19] Walker, "Love Alone", p. 522.
[20] Ibid., p. 524.

itself into the finite and concrete, while finite entities in turn are able to receive and retain it, as it is in itself, only as that which does not hold onto itself. Finite beings are thus trained by it in giving themselves away in love."[21] That passage refers to the "non-subsistence" of *esse* in its pouring out by God, described most fully by Balthasar in the fourth volume of the theological aesthetics. Though the language has undergone a sea change in the lexically and syntactically demanding German of the mid-twentieth-century Thomists Gustav Siewerth and Ferdinand Ulrich, Aquinas would have recognized here a version of his own creation metaphysics.[22] For the Thomas of the *Disputed Questions on the Power of God*, "being signifies something complete and simple yet non-subsisting".[23] On this basis, Siewerth speaks of how being is no existent, yet makes existents what they are. As the mediation of divine—self-subsistent—being to beings at large, it is at once unsurpassable yet groundless.[24]

Via Siewerth, Balthasar builds on Thomas' "real distinction" between essence and existence in creatures: the distinction that, by its absence, marks out in contrast the "Godness" of God. This is the thesis about created (and uncreated) reality so often taken as the defining thesis of Thomasian ontology.[25] But, drawing on Siewerth, Balthasar does not leave matters there.

> While insisting with Thomas that creaturely essences have no reality without the *actus essendi*, Balthasar also points out that these essences, while depending de facto on *esse creatum* [created being] for their very existence, nonetheless have their *ultimate* origin in God. If creaturely essence is not absolute, neither is creaturely *esse*, and the latter depends in its own way on the former as much as the former does on the

---

[21] Von Balthasar, *Love Alone Is Credible*, pp. 143–44.

[22] Gustav Siewerth, *Das Schicksal der Metaphysik von Thomas zu Heidegger* (Einsiedeln: Johannes Verlag, 1959); Gustav Siewerth, *Das Sein als Gleichnis Gottes* (Heidelberg: Kerle, 1958); and Ferdinand Ulrich, *Homo abyssus: Das Wagnis der Seinsfrage* (Einsiedeln: Johannes Verlag, 1961).

[23] Thomas Aquinas, *Quaestiones disputatae de potenti Dei*, q. 1, a. 1.

[24] Siewerth's ontology is expounded in Manuel Cabada Castro, *Sein und Gott bei Gustav Siewerth* (Düsseldorf: Patmos, 1971); a comparable survey of Ulrich's philosophy is found in Stefan Oster, *Mit-Mensch-Sein: Phänomenologie und Ontologie der Gabe bei Ferdinand Ulrich* (Freiburg-Munich: Karl Alber, 2004).

[25] See, for instance, Norbert del Prado, *De veritate christianae philosophiae* (Fribourg: Consociatio Sancti Pauli, 1911).

latter.... The result is the following structure: *esse* makes essences be as their quasi- or supra-formal cause [i.e., is fully efficacious in them without, however, entering into identity with them] and, in so doing, depends on them; essences, thus affirmed in their otherness from *esse*, are caught up into the dynamic of gift carried in *esse* as "dependent actualization", so that the creature's exercise of *esse*, its subsistence, is a "having-received-oneself-from-God-into-a-dynamic-of-self-gift".[26]

Here not only is adjustment made to Gilson's "Existentialist Thomism", as Balthasar seeks to do fuller justice to the realm of essence, illustrating thereby the balanced ontology he once sought to draw from Gregory of Nyssa, with existence and essence sharing the place of honour at the table of being.[27] More importantly, the theme is sounded of the inherently self-offering character of being, which is precisely what had enabled Siewerth to write, in his overview of the "fate of metaphysics" from Aquinas to Heidegger: "being, in its ultimate nature, is love."[28]

In the theological aesthetics, Balthasar had described the "philosophical act"—man's basic response to Being—in terms indebted to Heidegger. "In the single word *ekstasis* Heidegger found, already joined, the two necessarily connected aspects of the philosophical act: the dread (*Ent-setzen*) and fear of the finite spirit that, by thinking, discovers in itself the opening up of infinity, and the rapture (*Ent-zücken*) at sighting the fullness of the fountain which bestows itself and gathers men into itself."[29] But, so Balthasar went on there, "when Being is confronted as love the threat which infinity poses to finitude vanishes."[30] On this basis, in *Love Alone Is Credible*, Balthasar lays down a personal programme. "One's consciousness, one's self-possession and possession of being, can grow only and precisely to the extent that one breaks out of being in and for oneself in the

---

[26] Walker, "Love Alone", p. 526, footnote 19.

[27] Balthasar would have seen the point of the ironic criticism of Gilson in R. Trent Pomplum's lengthy essay, "John Duns Scotus in the History of Medieval Philosophy from the Sixteenth Century to Etienne Gilson", *Bulletin de philosophie médiévale* 58 (2016): 355–455: "The Angelic Doctor rises above the long tradition of essentialism, like a star rising out of the sea." Ibid., p. 442.

[28] Siewerth, *Schicksal der Metaphysik*, p. 397.

[29] Von Balthasar, *Seeing the Form*, p. 158.

[30] Ibid., p. 159.

act of communication, in exchange, and in human and cosmic *sympatheia*."[31] The creation, at its high point (both affective and rational) in mankind, calls for attunement to the original—and continuing— bestowal of being.

This sets the scene for the supreme divine gift—God's own self-gift—the flesh-taking of the Word whence the Paschal Mystery takes its rise. That gift event, so it now turns out, grounds the act of Christian faith in which this entire ontology becomes fully perspicuous for the first time. If the "integrated philosophical/theological vision" is to be Christocentric, as Balthasar has insisted in Bonaventurian style throughout the Trilogy, then its keystone will have to be the Incarnation along with the presupposition of the Incarnation— the eternal generation of the Word from the Father, himself the ultimate source of uncreated Being and created being alike. But this Christocentrism must be married with a Thomasian analysis of the metaphysical makeup of the Word-made-flesh if the unique Incarnation gift event is to illuminate universally that ontology of "self-offering" in being at large. This is the conceptual marriage Adrian Walker on Balthasar's behalf seeks to celebrate. At the Incarnation, the Son's *esse*, his act of existing, personally unique to himself in his hypostatic distinctiveness, for he is the Father's only-begotten beloved, was "communicated to the assumed humanity at the same point where created *esse* would normally be, 'taking over' from created *esse* all the functions that created *esse* normally would perform for it, realizing it as a subsisting, individual, complete, fully operational human nature—in which the person of the Son of God can then subsist for the temporal expression of his eternal being in the context of his visible mission."[32] That reflects the teaching of Thomas in the crucial metaphysical preamble to his account of the mysteries of the life of Christ.[33]

To that Thomasian understanding in Walker's account a characteristically Bonaventurian dual note of "expressiveness" and "liberality" is now added. "The Son's hypostatic *esse* 'stands in' for created *esse*, not only in its completeness and simplicity, but also in

[31] Von Balthasar, *Love Alone Is Credible*, p. 144.

[32] Walker, "Love Alone", p. 526, footnote 19.

[33] *ST* IIa, q. 17, a. 2. For its importance, in the context of the conciliar Christology, for an account of divine agency in those mysteries, see Aidan Nichols, O.P., *Deep Mysteries: God, Christ, and Ourselves* (Lanham, MD: Lexington Books, 2019), p. 23.

its non-subsistence, insofar as this non-subsistence is an expression
of divine liberality.... The Son's hypostatic *esse* therefore makes
his assumed humanity subsist constitutively in the dynamic of gift,
as even created *esse* would, while simultaneously transforming that
subsistence-as-gift into a temporal expression of the Son's eternal act
of letting himself be generated."[34] The Incarnation, by that necessary
back reference to its own presupposition in the eternal generation of
the Father's Word, "not only re-lives the 'given-awayness' of nonsubsistent *esse* and its reception by the creature" in a recapitulation of
God's creative act. The Incarnation also "precedes", and in preceding
"justifies, and defines" the "structure of the communication of creaturely being", not simply presupposing it—for the Son in entering
the realm of the created must necessarily be bounded by its nature,
but actually grounding it—for the Son, in whom all things were
made, has his own constitutive origin from the Father's "whyless"
love. Thus the Incarnation, "the 'ultimate mystery of God's kenosis
in Christ', without losing for an instant its character as a singular
event derived from an un-anticipatable free divine grace, 'is analogically prepared in the metaphysical mystery of being'."[35] That "metaphysical mystery", like its primordial analogate, the Holy Trinity, is
a mystery of gratuitous gift, and therefore a mystery of love, and is so
from the foundation of the world. Here the Franciscan and Dominican schools come together and embrace in Balthasar's simultaneously
Christocentric yet universally ontological thought.

Love as the principle of theological understanding

But Adrian Walker would go further still, arguing that "love alone"
should be considered "not just an *object* of theological reflection"—
its supreme object if the above is at all correct—but also "the very
principle of theological intelligence itself *as intelligence.*"[36] This, once
again, is an audacious claim, but it coheres with Balthasar's insistence,
learned from the Alexandrians and behind them from Saint John, that

---

[34] Walker, "Love Alone", p. 526, footnote 19.
[35] Ibid., p. 527, footnote 19.
[36] Ibid., p. 522; emphasis in original.

believing love is the highest gnosis of all. Before even Thomas and Bonaventure on the substance of Christological-trinitarian thinking about human salvation—not to be divorced from the wider issues of ontology just mooted—lie even more ancient sources on the theological epistemology of how all this may come to be known. As was noted in chapter 6, Balthasar had learned from the Alexandrian theology of Clement and Origen—and behind them, from Saint John. "For John, a love that believes is itself unsurpassable gnosis."[37] This is why the saint instantiates Christian knowing: such knowing is embodied in a Christomorphic—and therefore loving—form of life.[38] Not for nothing had Balthasar long insisted on the interconnexion between theology and—of all things—holiness.[39]

The aim now is to show how love, taken (as above) to be "constitutive of the *ratio entis*", can also act as "the principle of theological intelligence without undermining theology's rational character".[40] This will be key not only to the claim for the desirable quality of Balthasar's theology for the Catholic Church, faith and reason walking, as she wishes, hand in hand, but also for any proposal that Balthasar's theology enjoys a fundamental affinity or family resemblance with that of Aquinas. For Thomas, after all, theology is an eminently reasonable endeavour, epistemically dependent throughout on God as the first truth.

But here we at once encounter a difficulty. By submerging the *ratio entis* in the *ratio boni*, rather than treating the former as equivalent to the *ratio veri*, it would seem that "Balthasarian 'love alone' makes it impossible to *think* the *ratio entis* in terms of the *verum* and thereby undermines the possibility of theology as a rational enterprise."[41] This is by no means a foolish objection. Walker does not want to deny the existence of a "special connection" between love and *bonum*, the good.[42] It is a connexion Balthasar himself acknowledges

[37] Von Balthasar, *Seeing the Form*, p. 235.

[38] Matthew A. Rothaus Moser, *Love Itself Is Understanding: Hans Urs von Balthasar's Theology of the Saints* (Minneapolis: Fortress Press, 2016).

[39] Hans Urs von Balthasar, "Theology and Sanctity", in *Explorations in Theology*, vol. 1, *The Word Made Flesh* (San Francisco: Ignatius Press, 1989), pp. 181–209.

[40] Walker, "Love Alone", p. 522.

[41] Ibid., p. 531.

[42] Ibid., p. 532, footnote 29.

when he makes *bonum* the transcendental peculiar to the theological dramatics—the central panel of the Trilogy, where it was shown that, in the action that spans the interval from the Annunciation to the Paschal Mystery, God comes to man as love. But, so Walker points out, the "aspect of love that Balthasar mainly associates with the good is not love's appetibility for a will, but what he calls its 'gratuity': its uncalculating 'whylessness', to borrow a term from Meister Eckhart".[43] "To claim that 'love alone' is the principle of theological intelligence is not, in fact, to confuse the *ratio entis* with the *ratio* of the good—or, indeed, with any of the transcendentals. It is rather to claim that love is intrinsic to the *ratio* of being, and so lies at the root, not only of the good, but also of the beautiful, the true, and the one."[44] In this "interplay", the good "goes to the root of the true, not in order to undermine its specificity and originality as truth, but to underscore the gratuity that is co-constitutive of the *verum* as an expression of the *ratio entis*—just as the true goes to the root of the good in order to underscore the sense that is co-constitutive of the *bonum* as an equi-primordial expression of that same *ratio*".[45] "For the True is 'in its way an aspect of the Good' (Thomas) because, in both aspects, being shows itself to be self-giving (and hence profoundly Beautiful)."[46] The gratuitousness "co-constitutive" of the true as an expression of the real—what is this if not the founding charity of the Trinity in rendering created being the image of its own groundless love?

---

43 Ibid., p. 532, footnote 28.

44 Ibid., pp. 532–33.

45 Ibid., pp. 533–34.

46 Hans Urs von Balthasar, *Theo-drama: Theological Dramatic Theory*, vol. 2, *Dramatis Personae: Man in God* (San Francisco: Ignatius Press, 1990), p. 425.

CONCLUSION

The centre of Balthasar's theology, we have discovered, is the Paschal Mystery, but behind and within that mystery lies one deeper still—the triune God. The question obviously arises, how are these concentric foci to be set forth, and how is the rest of revelation—and of reality—to be ordered around them? "By the faith that loves" is always a correct answer but, *pace* Walker, it is not by itself a sufficient one. Balthasar does not deny that—in a version of the Scholastic mind-set—it is the task of theology to "make evident the logical inter-connection and necessity of the historical and accidental aspects of revelation", a rational task.[1] Then there is the need for theology to "deepen *pistis* into *gnosis* so far as this is possible on earth", by way of in-depth "penetration of individual facts", pre-eminent among which, surely, are the deeds of the Lord in the flesh, and this is a more especially contemplative labour.[2] Furthermore, in the service of "Christian praxis" Balthasar names a third work in hand: "the clarification of the structure of Christian faith for the Church as a whole and for her proclamation, and also for the individual in his Christian meditation and existence";[3] we can call that a kerygmatic and spiritual task. A final statement, more of the limits than of the purpose of theology, is less easy to decode. Theology, he remarks at the close of the aesthetics, must recognize its "measure" in the communication of the "charism of faith and knowledge" by Christ through the Spirit. Divine knowledge is measured out in such a way that Catholic theology will always be "differentiated", ordered diversely according to the multiplicity of "callings", vocations or missions, in the Church. Theology cannot, therefore, expect to find its own total unity (its "univocity") here and now:

---

[1] Hans Urs von Balthasar, *The Glory of the Lord: A Theological Aesthetics*, vol. 1, *Seeing the Form* (San Francisco: Ignatius Press, 1976), p. 600.
[2] Ibid., p. 601.
[3] Ibid.

it cannot be more eschatological than is faith itself.[4] The absolute unity of Catholic theology—as distinct from its legitimate, because bounded, plurality—is a goal to be aimed at only in an asymptotical fashion, since its full realization belongs with the parousial completion of revelation at the cosmic end, when all things will be laid bare and we shall see him whom we have pierced. Meanwhile, so Balthasar suggests, as in the epigraph which prefaces this book, there is overall growth in understanding—at least in the sense of a mounting awareness of revelation's inexhaustibility.

Such incremental developing awareness is, however, impossible unless there is in the Church, at all periods of her history, a Christian memory in full working order. Saint Thomas' project could be described, in terms used by the Balthasar scholar Cyril O'Regan, as a work of both "remembering, on the one hand, and providing an anatomy of misremembering, on the other".[5] In Thomas' case, the remembering is, for postbiblical writers, of the Church Fathers and the more recent spirituals and Doctors of the mediaeval period. The corrected misremembering is of the philosophers: above all, Aristotle and Plato, who were, as to Aristotle, misconstrued by the Arab thinkers of the early mediaeval period,[6] and, as to Plato, happily interpreted— so far as *sacra doctrina* is concerned—by those in the later Platonist schools (the Neoplatonists, not that Thomas would have recognized that term).[7] In Balthasar's case—and it is Balthasar for whom this language has been forged—the remembering is not only of Scripture, the Fathers, and the mediaevals (including Thomas himself), but of many later voices in the Tradition (not excluding the occasional Orthodox, as with Vladimir Soloviev, or Lutheran, as with Johann Georg Hamann), while the misremembering is above all of Hegel, and behind

[4] Ibid.

[5] Cyril O'Regan, *The Anatomy of Misremembering: Von Balthasar's Response to Philosophical Modernity*, vol. 1, *Hegel* (New York: Crossroad, 2014), p. 40.

[6] Not necessarily by all; for Thomas' debt to Avicenna, see David Burrell, C.S.C., *Knowing the Unknowable God: Ibn-Sina, Maimonides, Aquinas* (Notre Dame, IN: University of Notre Dame Press, 1986); David Burrell, C.S.C., *Freedom and Creation in the Abrahamic Traditions* (Washington, DC: Georgetown University Press, 1995).

[7] Wayne J. Hankey, "Aquinas and the Platonists", in *The Platonic Tradition in the Middle Ages: A Doxographic Approach*, ed. Stephen Gersch and Maarten J. F. M. Hoenen (Berlin: De Gruyter, 2002), pp. 279–324; Fran O'Rourke, "Aquinas and Platonism", in *Contemplating Aquinas: The Varieties of Interpretation*, ed. Fergus Kerr, O.P. (London: SCM Press, 2003), pp. 247–79.

him the Gnostics, though O'Regan intends to extend his project by describing, in a further volume, how Balthasar invokes Augustine so as to correct the philosophical inheritance of Heidegger.[8]

Balthasar was not alone among more traditionally minded Catholic theologians in seeing a return of Gnosticism in the modern age, whether via the Idealist "total subject" or the Socialist "collective destiny". The French Dominican Marie-Jean Le Guillou had come more or less independently to the same conclusion.[9] After referencing Le Guillou, Balthasar wrote, "The tragic side of personal freedom is so absorbed into the overriding interest in mankind's total development that anyone who refuses to surrender his personal drama to the latter is regarded as immoral and ripe for liquidation."[10] Only the biblical Absolute, the living God, really offers ultimate meaning to human life. But who in the contemporary high culture credits this, or even recalls how once it had inspired Christendom? If Balthasar is more generous with extended citations than is Thomas (and The Glory of the Lord includes those twelve entire monographs on Christian theologians—and poet theologians—from the past), that is because "the provocation is modernity's amnesia with regard to the gift of Christianity, and Balthasar's response is to be the choreographer of memory who puts into play as many Christian voices as possible, which if they are together symphonic, nonetheless individually strike very different notes."[11] (There is a reference there to Balthasar's essay collection illustrating ways of bringing unity out of pluralism, Truth is Symphonic.[12]) The misremembering in Balthasar's case takes the form of undoing Hegel's inheritance and influence, the power of which must first be gauged before it can be unpicked as a revalorization of ancient (Gnostic and Valentinian) heresies.

---

[8] Meanwhile, there is Cyril O'Regan, "Von Balthasar's Valorization and Critique of Heidegger's Genealogy of Modernity", in Christian Spirituality and the Culture of Modernity: The Thought of Louis Dupré, ed. George P. Schner, S.J., and Peter Cassarella (Grand Rapids, MI: Eerdmans, 1998), pp. 123–58.

[9] Marie-Jean Le Guillou, O.P., Le mystère du Père: Foi des apôtres, gnoses actuelles (Paris: Fayard, 1973).

[10] Hans Urs von Balthasar, Theo-drama: Theological Dramatic Theory, vol. 2, Dramatis Personae: Man in God (San Francisco: Ignatius Press, 1990), p. 40.

[11] O'Regan, Hegel, p. 40.

[12] Hans Urs von Balthasar, Truth Is Symphonic: Aspects of Christian Pluralism (San Francisco: Ignatius Press, 1987).

In his Trilogy, and indeed his wider oeuvre, Balthasar draws on such resources of art, philosophy, and theology as were available to him (and they were richly available) so as to achieve these aims: aims rational, contemplative, kerygmatic, and spiritual, bearing in mind, however, the caveat that, while the Church is still on pilgrimage, the perfect integration of a total theology will not be yet. In the context of "Balthasar for Thomists", it is of course the philosophy and theology that have commanded our attention—though reference to the arts was hardly avoidable if the manner of the Swiss theologian's "aesthetics" and "dramatics" were to be explained.

As to philosophy, O'Regan reports how at the end of the fourth volume of the theological aesthetics Aquinas is "praised as a philosopher who, for all his Aristotelianism, is continuous with the great Platonic and Neoplatonic tradition of inquiry and thoroughly invested in giving a comprehensive account of the participation of all in *esse*."[13] And the same writer went on to underline how "in Plato and Neoplatonism, [Balthasar] finds a form of philosophical thought that is responsive to excess, mystery and giftedness, and that underscores the humility that makes responsiveness possible."[14] Already in *Wahrheit*, "the Neoplatonic understanding of the fecundity and mystery of the 'really real' provides the context for the articulation of the dynamic self-transcendence of human being defined as spirit. That the embrace of Platonism and Neoplatonism is made with certain caveats ... does not mean in the slightest that it is not made with significant enthusiasm."[15] These words in praise of the Platonic do not imply Balthasarian distance from Aquinas. Balthasar had never thought Thomas simply a Christian Aristotelian. In his Nyssa book from 1942, he had called Thomas "the fruit of the meeting between Augustinianism and Aristotelianism"—which had to include indebtedness to the *Platonici*.[16] In the words of Fran O'Rourke, "Aquinas follows, *grosso modo*, Aristotle's explanation of the scope and nature of knowledge, yet many of his deepest metaphysical intuitions are

---

[13] O'Regan, *Hegel*, pp. 63–64.
[14] Ibid., p. 67.
[15] Ibid.
[16] Hans Urs von Balthasar, *Presence and Thought: Essay on the Religious Philosophy of Gregory of Nyssa* (San Francisco: Ignatius Press, 1995), p. 17.

unmistakenly Platonist."[17] As to those "intuitions" O'Rourke gives
two principal examples. In the first, "what [Plato] ultimately affirms
as the transcendent and infinite plenitude, the Good in itself, is ...
an adumbration of Aquinas's *ipsum esse subsistens*, the self-subsisting
plenitude of existence",[18] and on the second, the doctrine of participation, O'Rourke writes, "Participation constitutes the central axis
of Plato's dialectic: it is the foundation and coping-stone of his entire
vision; it becomes the same for Aquinas. Plato and Aquinas share comparable principles, applied analogously within distinctive intellectual
and existential environments. The ultimate metaphysical explanation
of individual beings is best accounted for each ... through the act of
participation, pointing ultimately to the existence of a unique transcendent plenitude of perfection, the source of all existence and intelligibility".[19] It was the Neoplatonic tradition which enabled Aquinas'
achievement in rendering the participation idea fruitful throughout
his philosophy and theology.

As to theology: following in O'Regan's footsteps, I have several times drawn attention to the Bonaventurian-Thomasian axis of
Balthasar's Trilogy. Reference has necessarily been made to
Thomas' theology at regular intervals throughout; the opportuni-
ties to point to Bonaventure have been fewer, or at any rate, less
often explored—this is "Balthasar for Thomists", not "Balthasar for
Bonaventurians"! Yet, taken overall, Balthasar's theology of the
Holy Trinity in its self-expression in the Paschal Mystery does have
an unmistakably Bonaventurian flavour. As Balthasar summarises
the doctrine of the Franciscan master in volume 2 of the aesthetics:

> The Father has given expression to himself in the Son, because he has
> the incomprehensible power to be one and the same God in another
> than himself; Bonaventure says that it is only this power that prevents
> him from ceasing to exist when he makes the total gift of his being
> as God. Thus it is again the same power which enables God to give
> expression to himself outside himself, in what is no longer the divine,
> because the Father has given expression in the Son to everything and

so to every possible world. Because the absolute expression is in God, he may dare to make expression in what is nothing, the act of descending into what is nothing in order to express himself is God's humility, his condescension, his going outside his own riches to become poor.[20]

The Cross is the supreme expression thereof, and in its imitation by individuals, "the crowning conclusion (and not the breaking-off) of [Bonaventure's] whole teaching about beauty, in as much as the ecstatic love which is enkindled by the forms of expression of the self-sacrificing love of God penetrates through to the ultimate source from which all beauty in its appearing flows".[21] This is just too close to the overall message of the Trilogy to have the character of coincidence.

By the end of the Trilogy, when he wrote the second and third volumes of the theological logic, Balthasar was perfectly aware that, in matters of Christ the "Trinitarian Son", Thomas is a master theologian. Though he had dealt with him in the logic's initial book simply as the provider of a general ontology, that ontology had remained invaluable, for as Balthasar's mentor Przywara showed him, the commitments of a Catholic philosopher-theologian to both analogy and mystery are not jarringly at war. Rather they are entirely compatible. That indeed was what opened the way to the Christological and trinitarian teaching found in the logic's remaining books. The teaching in question resumed what Balthasar had earlier laid out in the theological dramatics. "Etched in Maximus and developed in a theological figure such as Bonaventure" it was shown there how "precisely in the person of Christ ... concreteness and difference are provided their authority. The very unrepeatability of Christ whose person is a function of an irreducible mission grounds the unrepeatability of each human person."[22] It was a claim altogether constitutive for *Theo-drama*'s message. In the last two volumes of the Trilogy, the "Bonaventurian-Thomasian axis" is powerfully recalled, as the "truth of God" and the "truth of the Spirit" throw their definitively illuminating light on the "truth of the World". "Given powerful,

---

[20] Hans Urs von Balthasar, *The Glory of the Lord: A Theological Aesthetics*, vol. 2, *Studies in Theological Style: Clerical Styles* (San Francisco: Ignatius Press, 1984), pp. 352–53.

[21] Ibid., p. 359.

[22] O'Regan, *Hegel*, p. 124.

if different, expressions, in Thomas and Bonaventure ... it is Trinitarian difference, that is, the distance and relation between the hypostases that grounds the concreteness and multiplicity of the world, which although without an immanent ground of synthesis ... is not without such a ground in transcendence."[23]

The Bonaventurian-Thomasian axis also explains Balthasar's balanced view of the relation between apophatic and cataphatic discourse about divine things. "The axiom of the incomprehensibility of God is a position that Balthasar finds articulated throughout the patristic and medieval periods, and which finds classic representatives in Maximus and Bonaventure."[24] In his monograph on Bonaventure in volume 2 of the theological aesthetics, Balthasar wrote: "The impossibility of mastering revelation does not give rise to doubt or an experience of anxious failure in Bonaventure: it is complete beatitude in the face of the inexhaustibility of God"; "in the face of this, the last word remains the experience of being out-trumped, of wonder, and of being transported out of oneself (*excessus*)."[25] As for Thomas, in the opening question of the *Summa theologiae* he had underlined that we cannot know God's quiddity, the "what" (*quid*) of who God is,[26] and in *Prima Pars* question 3 he famously asserts that "we cannot know of God how he is, but how he is not."[27] The utter "simplicity" of God for Thomas, the denial in God of "composition", follows from the way the patterns familiar to us from created reality, such as nature and existence, nature and subject, genus and difference, substance and accidents, form and matter, are useless here. The specifically Balthasarian connotations of the repeated word "mystery" should, however, always be borne in mind in the context of Thomas-Balthasar comparison and contrast. As the second volume of the theological logic illustrates, in Balthasar's writing "mystery" is typically "defined positively rather than negatively, or more specifically as ontologically excessive rather than epistemologically unavailable".[28] Here alongside Bonaventure, Thomas the

---

[23] Ibid.
[24] Ibid., p. 135.
[25] Von Balthasar, *Studies in Theological Style*, pp. 267, 266.
[26] *ST* Ia, q. 1, a. 7 ad 1.
[27] *ST* Ia, q. 3, introduction.
[28] O'Regan, *Hegel*, p. 542, endnote 22.

commentator on Denys the Areopagite (not much studied, one suspects, in "Analytical Thomism") could serve Balthasar's turn.

> The God of natural theology, distanced from all worldly being by the *major dissimilitudo* of his act of being, is primarily negatively incomprehensible; he slips through all the mind's instrumental categories that try to pin him down with their "what?" and "how?". However, when God, whom no man has ever seen, is "interpreted" (John 1:18) by his Son in human words and deeds, we find that the negative incomprehensibility turns into a positive one. For it is far more incomprehensible that the Eternal God, in his freedom, should set forth to come to us, caring for us by means of his Incarnation, Cross and Eucharist, and opening up to us his own realm of freedom so that, in it, we can attain the fullness of our own freedom.[29]

But, as all Thomists agree, the escape of the divine Essence from the grid of concepts does not prevent the analogical use of the "perfections" found in his handiwork in order to furnish "Names" with which to gesture towards him, even prior to his coming forth from his mystery in the wondrous missions of the Spirit and the Son. "In general it can be affirmed that the influence of Thomas on the 'style' and framework of Balthasar's theology prevents it from shying away from the analogy of being despite the considerable presence of authors such as Hegel and Barth. This emerges above all in the space that philosophy assumes next to theology in his thought, and in the typically Thomistic equilibrium between the two, and further in the metaphysical conception of the relation between God and the world."[30] Yet Balthasar is not Thomas. We recall here (from chapter 4) the specifically Balthasarian version of *analogia entis* in the theological logic—not only in its eventual Christological recentering but also in its more immediate interpretation in terms of the inherent relation of disclosure and mystery in both the world and God. In chapter 2 of this study we saw the creative reworking of the analogy of being in the theological aesthetics as an analogy of beauty, and in chapter 3, on the theological dramatics, how the

[29] Von Balthasar, *Man in God*, p. 260.
[30] Angelo Campodonico, "Hans Urs von Balthasar's Interpretation of the Philosophy of Thomas Aquinas", *Nova et Vetera* 8, no. 1 (2010): 34; see pp. 33–53.

analogy of being reemerges yet again as an "analogy of freedom", leading through engracement to an "analogy of charity". Above all, the analogy of being is now—at Balthasar's hands but in the manner of Bonaventure—the "analogy of Christ". We would look in vain in Bonaventure's corpus for this precise phrase. Its sense, however, is given in the Franciscan master's distinctive formula for the being of Christ in relation to all other reality: *medium reducens*; the incarnate Word is the instrument for unifying in the epistemic and metaphysical order all that is known, and, in the order of life, for unifying man himself.[31] For his part, Balthasar explains what he means by calling Christ the "concrete analogy of being" when he writes, "The philosophical formulation of the analogy of being is related to the measure of Christ precisely as is world history to his history—as promise to fulfillment, the preliminary to the definitive. He is so very much what is most concrete and most central that in the last analysis we can only think by starting with him; every question as to what might be if he did not exist, or if he had not become man, or if the world had to be considered without him, is now superfluous and unnecessary."[32] The foundation of the universe in the "concrete analogy of being" is established by the Father in the cosmic creative act, but Balthasar does not neglect to add that the universalisation of Christ's historical being—the life, death, and Resurrection of the Redeemer—so as to become the "immediate norm of every individual existence", is the work of the Holy Spirit, the One who takes what is Christ's and gives it to the disciples (cf. Jn 16:13–14), spreading Christlikeness through the Church in the world.[33]

As to their theology as a whole in its living bond with the persons of its practitioner: where Thomas would speak of the significance of "connaturality",[34] Balthasar writes of an interconnexion of theology and holiness that takes the theologian to the heart of

---

[31] J. Guy Bougerol, O.F.M., *Introduction to the Works of Bonaventure* (Paterson, NJ: Saint Anthony Guild Press, 1963), p.164.

[32] Hans Urs von Balthasar, *A Theology of History* (1963; San Francisco: Ignatius Press, 1994), p. 70, footnote 5.

[33] Ibid., pp. 81–82.

[34] Evidence for the role of connaturality in the making of Thomas' theology is provided in Paul Murray, O.P., *Aquinas at Prayer: The Bible, Mysticism, and Poetry* (London: Bloomsbury, 2013).

revelation.[35] Holiness is implicit in any theology that is truly fruitful for the Church, just as all theology must learn from the witness
of the saints, finding in them the living monuments of Tradition,
expressions of the apostolic *paradosis* not so much in words as in life.

According to Balthasar, the attunement of every saint to the
divine "Other" gives him or her a "nuptial" and a "Marian" character. But in his writing the Marian theme, which is simultanesouly
a bridal theme, always calls to mind the Church, just as it tends ever
to find its climax in the Mother of the Lord's "standing-by" at the
foot of the Cross. That action or passion—shall we say that "active
receptivity?"—at one and the same time renewed the humility of
her Annunciation *fiat* and constituted the true ground of her glorification. There, at the Cross, she brought to "finally fulfilled expression ... the faith of Abraham and of Israel as a whole", giving back
to God "her Son, the Son of the fulfillment, in darkness of faith
that she cannot comprehend or penetrate".[36] Yet that darkness was
a *luminous* darkness—as would be the faith of the Church she triumphantly personifies. "Christian knowledge cannot master the excess
of Being which shines through the crucified one."[37]

The closing words of the introductory volume of the Trilogy
are, printed in capitalized Greek letters, "Hail Mary, the Mother of
Light". Saint Thomas acclaimed the Nativity of the Blessed Virgin
in the sermon *Lux orta est*, "Light is risen for the just and joy for the
upright of heart."[38] For Thomas, preaching in the spirit of Bonaventure, Mary's Son was the Light, but light comes from light. And the
incarnate Word is son of Mary as well as Son of God. So, thought
Thomas, the title must be hers too.

---

[35] Hans Urs von Balthasar, "Theology and Sanctity", in *Explorations in Theology*, vol. 1, *The Word Made Flesh* (San Francisco: Ignatius Press, 1989).

[36] Hans Urs von Balthasar, with Joseph Ratzinger, *Mary—the Church at the Source* (San Francisco: Ignatius Press, 2005), p. 104.

[37] O'Regan, *Hegel*, p. 136.

[38] Psalm 97:11, the incipit of the sermon. On this, see Aidan Nichols, O.P., "The Mari-
ology of St. Thomas", in *Aquinas on Doctrine: A Critical Introduction*, ed. Thomas Weinandy, Daniel Keating, and John Yocum (London and New York: T&T Clark, 2004), p. 251; see pp. 214–60.

BIBLIOGRAPHY

Aertsen, Jan A. *Medieval Philosophy and the Transcendentals: The Case of Thomas Aquinas*. Leiden: Brill, 1996.

Albus, Michael. "Geist und Feuer: Ein Gespräch mit Hans Urs von Balthasar". *Herder-Korrespondenz* 30 (1976): 72–82.

Aulén, Gustaf. *Christus Victor: A Study of the Three Main Types of the Idea of the Atonement*. London: Society for the Promotion of Christian Knowledge, 2003. First published 1953.

Backus, Irena, ed. *The Reception of the Church Fathers in the West: From the Carolingians to the Maurists*, 1:337–66. Leiden: Brill, 1997.

Bardy, Gustave. "Sur les sources patristiques grecques de saint Thomas". *Revue des sciences philosophiques et théologiques* 12 (1923): 493–502.

Berger, David. *Thomas Aquinas and the Liturgy*. Naples, FL: Sapientia Press, 2004.

Blankenhorn, Bernhard, O.P. "Aquinas as Interpreter of Augustinian Illumination in Light of Albertus Magnus". *Nova et Vetera* 10, no. 3 (2012): 689–713.

Bougerol, J. Guy, O.F.M. *Introduction to the Works of Bonaventure*. Paterson, NJ: Saint Anthony Guild Press, 1963.

Bressan, Fabio Angelo. *Lo sfondo mistico della teologia: La lezione breve di Anselm Stolz*. Padua: Edizione Messagero, 2004.

Buckley, James J. "Balthasar's Use of the Theology of Aquinas". *The Thomist* 59 (1995): 517–45.

Bulgakoff, Serge. *Le Paraclet*. Paris: Aubier, 1946.

Burrell, David, C.S.C. *Freedom and Creation in the Abrahamic Traditions*. Washington, DC: Georgetown University Press, 1995.

———. *Knowing the Unknowable God: Ibn-Sina, Maimonides, Aquinas*. Notre Dame, IN: University of Notre Dame Press, 1986.

Butler, Cuthbert, O.S.B. *Western Mysticism: The Teaching of SS Augustine, Gregory and Bernard on the Contemplative Life; Neglected Chapters in the History of Religion*. 2nd ed. London: Constable, 1927.

Campodonico, Angelo. "Hans Urs von Balthasar's Interpretation of the Philosophy of Thomas Aquinas". *Nova et Vetera* 8, no. 1 (2010): 33–53.

Candler, Peter. *Theology, Rhetoric and Manuduction or Reading Scripture Together on the Path to God*. Grand Rapids, MI: Eerdmans, 2006.

Carpenter, Anne. *Theo-poetics: Hans Urs von Balthasar and the Risk of Art and Being*. Notre Dame, IN: University of Notre Dame Press, 2015.

Castro, Manuel Cabada. *Sein und Gott bei Gustav Siewerth*. Düsseldorf: Patmos, 1971.

Chapp, Larry S. "The Primal Experience of Being in the Thought of Hans Urs von Balthasar: A Response to Theodore Kepes, Jr." *Philosophy and Theology* 20, no. 1/2 (2008): 291–305.

Chenu, Marie-Dominique, O.P. *Introduction a l'étude de saint Thomas d'Aquin*. Paris: Cerf, 1950.

————. *Une Ecole de théologie: Le Saulchoir*. Paris: Cerf, 1985. First published 1937.

Chesterton, G.K. *Orthodoxy*. London: John Lane, 1909.

————. *St. Thomas Aquinas*. London: Hodder and Stoughton, 1943. First published 1933.

Clarke, W. Norris, S.J. "Metaphysical Reflections". In *The Universe as Journey: Conversations with W. Norris Clarke, S.J.*, edited by Gerald A. McCool, S.J., pp. 49–92. New York: Fordham University Press, 1988.

————. *The Philosophical Approach to God: A Neo-Thomist Perspective*. 2nd ed. New York: Fordham University Press, 2007.

Corbin, Michel. *Le chemin de la théologie chez Thomas d'Aquin*. Paris: Beauchesne, 1974.

Dauphinais, Michael, ed. *Thomas Aquinas and the Greek Fathers*. Naples, FL: Sapientia Press, 2018.

————, and Matthew Levering. *Reading John with St. Thomas: Theological Exegesis and Speculative Theology*. Washington, DC: Catholic University of America Press, 1995.

De Lubac, Henri. *Corpus mysticum: Essai sur l'Eucharistie et l'Eglise au moyen âge*. Paris: Aubier, 1944.

————. *Exégèse mediévale: Les quatre sens de l'Ecriture*. 4 vols. Paris: Editions Montaigne, 1958–1969.

————. *La posterité spirituelle de Joachim de Flore*. Paris: Lethellieux & Namur: Culture et Verité, 1979.

————. *The Mystery of the Supernatural*. New York: Crossroad, 1998. First published 1967.

————. "A Witness of Christ in the Church: Hans Urs von Balthasar". In *The Church: Paradox and Mystery*, pp. 103–21. Shannon, IE: Ecclesia Press, 1969.

Del Prado, Norbert, O.P. *De veritate christianae philosophiae*. Fribourg: Consociatio Sancti Pauli, 1911.

Dickens, W.T. *Hans Urs von Balthasar's Theological Aesthetics: A Model for Post-Critical Biblical Interpretation*. Notre Dame, IN: University of Notre Dame Press, 2003.

Dulles, Avery, S.J. *Church and Society: The Laurence J. McGinley Lectures, 1988–2007*. New York: Fordham University Press, 2008.

Dupont, Jacques. *Gnosis: La connaissance religieuse dans les épitres de saint Paul*. Louvain: Nauwaelerts, 1949.

Duroux, Benoit, O.P. *La Psychologie de la Foi chez saint Thomas d'Aquin*. Paris: Desclée de Brouwer, 1963.

Eco, Umberto. *The Aesthetics of Aquinas*. Boston: Harvard University Press, 1988.

Elders, Leo. "Thomas Aquinas and the Fathers of the Church". In *The Reception of the Church Fathers in the West: From the Carolingians to the Maurists*, edited by Irena Backus, 1: 337–66. Leiden: Brill, 1997.

———. "The Ecclesial Fruit of the Eucharist in St. Thomas Aquinas". *Nova et Vetera* 2, no. 1 (2004): 43–60.

———. *La Trinité créatrice: Trinité et création dans les commentaires aux "Sentences" de Thomas d'Aquin et de ses précurseurs Albert le Grand et Bonaventure*. Paris: Vrin, 1995.

———. "Trinité et creation". *Revue des sciences philosophiques et théologiques* 79 (1995): 405–30.

———. *Trinity in Aquinas*. Ypsilanti, MI: Sapientia Press, 2003.

Farrer, Austin. *The Glass of Vision*. Westminster: Dacre Press, 1948.

Flannery, Michael A. *Alfred Russel Wallace's Theory of Intelligent Evolution: How Wallace's World of Life Challenged Darwinism*. Rev. ed. Riesel, TX: Erasmus Press, 2011.

Franks, Angela. "Trinitarian *analogia entis* in Hans Urs von Balthasar". *The Thomist* 62, no. 4 (1998): 533–59.

Friesenhavn, Jacob H. *The Trinity and Theodicy: The Trinitarian Theology of von Balthasar and the Problem of Evil*. Farnham: Ashgate, 2011.

Garrigou-Lagrange, Réginald, O.P. *Perfection chrétienne et contemplation selon S. Thomas d'Aquin et S. Jean de la Croix*. Saint-Maximin, Editions de la Vie spirituelle, 1923.

Geenen, Godefrid. "Saint Thomas et les Pères". *Dictionnaire de théologie catholique* XV.1, cols. 738–61. Paris: Letouzey et Ané, 1946.

Gilby, Thomas, O.P. "Sacra Doctrina". In *St. Thomas Aquinas, Summa Theologiae*. Vol. 1, *Christian Theology, Ia.1*, pp. 57–66. London: Eyre and Spottiswoode, 1964.

Gilson, Etienne. *The Christian Philosophy of St. Bonaventure*. London: Sheed and Ward, 1940.

———. *The Christian Philosophy of St. Thomas Aquinas*. London: Gollancz, 1957.

———. *L'esprit de la Philosophie médiévale*. Paris: Vrin, 1932.

———. *Jean Duns Scot: Introduction à ses positions fondamentales*. Paris: Vrin, 1952.

Gondreau, Paul. *The Passions of Christ's Soul in the Theology of St. Thomas Aquinas*. Scranton, PA: University of Scranton Press, 2009.

Griffiths, Paul. "Is There a Doctrine of the Descent into Hell?", *Pro Ecclesia* 17, no. 3 (2008): 257–68.

Guardini, Romano. *The Church and the Catholic*. New York: Sheed and Ward, 1935.

————. *Glaubenserkenntnis: Versuche zur Unterscheidung and Ertiefung*. Freiburg: Herder, 1983. First published 1949.

Guerriero, Elio. *Hans Urs von Balthasar*. Cinisello Balsamo: Edizioni Paoline, 1991.

Hadot, Pierre. *Philosophy as a Way of Life*. Chicago: University of Chicago Press, 1995.

Hankey, Wayne J. "Aquinas and the Platonists". In *The Platonic Tradition in the Middle Ages: A Doxographic Approach*, edited by Stephen Gersch and Maarten J. F. M. Hoenen, pp. 279–324. Berlin: De Gruyter, 2002.

Healy, Nicholas. *The Eschatology of Hans Urs von Balthasar: Being as Communion*. New York: Oxford University Press, 2005.

Hibbs, Thomas. *Dialectic and Narrative in Aquinas: An Interpretation of the Summa contra Gentiles*. Notre Dame, IN: University of Notre Dame Press, 1995.

Hittinger, Russell. "Theology and Natural Law Theory". *Communio* 17 (1990): 402–8.

Howsare, Rodney. "What You Need to Know about Hans Urs von Balthasar". *Front Porch Republic*, August 19, 2013. https://www.frontporch republic.com/2013/08/what-you-need-to-know-about-hans-urs -von-Balthasar/.

Hunt, Anne. *The Trinity and the Paschal Mystery*. Wilmington, DE: Michael Glazier, 1997.

Johnson, Junius. *Christ and Analogy: The Christocentric Metaphysics of Hans Urs von Balthasar*. Minneapolis: Fortress, 2013.

Jones, David. *Epoch and Artist*. London: Faber and Faber, 1959.

Jordan, Mark D. *Ordering Wisdom: The Hierarchy of Philosophical Discourses in Aquinas*. Notre Dame, IN: University of Notre Dame Press, 1986.

Kaliba, Clemens. *Die Welt als Gleichnis des dreieingen Gottes*. Salzburg: Müller, 1952.

Kasper, Walter. *The Absolute in History: The Philosophy and Theology of History in Schelling's Late Philosophy*. New York; Mahwah, NJ: Paulist, 2018.

Kerr, Fergus, O.P., ed. *Contemplating Aquinas: On the Varieties of Interpretation*. London: SCM, 2003.

Kockelmans, Joseph. *The Metaphysics of Aquinas: A Systematic Presentation*. Leuven: Bibliotheek van de Faculteit Godgeleerdheid, 2001.

Lafont, Ghislain, O.S.B. *Structures et méthode dans la Somme théologique de S. Thomas d'Aquin*. Paris: Desclée de Brouwer, 1961.

Laporte, Jean-Marc. "Christ in Aquinas' *Summa theologiae*: Peripheral or Pervasive?" *The Thomist* 67 (2003): 221–48.

Leahy, Brendan. *The Marian Profile in the Ecclesiology of Hans Urs von Balthasar*. London: New City, 2000.

Le Guillou, Marie-Jean, O.P. *Le mystère du Père: Foi des apôtres, gnoses actuelles*. Paris: Fayard, 1973.

Lochbrunner, Manfred. *Hans Urs von Balthasar als Autor, Herausgeber und Verleger*. Würzburg: Echter, 2002.

————. *Hans Urs von Balthasar und seine Literatenfreunde*. Würzburg: Echter, 2007.

————. *Hans Urs von Balthasar und seine Philosophenfreunde*. Würzburg: Echter, 2005.

————. *Hans Urs von Balthasar und seine Theologiekollegen*. Würzburg: Echter, 2009.

Long, D. Stephen. *Saving Karl Barth: Hans Urs von Balthasar's Preoccupation*. Minneapolis: Fortress, 2014.

Löser, Werner. *Geschenkte Wahrheit: Annäherungen an das Werk Hans Urs von Balthasars*. Würzburg: Echter, 2015.

Louth, Andrew. *St. John Damascene: Tradition and Originality in Byzantine Theology*. Oxford: Oxford University Press, 2004.

Maidl, Lydia. *Desiderii interpres: Genese und Grundstruktur des Gebetstheologie des Thomas von Aquin*. Paderborn: Schöningh, 1994.

Maritain, Jacques. *Art et scolastique*. Paris: Librairie de l'Art catholique, 1920.

————. *Distinguer pour unir, ou Les Degrés du savoir*. Paris: Bibliothèque de la philosophie française, 1932.

————. *On the Church of Christ: The Person of the Church and Her Personnel*. Notre Dame, IN: University of Notre Dame Press, 1973.

————. *La Personne et le bien commun*. Paris: Desclée de Brouwer, 1947.

Martin, Raymond, O.P. "Le principe formel immédiate de la contemplation surnaturelle". *Revue Thomiste* 17 (1909): 587–608.

McCool, Gerald A., S.J. "An Alert and Independent Thomist: William Norris Clarke, S.J." In *The Universe as Journey: Conversations with W. Norris Clarke, S.J.*, pp. 13–48. New York: Fordham University Press, 1988.

————. *Catholic Theology in the Nineteenth Century: The Quest for a Unitary Method*. New York: Seabury, 1977.

————. *From Unity to Pluralism: The Internal Evolution of Thomism*. New York: Fordham University Press, 1989.

McInroy, Mark. *Balthasar on the Spiritual Senses: Perceiving Splendor*. New York: Oxford University Press, 2014.

Mongeau, Gilles. *Embracing Wisdom: The* Summa theologiae *as Spiritual Pedagogy.* Toronto: Pontifical Institute of Mediaeval Studies, 2015.

Mongrain, Kevin. *The Systematic Thought of Hans Urs von Balthasar: An Irenaean Retrieval.* New York: Crossroad, 2003.

Moser, Matthew A. Rothaus. *Love Itself Is Understanding: Hans Urs von Balthasar's Theology of the Saints.* Minneapolis: Fortress Press, 2016.

Mulchahey, M. Michèle. *"First the Bow Is Bent in Study": Dominican Education before 1350.* Toronto: Pontifical Institute of Mediaeval Studies, 1998.

Murray, Paul, O.P. *Aquinas at Prayer: The Bible, Mysticism, and Poetry.* London: Bloomsbury, 2013.

Narcisse, Gilbert. *Les raisons de Dieu: Arguments de convenance et esthétique théologique selon saint Thomas d'Aquin et Hans Urs von Balthasar.* Fribourg: Editions universitaires, 1997.

Nichols, Aidan, O.P. *Beyond the Blue Glass: Catholic Essays in Faith and Culture.* Vol. 1. London: Saint Austin Press, 2002.

———. *Deep Mysteries: God, Christ, and Ourselves.* Lanham, MD: Lexington Books, 2019.

———. *Discovering Aquinas: An Introduction to His Life, Work, and Influence.* London: Darton, Longman and Todd, 2002.

———. *Divine Fruitfulness: Balthasar's Theology beyond the Trilogy.* London: Continuum, 2007.

———. *A Key to Balthasar: Hans Urs von Balthasar on Beauty, Goodness, and Truth.* London: Darton, Longman and Todd, 2011.

———. "The Mariology of St. Thomas". In *Aquinas on Doctrine: A Critical Introduction,* edited by Thomas Weinandy, Daniel Keating, and John Yocum, pp. 214–60. London and New York: T&T Clark, 2004.

———. *No Bloodless Myth: A Guide through Balthasar's Dramatics.* Edinburgh: T&T Clark, 2000.

———. "St. Thomas Aquinas on the Passion of Christ: A Reading of Summa Theologiae IIIa., q. 46". *Scottish Journal of Theology* 43 (1990): 447–59.

———. *Say It Is Pentecost: A Guide through Balthasar's Logic.* Edinburgh: T&T Clark, 2001.

———. *Scattering the Seed: A Guide through Balthasar's Early Writings on Philosophy and the Arts.* London: Continuum, 2006.

———. "Thomism and the *nouvelle théologie*". *The Thomist* 64 (2000): 1–19.

———. "Von Balthasar's Aims in His Theological Aesthetics". *Heythrop Journal* 40 (1999): 409–23. Republished in *Beyond the Blue Glass: Catholic Essays in Faith and Culture,* by Aidan Nichols, O.P., 1:87–106. London: Saint Austin Press, 2002.

———. *The Word Has Been Abroad: A Guide through Balthasar's Aesthetics.* Edinburgh: T&T Clark, 1998.

Oakes, Edward T. "Balthasar and *Ressourcement*: An Ambiguous Relationship". In *Ressourcement: A Movement for Renewal in Twentieth Century Catholic Theology*, edited by Gabriel Flynn and Paul D. Murray, pp. 278–88. Oxford: Oxford University Press, 2014.

———. "Descensus and Development: A Response to Recent Rejoinders". *International Journal of Systematic Theology* 13, no. 1 (2011): 3–24.

———. "The Internal Logic of Holy Saturday in the Theology of Hans Urs von Balthasar". *International Journal of Systematic Theology* 9, no. 2 (2007): 184–99.

———. *The Pattern of Redemption: The Theology of Hans Urs von Balthasar.* London: Bloomsbury, 1997.

———. "What I Learned about Prayer from Hans Urs von Balthasar". *America: The Jesuit Review*, August 1, 2005. https://www.america magazine.org/faith/2005/08/01/what-i-learned-about-prayer-hans -urs-von-Balthasar.

Ochagavia, Juan, S.J. *Filius visibile Patris: A Study of St. Irenaeus' Teaching on Revelation and Tradition.* Rome: Pontifical Institute of Oriental Studies, 1964.

O'Hanlon, Gerard F., S.J. *The Immutability of God in the Theology of Hans Urs von Balthasar.* Cambridge: Cambridge University Press, 1990.

O'Neill, Colman, O.P. *Meeting Christ in the Sacraments.* Staten Island, NY: Alba House, 1964.

———. *Sacramental Realism: A General Theory of the Sacraments.* Wilmington, DE: Michael Glazier, 1983.

O'Regan, Cyril. *The Anatomy of Misremembering: Von Balthasar's Response to Philosophical Modernity.* Vol. 1, *Hegel.* New York: Crossroad, 2014.

———. "Von Balthasar's Valorization and Critique of Heidegger's Genealogy of Modernity". In *Christian Spirituality and the Culture of Modernity: The Thought of Louis Dupré*, edited by George P. Schner, S.J., and Peter Cassarella, pp. 123–58. Grand Rapids, MI: Eerdmans, 1998.

O'Rourke, Fran. "Aquinas and Platonism". In *Contemplating Aquinas: The Varieties of Interpretation*, edited by Fergus Kerr, O.P., pp. 247–79. London: SCM Press, 2003.

Oster, Stefan. *Mit-Mensch-Sein: Phänomenologie und Ontologie der Gabe bei Ferdinand Ulrich.* Freiburg-Munich: Karl Alber, 2004.

Ouellet, Marc. "The Foundation of Christian Ethics according to Hans Urs von Balthasar". *Communio* 16 (1990): 379–401.

Peddicord, Richard, O.P., *The Sacred Monster of Thomism: An Introduction to the Life and Legacy of Reginald Garrigou-Lagrange, O.P.* South Bend, IN: St. Augustine's Press, 2005.

Pesch, Otto-Hermann. "Thomismus: Geschichtliche Durchblick". In *Lexikon für Theologie und Kirche*. Vol. 10, *Teufel bis Zypem*, edited by Michael Buchberger, Joseph Hofer, and Karl Rahner, pp. 157–59. Freiburg: Herder, 1965.

Peterson, Paul Silas. *The Early Hans Urs von Balthasar: Historical Contexts and Intellectual Formation.* Berlin: De Gruyter, 2015.

Pinckaers, Servais, O.P. "Recherche de la signification véritable du terme 'speculatif' ". *Nouvelle Revue Théologique* 81, no. 17 (1959): 673–95.

———. *The Sources of Christian Ethics.* Washington, DC: Catholic University of America Press, 1995.

———. "Le thème de l'image de Dieu en l'homme et l'anthropologie". In *Humain à l'image de Dieu*, edited by Pierre Bühler, pp. 147–63. Geneva: Labor et fides, 1989.

Pitstick, Alyssa Lyra. *Christ's Descent into Hell: John Paul II, Joseph Ratzinger and Hans Urs von Balthasar on the Theology of Holy Saturday.* Grand Rapids, MI: Eerdmans, 2016.

———. *Light in Darkness: Hans Urs von Balthasar and the Catholic Doctrine of Christ's Descent into Hell.* Grand Rapids, MI: Eerdmans, 2007.

Plested, Marcus. *Orthodox Readings of Aquinas.* Oxford: Oxford University Press, 2012.

Pomplum, R. Trent. "John Duns Scotus in the History of Medieval Philosophy from the Sixteenth Century to Etienne Gilson". *Bulletin de philosophie médiévale* 58 (2016): 355–455.

Porter, Jean. *Natural and Divine Law: Reclaiming the Tradition for Christian Ethics.* Ottawa: Novalis, 1999.

Przywara, Erich. *Analogia Entis: Metaphysics; Original Structure and Universal Rhythm.* Grand Rapids, MI: Eerdmans, 2014.

———. *Summula.* Nuremberg: Glock & Lutz, 1947.

Raffl, Albert. "Balthasar-Rahner: eine 'Vergegnung'?". In *Logik der Liebe und Herrlichkeit Gottes. Hans Urs von Balthasar im Gespräch*, edited by Walter Kasper. Ostfildern: Matthias-Grünewald Verlag, 2006.

Rahner, Karl. *The Trinity.* New York: Crossroad, 1970.

Ratzinger, Joseph. " 'Consecrate Them in the Truth': A Homily for St. Thomas' Day". *New Blackfriars* 68, no. 803 (1987): 112–15.

Rikhof, Herwi. "Thomas on the Church: Reflections on a Sermon". In *Aquinas on Doctrine: A Critical Introduction*, edited by Thomas Weinandy, Daniel Keating, and John Yocum, pp. 199–223. London and New York: T&T Clark, 2004.

————. "Thomas at Utrecht". In *Contemplating Aquinas: On the Varieties of Interpretation*, edited by Fergus Kerr, O.P., pp. 105–36. London: SCM, 2003.

Rogers, Eugene. *Thomas Aquinas and Karl Barth: Sacred Doctrine and the Natural Knowledge of God*. Notre Dame, IN: University of Notre Dame Press, 1995.

Rousselot, Pierre. *The Eyes of Faith, with Answers to Two Attacks*. New York: Fordham University Press, 1990.

Sabra, George. *Thomas Aquinas' Vision of the Church: Fundamentals of an Ecumenical Ecclesiology*. Mainz: Matthias-Grünewald Verlag, 1987.

Sammon, Brendan Thomas. *The God Who Is Beauty: Beauty as a Divine Name in Thomas Aquinas and Dionysius the Areopagite*. Eugene, OR: Pickwick, 2013.

Sara, Juan M. "*Descensus ad inferos*, Dawn of Hope: Aspects of the Theology of Holy Saturday in the Trilogy of Hans Urs von Balthasar". *Communio* 32 (2005): 541–72.

Schindler, David C. *Hans Urs von Balthasar and the Dramatic Structure of Truth: A Philosophical Investigation*. New York: Fordham University Press, 2004.

Schumacher, Lydia. *Divine Illumination: The History and Future of Augustine's Theory of Knowledge*. Oxford: Wiley-Blackwell, 2011.

Schumacher, Michele. *A Trinitarian Anthropology: Adrienne von Speyr and Hans Urs von Balthasar in Dialogue with Thomas Aquinas*. Washington, DC: Catholic University of America Press, 2014.

Schürmann, Heinz, Joseph Ratzinger, and Hans Urs von Balthasar. *Principles of Christian Morality*. San Francisco: Ignatius, 1986.

Sciglitano, Anthony. *Marcion and Prometheus: Balthasar against the Expulsion of Jewish Origins in Modern Christian Thought*. New York: Crossroad, 2014.

Siewerth, Gustav. *Das Schicksal der Metaphysik von Thomas zu Heidegger*. Einsiedeln: Johannes Verlag, 1959.

————. *Das Sein als Gleichnis Gottes*. Heidelberg: Kerle, 1958.

Smalley, Beryl. *Historians in the Middle Ages*. New York: Charles Scribner, 1975.

Steck, Christopher, S.J. *The Ethical Thought of Hans Urs von Balthasar*. New York: Crossroad, 2001.

Stolz, Anselm, O.S.B. *The Doctrine of Spiritual Perfection*. St. Louis, MO: Herder, 1948.

Te Velde, Rudi A. "Understanding the *Scientia* of Faith: Reason and Faith in Aquinas's *Summa theologiae*". In *Contemplating Aquinas: On the Varieties of Interpretation*, edited by Fergus Kerr, O.P., pp. 55–74. London: SCM, 2003.

Torrell, Jean-Pierre, O.P. *Le Christ en ses Mystères: La vie et l'oeuvre de Jésus selon saint Thomas d'Aquin*. 2 vols. Paris: Desclée de Brouwer, 1999.

―――. *Pour nous les hommes et pour notre Salut*. Paris: Cerf, 2014.

―――. *Saint Thomas Aquinas*. Vol. 1, *The Person and His Work*, translated by Robert Royal. Washington, DC: Catholic University of America Press, 1996.

―――. *Saint Thomas Aquinas*. Vol. 2, *Spiritual Master*, translated by Robert Royal. Washington, DC: Catholic University of America Press, 2003.

―――. "*Spiritualitas* chez S. Thomas d'Aquin: Contribution à l'histoire d'un mot". *Revue des sciences philosophiques at théologiques* 73 (1989): 575–84.

Turner, Denys. *Julian of Norwich, Theologian*. New Haven, CT; London: Yale University Press, 2011.

Ulrich, Ferdinand. *Homo abyssus: Das Wagnis der Seinsfrage*. Einsiedeln: Johannes Verlag, 1961.

Valkenburg, Wilhelmus G. B. M. *Words of the Living God: Place and Function of Holy Scripture in the Theology of St. Thomas Aquinas*. Louvain: Peeters, 1999.

Venard, Olivier-Thomas. *Thomas d'Aquin, Poète théologien*, I-II. Geneva: Ad Solem, 2003–2004.

Vetö, Etienne. *Du Christ à la Trinité: Penser les mystères du Christ après Thomas d'Aquin et Balthasar*. Paris: Cerf, 2012.

Von Balthasar, Hans Urs. *Apokalypse der deutschen Seele: Studien zu einer Lehre von letzten Haltungen*. 3 vols. Salzburg: Pustet, 1937–1939.

―――. "Beyond Contemplation and Action?" In *Explorations in Theology*. Vol. 4, *Spirit and Institution*, pp. 299–308. San Francisco: Ignatius Press, 1995.

―――. *The Christian State of Life*. San Francisco: Ignatius Press, 1983.

―――. *Cosmic Liturgy: The Universe according to Maximus the Confessor*. San Francisco: Ignatius Press, 2013.

―――. *Dare We Hope "That All Men Be Saved"? With a Short Discourse on Hell*, translated by David Kipp and Lothar Krauth. San Francisco: Ignatius Press, 1988.

―――. *Elizabeth of Dijon*. London: Harvill Press, 1956.

―――. *Epilogue*. San Francisco: Ignatius Press, 2004.

―――. "Erich Przywara". In *Tendenzen der Theologie im 20: Jahrhundert: Eine Geschichte in Porträts*, edited by Hans Jürgen Schultz, pp. 354–59. Stuttgart-Berlin: Kreuz-Verlag; Olten-Freiburg: Walter Verlag, 1966.

―――. "Fides Christi". In *Explorations in Theology*. Vol. 2, *Spouse of the Word*, pp. 43–79. San Francisco: Ignatius Press, 1991.

————. *First Glance at Adrienne von Speyr.* San Francisco: Ignatius Press, 1981.

————. *Geschichte des eschatologischen Problems in der modernen deutschen Literatur.* Zurich: Selbstverlag des Verfassers, 1930.

————. *The Glory of the Lord: A Theological Aesthetics.* Vol. 1, *Seeing the Form.* Translated by Erasmo Leiva-Merikakis. San Francisco: Ignatius Press, 1982.

————. *The Glory of the Lord: A Theological Aesthetics.* Vol. 2, *Studies in Theological Style: Clerical Styles.* San Francisco: Ignatius Press, 1984.

————. *The Glory of the Lord: A Theological Aesthetics.* Vol. 3, *Lay Styles.* San Francisco: Ignatius Press, 1986.

————. *The Glory of the Lord: A Theological Aesthetics.* Vol. 4, *The Realm of Metaphysics in Antiquity.* San Francisco: Ignatius Press, 1989.

————. *The Glory of the Lord: A Theological Aesthetics.* Vol. 5, *The Realm of Metaphysics in the Modern Age.* San Francisco: Ignatius Press, 1991.

————. *The Glory of the Lord: A Theological Aesthetics.* Vol. 6, *Theology: The Old Covenant.* San Francisco: Ignatius Press, 1990.

————. *The Glory of the Lord: A Theological Aesthetics.* Vol. 7, *Theology: The New Covenant.* San Francisco: Ignatius Press, 1989.

————. *The Grain of Wheat: Aphorisms.* San Francisco: Ignatius Press, 1995.

————. *Love Alone Is Credible.* Translated by D.C. Schindler. San Francisco: Ignatius Press, 2004.

————, with Joseph Ratzinger. *Mary—the Church at the Source.* San Francisco: Ignatius Press, 2005.

————. *Mysterium Paschale: The Mystery of Easter.* Translated by Aidan Nichols, O.P. 2000. Reprint, San Francisco: Ignatius, 2005.

————. "Nine Propositions in Christian Ethics". In *Principles of Christian Morality,* by Heinz Schürmann, Joseph Ratzinger, and Hans Urs von Balthasar, pp. 77–104. San Francisco: Ignatius Press, 1986.

————. *The Office of Peter and the Structure of the Church.* San Francisco: Ignatius Press, 1986.

————, ed. *Origen: Spirit and Fire; A Thematic Anthology of His Writings.* Washington, DC: Catholic University of America Press, 1984.

————. *Parole et mystère chez Origène.* Geneva: Ad Solem, 1998. First published 1957.

————. "Peace in Theology". *Communio* 12 (1985): 398–407.

————. *Prayer.* San Francisco: Ignatius Press, 1986. First published 1961.

————. *Presence and Thought: Essay on the Religious Philosophy of Gregory of Nyssa.* San Francisco: Ignatius Press, 1995.

————. *Romano Guardini: Reform from the Source.* San Francisco: Ignatius Press, 2010.

————. *The Scandal of the Incarnation: Irenaeus against the Heresies*. San Francisco: Ignatius Press, 1990.

————. "The Scholastics, the Fathers, and Ourselves". *Communio* 24 (1997): 347–96.

————. "Scholastik, Patristik und wir". *Theologie der Zeit* 3 (1939): 65–104.

————. *Theo-drama: Theological Dramatic Theory*. Vol. 1, *Prolegomena*, translated by Graham Harrison. San Francisco: Ignatius Press, 1988.

————. *Theo-drama: Theological Dramatic Theory*. Vol. 2, *Dramatis Personae: Man in God*, translated by Graham Harrison. San Francisco: Ignatius Press, 1990.

————. *Theo-drama: Theological Dramatic Theory*. Vol. 3, *Dramatis Personae: The Person in Christ*, translated by Graham Harrison. San Francisco: Ignatius Press, 1992.

————. *Theo-drama: Theological Dramatic Theory*. Vol. 4, *The Action*, translated by Graham Harrison. San Francisco: Ignatius Press, 1994.

————. *Theo-drama: Theological Dramatic Theory*. Vol. 5, *The Last Act*, translated by Graham Harrison. San Francisco: Ignatius Press, 1998.

————. *Theo-logic. Theological Logical Theory*. Vol. 1, *Truth of the World*, translated by Adrian J. Walker. San Francisco: Ignatius, 2000.

————. *Theo-logic: Theological Logical Theory*. Vol. 2, *Truth of God*, translated by Adrian J. Walker. San Francisco: Ignatius Press, 2004.

————. *Theo-logic: Theological Logical Theory*. Vol. 3, *The Spirit of Truth*, translated by Graham Harrison. San Francisco: Ignatius Press, 2005.

————. *A Theological Anthropology*. New York: Sheed and Ward, 1967.

————. *The Theology of Henri de Lubac*. San Francisco: Ignatius Press, 1991.

————. *A Theology of History*. San Francisco: Ignatius Press, 1994. First publication: New York and London: Sheed and Ward, 1963.

————. *The Theology of Karl Barth: Exposition and Interpretation*. Translated by Edward T. Oakes, S.J. San Francisco: Communio Books; Ignatius Press, 1992.

————. "Theology and Sanctity". In *Explorations in Theology*. Vol. 1, *The Word Made Flesh*, pp. 181–209. San Francisco: Ignatius Press, 1989.

————. *Thérèse of Lisieux: A Story of a Mission*. London: Sheed and Ward, 1953.

————. *Thomas und die Charismatiker: Kommentar zu Thomas von Aquin, Summa Theologica Quaestiones II II 171–182: Besondere Gnadenlehre und die zwei Wege menschlichen Lebens*. Einsiedeln: Johannes, 1996. First published 1954.

————. *The Threefold Garland: The World's Salvation in Mary's Prayer*. San Francisco: Ignatius Press, 1985.

————. *Truth Is Symphonic: Aspects of Christian Pluralism*. San Francisco: Ignatius Press, 1987.

———. "Understanding Christian Mysticism". In *Explorations in Theology.* Vol. 4, *Spirit and Institution*, pp. 309–36. San Francisco: Ignatius Press, 1995.

———. *Wahrheit: Wahrheit der Welt.* Einsiedeln: Benzinger, 1947.

———. "Who Is the Church?" In *Explorations in Theology.* Vol. 2, *Spouse of the Word*, pp. 143–91. San Francisco: Ignatius Press, 1991.

Von Speyr, Adrienne. *Das Wort und die Mystik.* 2 vols. Einsiedeln: Johannesverlag, 1970.

Walatka, Todd. *Von Balthasar and the Poor: Theo-dramatics in the Light of Liberation Theology.* Washington, DC: Catholic University of America Press, 2017.

Walker, Adrian J. "Love Alone: Hans Urs von Balthasar as a Master of Theological Renewal". *Communio* 32 (2005): 517–40.

Walz, Angelus, O.P. "De genuine titulo *Summae theologiae*". *Angelicum* 18 (1941): 142–51.

Weinandy, Thomas, Daniel Keating, and John Yocum, eds. *Aquinas on Doctrine: A Critical Introduction.* London and New York: T&T Clark, 2004.

———. *Aquinas on Scripture: An Introduction to His Biblical Commentaries.* London and New York: T&T Clark, 2005.

Wippel, John. *The Metaphysical Thought of Thomas Aquinas: From Finite Being to Uncreated Being.* Washington, DC: Catholic University of America Press, 2000.

Wojtyła, Karol. "Thomistic Personalism". In *Person and Community: Selected Essays*, edited by Andrew N. Woznicki, pp. 165–75. New York: Peter Lang, 1993.

Yocum, John P. "Sacraments in Aquinas". In *Aquinas on Doctrine: A Critical Introduction*, edited by Thomas Weinandy, Daniel Keating, and John Yocum, pp. 159–82. London and New York: T&T Clark, 2004.

INDEX

active and contemplative lives, 155,
171, 172, 191–95
Ad Magnesios (Ignatius of Antioch),
185
aesthetics, theological. *See Glory of
the Lord*
Aeterni Patris (encyclical, 1879), 24
Albert the Great, 27, 185
Alexander of Hales, 193
analogia entis (analogy of being), 23,
98, 108–11, 113, 114, 216–17
Analogia entis (Przywara), 23, 98
Analytical Thomism, 216
The Anatomy of Misremembering
(O'Regan), 5
angels, 72, 81, 82, 107, 184, 185, 193
anger, of God, 87, 88
animal world, and eschatology, 149
Annunciation, 83, 85, 115, 208, 218
Anselm of Milan, 27, 72, 87, 138,
170
anthropology, 121, 131–36, 138, 163,
190
Apokalypse der deutschen Seele
(Balthasar), 21, 128
apologetics, 39, 44–45, 90, 133
Apostles' Creed, Thomas's
commentary on, 92, 152
Aquinas. *See* Thomas Aquinas
Aristotle/Aristotelian philosophy
ethics and, 166
influence on Balthasar, 16, 23
spirituality and, 172, 191, 192, 194
Thomas and, 210, 212
in Trilogy, 40, 43, 50, 64, 104, 106
Atonement theology, 52, 72, 73, 75,
87–91, 126, 138
attunement (*Stimmung*), 47

Augustine of Hippo
Balthasar's *Theo-drama* and, 60, 75,
76, 77, 78, 82
Balthasar's *Theo-logic* and, 103–4
City of God, 151
on contemplative life, 191, 192
eschatology of, 147
on faith seeking understanding,
170
on gift of tongues, 190
Heidegger and, 211
on prophecy and mysticism,
180–81
on *raptus*, 188, 189
Thomas as fruit of meeting
between Augustianianism and
Aristotelianism, 212
Thomas on manuduction and, 31
on Trinity, 122
on virtue as ordered love, 161–62
Aulén, Gustaf, 72, 138
Averroes, 64
Avicenna, 177, 210n6

Balthasar, Hans Urs von, 13–35.
See also doctrinal considerations
of Balthasar and Thomas;
fundamental principles of
Balthasar's theology; spirituality
advanced studies undertaken by,
16–24
birth, family, youth, and vocation,
13–16
cardinalate, 30
influences and sources, 16–30
Jesuit life and Ignatian spirituality
for, 10–11, 14–15, 30
nouvelle théologie and, 24–28